SISU, One American Boy's Life in the 1940's

SISU, One American Boy's Life in the 1940's

Tracy R. Gran Sr.

Copyright © 2017 Tracy R. Gran Sr.
All rights reserved.

ISBN: 1546392971
ISBN 13: 9781546392972
Library of Congress Control Number: 2017906989
CreateSpace Independent Publishing Platform
North Charleston, South Carolina

To my brother, Russell, who suffered all his life.

Contents

Sisu

THE FINNISH WORD FOR TENACITY of purpose, perseverance, rational planning, and courage is *sisu*. My father, of Finnish descent, was committed to its basic tenants and determined to instill *sisu* into the lives of his family. He demanded that my brother Russell and I (as well as our mom) hold to his standards. Failure to follow his rules was disrespectful. To do anything contrary was impertinent.

Dad believed that childhood was a time to learn to become an adult. Frivolous imagination, playing games, and fantasizing were barriers to maturity. He proclaimed life must be one of "measured courage." Dad had little tolerance for self-centered emotionalism, reliance on luck, fate, or passivity. Dad believed success was only truly achieved through reasoned efforts and hard work.

Dad told us not to believe in "luck." Accepting the false dichotomy of "bad" versus "good" luck was foolish. "Bad luck," he maintained, "was the consequence of weak or no planning. Good luck was simply the outcome of diligent and rational preparation."

As youths, dad's primary concern for our faithful commitment to the virtues of *sisu* involved the state of our bowels and teeth. Adherence to a productive schedule of bodily tasks was central to dad's way of thinking. Every day we were asked, "Have you boys brushed and grunted?" There was only one acceptable answer: a definite: "YES!" We dreaded the consequence of voicing a contrary response.

Any doubt on his part meant an immediate trip to the upstairs bathroom. Dad would be at our heels scolding us for the disservice to our teeth and/or bowels.

If we neglected to brush our teeth, out from the cabinet came the small canister of Arm and Hammer baking soda tooth powder. Dad meticulously sprinkled a white mound of the mixture on each of our brushes and watched us clean our teeth. We had to brush our "bottoms" for three minutes and then our "uppers" for an equal amount of time. I detested the entire process. The tooth powder was dry and chalky, and bland in flavor. I felt like I was scrubbing my teeth with sand.

Dad made us feel guilty about cavities, insisting they were the consequence of laziness. When our family dentist, Orien Anderson, found decay in our teeth, we were marked children. Cavities in our mouths symbolized our disregard for dad's rules (with an equal measure of blame directed at mom's lack of discipline). To dad, repairing teeth was an avoidable expense. To lessen the cost (and add to our discomfort), dad insisted our dentist omit the use of Novocain.

Failing the "grunt" regulation subjected us to a spoonful of the hated elixir: COD LIVER OIL! The vile tasting fish liquid was dad's (and the devil's) intestinal bromide for constipation and our lack of appreciation for *susi*. Our father believed that if his offspring were brushing and defecating regularly, then he was fulfilling an essential responsibility of Finnish parenthood.

Every Minnesota spring, as the snow melted away and the days lengthened and warmed, it was a time for a generalized "cleansing." Even if Butch and I were awarded an "all-city gold medal for the greatest quantity of stools produced during the winter months," the horrendous oily mixture had to be swallowed once a week until school was over. I remember asking Butch why "they" couldn't make such poison tolerable by bottling it with a delicious soda pop? I guess suffering was considered therapeutic and educational.

Regrettably, as with many other tenants of *sisu* espoused by dad, I never seemed able to fully satisfy his mandates. On a regular basis, dad would admonish my failures with the phrase: "*Sisu*, son, *sisu!*" Butch suffered the same terse sermon.

Roots

I CAN STILL SMELL THE odor of stale milk inside Mr. Andersen's creamery truck where my brother hid me when he saw dad clumsily staggering toward us. Dad was waving a pistol above his head. Our father was drunk and screaming at Mr. Anderson. My brother whispered that dad had discovered Mr. Anderson, our milkman, was having an affair with mom. I had no idea what he meant by an affair. I did know we were both scared to death.

Peeking through the backdoor of the small truck, we watched in fear as dad lunged at Mr. Anderson and hit him with the barrel of the gun. Mr. Anderson wrestled the weapon away from dad and threw him to the ground. He then straddled dad and slapped him back and forth on the face. Dad was too drunk to fight back. The neighborhood police were called and dad spent the night in the local drunk tank.

The incident happened in 1943, when I was four years old. A few years later, my brother informed me that the sex between mom and Mr. Anderson occurred in the very truck in which we had hidden. To balance this adulterous saga, he also alleged that Mr. Anderson's wife, Millie—a Rita Hayworth look-alike—had "serviced" dad on numerous occasions.

Such experiences involving mom and dad were frequent. My brother and I lived with parents who were absent, unfaithful, drunk (or at least tipsy), and argumentative. Anxiety typified our youth.

Dad and mom came from very different backgrounds. Dad's father (my Grandpa Victor Herman Gran), migrated to America from Finland in the last decade of the nineteenth century. He tenaciously worked his way through undergraduate and law school. By the time grandpa was in his early thirties, he had a well-established practice in Duluth. Grandpa Gran would eventually serve sixteen years within the offices of the Attorney General of Minnesota. He knew, and represented, many successful people.

My father's biological mother, Olga, migrated from Sweden. She bore three children with Grandpa Gran (Mildred in 1907, Robert in 1908, and my dad, Russell, in 1912). Mildred died from the flu in 1914. A few years after my father was born, Grandma Olga confessed to committing adultery. Grandpa Gran abruptly divorced her. He refused to allow his children to communicate with their mother. She died, apparently alone, of tuberculosis in 1916. Although he retained only a vague memory of her, dad always kept a small picture of Grandma Olga on his writing desk in our living room. I always liked that picture and thought she was beautiful. I wish I had known her.

Grandpa Gran married again in 1917. His second wife (my brother and I never learned her first name), was a native of Duluth and the daughter of a wealthy businessman. The new Mrs. Gran had earned a graduate degree in teacher education in 1916, a marked achievement given the times. Prominent within the social and cultural circles of the city, she served on the Duluth School Board for decades. One child, my Aunt Rhea, was produced from this marriage in 1919.

Dad, Uncle Bob, and Aunt Rhea were reared in a privileged household. The family home was a large three-story house on hillside Duluth, above Central High School. Two live-in domestic servants were employed to meet daily needs: a maid-cook-servant girl from Finland and a butler-handyman-chauffer from England. Adherence to the values and expectations of Grandpa Gran, who dominated family life, were methodically drilled into the minds of the children, especially the boys.

While money was never a problem, dad's father and stepmother strictly managed their finances. Grandpa Gran demanded that his male offspring be entirely independent after high school. He asserted one must earn, and not be given, the right to success. Grandpa Gran adhered to the values of planning, endless effort, sacrificing for the future, and striving for the best in life. One must achieve status and wealth by a strong work ethic, reasoned choices, and diligence. This model for living was expected of grandpa's two sons.

Grandpa Gran was staunchly conservative and had little sympathy for people whom he felt were lazy and on the public dole. Society did not owe anyone a living. He was opposed to governmental welfare. He was not an advocate of the New Deal programs enacted in the 1930's by President Roosevelt. Grandpa was convinced that Roosevelt was a socialist and his administration threatened rugged individualism and self-reliance. My dad was a faithful disciple of grandpa's convictions.

Mom's mother, Edith Reid, was born in 1892 in Iowa. Her parents had migrated to Iowa from England in the 1870s. Wed in her late teens to John Kier, grandma and her husband moved to St. Paul, Minnesota where my mother, Mary, was born in 1914. Mom's sister, and grandma's namesake, Edith, was born in 1921. Grandpa Kier died in 1923. Grandma Kier never remarried. She had numerous relationships over the next eight years. The "attachments" were brief and trauma-filled (the final "daddy" being partial to domestic acts of child molestation). With no male "breadwinner," the family had little money and constantly flirted with poverty.

Grandma Kier's variety of and separations from a string of partners proved to be emotionally damaging as well as geographically disruptive to mom and Aunt Edith. Because of their mobile youth, attempts at friendships were sporadic and temporary. In later years, Grandma Kier often talked of her two daughters as "father-less" brats. Mom and Aunt Edith had never known a lasting and endearing paternal figure. Such a rearing served to create a close "sisterhood" among the three women. They were very dependent upon one other.

Grandma Kier moved to Duluth in 1931 and started a seamstress business. In due time, her father (my Great-Grandfather Reid) joined the family. Great-Grandfather Reid improved the economic status of the household during the height of the Depression. He was employed as an engineer on the Great Northern Railroad and ranked high in seniority. Great-Grandfather

Reid (a recent widower), Grandma Kier, Aunt Edith, and mom soon rented a small flat near my grandma's business.

My parents graduated from Duluth Central High School, dad in 1929 and mom in 1932. As a transfer student, mom spent only her senior year at Central. After graduation, and a failed attempt at patenting a new type of clothes pin, Dad enrolled in pre-law classes at Duluth Junior College. His quest to follow his father into the legal profession was quickly squelched. Dad had little money and any thought of his father financially assisting him in his studies was never entertained. Dad knew backing from Grandpa Gran would run counter to "the old man's" personal philosophy. Consequently, with his meager savings depleted after the freshman year, dad dropped out of college. He would never continue his college studies.

In 1930, dad found a job as an assistant manager at the Garrick, a local movie theater. The 40 hours a week job paid $19.

Parents

My parents met at the Garrick theater in late 1932. Their courtship was brief. No pictures exist of their 1933 wedding. I later learned that mom's sister, Aunt Edith, served as mom's maid of honor. Dad's brother, Uncle Bob, was the best man. Great-Grandfather Reid escorted mom down the aisle.

Dad's parents neither condoned nor attended the ceremony. Grandpa and Grandma Gran felt their son's new bride was "far below" them in education, ambition, sophistication, and social class. They were not accepting of my mother or any member of her side of the family. My father's parents believed the hasty marital bond of our parents was doomed to failure. History would prove them correct.

Mom and dad eventually resided in a "blue collar" neighborhood in West Duluth. They rented one side of a two-story, red brick duplex at 219 North Fifty-First Avenue West. My older brother and only sibling, Russell Jr. (everyone called him "Butch"), was born in 1936. I was born in 1939, one week before the start of World War II.

Dad spent the 1930's as a movie theater employee. By the time I was born, he had worked his way up to an evening projectionist at numerous theaters in Duluth, including the Doric, West, Garrick, Granada, Lyceum, Lyric, and Strand movie houses. During the day, he "freelanced" as a laborer, working at any job he could get. His employment status changed when the United States entered World War II. Rejected for military service, he was hired in 1942 as a machinist at the Duluth Brass Works. Dad worked nine hours a day at the Works and four hours at night as a movie projectionist, six days a week. Sunday's were spent on temporary jobs in the neighborhood. Mom said his three jobs paid a combined weekly wage of around $47.00. With my weekly allowance of a nickel, I thought dad was a rich man! I had no idea he worked over 80 hours a week for that income.

We had no car. Like most working men, dad walked to his job. Fortunately, Duluth Brass Works was just a block away from our house. Dad's nightly employment at the West and Doric theaters was reachable by foot. When he worked in downtown Duluth, dad hitchhiked to and from the theaters.

One of my happiest recollections was a trip to dad's job at the Brass Works on my fourth birthday in 1943. I had received a new pair of long jeans. For once, I didn't have to don my coveralls. I was also given a belt that had four holes in it, a large shiny buckle, and smelled like leather! When I strapped the belt around my waist, I "became" Gene Autry or Roy Rogers. They wore belts just like mine.

Mom arranged a luncheon date with dad to show off my new clothing. I remember going with her to the gated work area of the Brass Works. When dad saw my jeans and belt, he boasted that I looked like a little man. I felt so proud!

The three of us ate our meal sitting on opposite sides of a heavy fence. We were not allowed in the work yard, so mom passed dad's lunch through the wire fencing. What I remember and treasure most from that day is the after lunch kiss my parents shared through the wire fence linkages. That kiss left me with the feeling that mom and dad were content with one another.

Mom was a housewife. While numerous women were employed to assist in the war effort, married women with a family typically did not work outside the home. During my preschool days, mom prepared the meals, cleaned the house, and cared for the needs of her husband and children. I cannot remember a day in my preschool years when mom was not home with me. Such stability changed when I started school.

In 1943-44, Butch was in the second grade at Irving Grade School. I didn't understand what "being in school" meant. I remember feeling grateful I could stay home all day with my mother. I was thankful I didn't have to go to this strange "Irving place." When mom said in another year (September 1944), I would be in school with Butch, I became scared. I did not want to leave the familiar comfort of my home.

Mom said Irving Grade School was a fun place and not to fear going there. Kindergarten days, she explained, were spent playing games, doing puzzles, listening to stories, and going outdoors to swing and teeter-totter. It would be fun, she promised. I wanted to believe her but my brother painted a different picture.

Butch said that most of the teachers were witches and hated children, especially boys. He claimed that Miss Lulu Carr, my future kindergarten teacher, had taken a male student home and put him in a basement cage! Butch swore she ate him for supper! I just knew when I started school, I would be one of Miss Carr's meals! My plan was to convince my parents I should stay at home for the rest of my life.

I began to bite my nails. I was so afraid of school. I was going to die at Irving!

DAD

My father was a tall, muscular man with Nordic features. He had silver blond hair, bright blue eyes, and the whitest skin I had ever seen. My mother was told by her friends how lucky she was to have married such a good-looking man, but I don't think mom always felt very lucky.

Dad rarely seemed happy. I recall him often being nervous and upset. Most of his male friends (including his brother, Bob), were in the armed forces. I think dad felt guilty for not being able to join up. Perhaps it was one of the reasons he drank so much?

He was also frustrated by his father's unwillingness to help him become a lawyer. While Grandpa Gran was chauffeured daily to his job at the state capital, dad walked to his low paying jobs. With the birth of two sons and the added burden of parental responsibility and expense, dad's dreams of going to law school faded. He must have realized his wish to become a lawyer would always be nothing but a wish.

Dad was very much affected by the social conditions of the time. America had struggled through a severe economic depression. Now the country was at war. There was real suffering; lives were out of sync with so many men and women away in battle. Marriages were strained, and it was increasingly difficult to maintain a normal home life for child rearing.

Being a kid, I was oblivious to what the Depression and war was doing to people. My world was limited to the outer edges of our front and backyards. But even as a tyke, I remember feeling sorry for dad's unhappiness. Dad was often quiet and kept to himself. He rarely played with my brother or me. He was too busy working, worrying, and drinking.

When dad drank, he became loud and combative. Our house often evolved into a battlefield of yelling and crying. Dad usually started the "war." Most arguments centered on money. Mom sometimes innocently ignited a tiff by asking dad for an increase in her "allowance" to run the house. Dad predictably responded by accusing mom of wasting the weekly dole (about $15), disparagingly adding the familiar line, "money doesn't grow on trees, you know!" Mom defended her position by claiming she was extremely efficient with her allotted sum of money. She chided that maybe if dad spent less time going to bars and fooling with other women, there would be more money to spend on household needs. Dad always exploded! He screamed back he only went to bars because the people there understood the pressures he was under and cared more about him than his "goddamned wife!" Dad never mentioned anything about the women he met at the bars.

Our parents' arguments often took place on a Sunday when the bars were closed, dad was not working, and he had been "nipping" in the basement. If a "disagreement" started, my brother and I scampered out the backdoor. We'd run down the alley until we could no longer hear the fighting. When dad stormed out the backdoor to head for the house of a drinking "buddy," it was our signal to safely return home.

If dad stayed at home, and our parents were arguing, we dreaded going inside when mom called us to eat. The supper table conversation was going to be mom and dad yelling at one another. Butch and I learned to eat quickly so that we could retreat to our room. I ate my food in record times. I hated the tension.

Mom and dad's worst fights ended in their bedroom at night. Such battles were the culmination of hours of arguing and dad being drunk. Mom was called a "whore" or a "neighborhood slut." I did not know what dad meant by his comments, but his angry voice told me that mom must have done something wrong. Sometimes, dad would hit mom. Mom would plead for dad to stop slapping her. It seemed the more she pleaded the more he hit her.

My brother and I could not escape the sounds of the nighttime battles. We would try to drown out what we were hearing by putting our heads under the pillows. I was so scared on those nights. I thought dad was going to kill mom. I cannot remember mom ever calling the police or running to the neighbors for help. She must have been fearful of what dad might do to her if she reported the abuse.

I never talked to my brother about our parents fighting. I thought my silence might make the arguments go away. Also, since dad and mom argued about money, I believed Butch and I were somehow to blame for the tension in our family. Mom always emphasized to dad that the two of us had to be fed and clothed. We must have taken up a lot of dad's paychecks. My guilt led to being quiet about what was going on in our house. I rarely expressed myself.

There were mornings when mom had bruises on her arms and face. I remember one time she had a black eye. Mom said she had fallen and hurt herself. Butch and I knew how she became bruised, and she knew we knew.

If dad had a hangover, our house became a tense, hostage-like setting. We all tiptoed around him. At any moment, the false atmosphere of peace and quiet might erupt into another stormy battle. When we could not escape to the outdoors on "hangover days," my brother and I communicated through whispers and crude sign language. We did our best not to inflame dad's anger. We knew he would treat any sudden movement or noise as being disrespectful. Our goal was to minimize contact with dad and avoid renewing the argument of the previous day.

There also were times when dad, following an eventful bender, claimed he was sorry about his most recent drinking spree. For a day or two, at most, our house became a cheerful place. Dad was unusually attentive and took an interest in us.

Sad for us, those happy days infrequently occurred. Typically, Butch and I lived in a desperate stillness when dad was around us. World War II was in full swing, but the only conflict we knew firsthand was taking place within the walls of our house, and, sometimes, with our neighbors.

On afternoon in 1943, I came home with blood stains on my new white shirt. I had just received the shirt as a present. When dad returned from his day job and saw my soiled shirt, he demanded to know: "What the hell happened?!" Trembling and in tears, I told him I was at the nearby New Duluth Laundry writing chalk figures on their cement walkways. One of the lady workers at the laundry came out of the building and yelled at me to stop messing up their sidewalks. In the process, she grabbed my collar to raise me up. Accidentally, one of her fingernails cut my neck and blood spurted onto my new shirt. I told dad that the lady felt bad for hurting me. She hugged me and apologized. She offered to wash my shirt for free. The lady then put Mercurochrome on the cut to sterilize it. My story ignited dad! He became furious and began ranting about the mistake of hiring women to fill men's jobs!

He screamed: "Your average woman can't handle the pressures of a workday! I'll be goddamned if I am going to allow some bitch to hurt one of my children!"

Mom told dad to calm down over what was, after all, an unfortunate accident. She would wash out the stains and the shirt would be fine. Mom reminded dad the lady had apologized, offered to launder the shirt, and cleaned my small wound.

Dad accused mom of "missing the point." I remember dad shouting that mom "was too stupid to realize what the laundry woman had done! She had no right to harm the kid!"

Mom cautiously said something to the effect that dad was making "a mountain out of a mole hill." Her suggestion only enraged dad more.

Dad left for his evening job cursing mom, female workers, and women in general. Early the next morning, dad apparently drank from one of his bottles in the basement. He then walked angrily to the New Duluth Laundry and began throwing freshly cleaned items out of a parked company truck. The nearby street and lawn were covered with shirts, trousers, and towels. The driver of the parked truck finally realized what was happening. He apparently told dad to leave the area or police would be called. Dad left cussing the laundry truck driver.

Mom easily got the blood stains out of my new white shirt. She suggested we only chalk our own sidewalks in the future.

Another occasion in 1943 involved a neighbor, dad, and me. When dad came home in late afternoon from the Brass Works, he would empty his trousers on the kitchen counter. I would jump onto the counter and separate his coins from other objects he had pulled out of his pockets. I called the coins "round circle money." After sorting the coins by their size, I would proudly deposit the money into an old ceramic coin bank. I loved this almost daily routine. I felt that somehow my actions helped dad relieve some of the burden of his long workday and upcoming evening job.

One day, dad had been sent home early from the Brass Works for getting into a fistfight with a co-worker, Mr. Samways. The scuffle was over the policies of President Roosevelt. Dad disliked Roosevelt and his social programs. Mr. Samways disagreed with dad and their argument evolved into physical blows.

After dad arrived home in late morning, he called the manager of West Theater and lied that he was sick and could not work that night. Predictably, he began drinking. I remember him sitting in the kitchen with his bottle and ranting about "the handouts for the lazy." Dad said Roosevelt was a "goddamn communist and dictator!"

Dad exhorted that "giveaways don't work! Why do we waste tax dollars on people who refuse to work? We are stealing from the hard-working people and giving the money to the unfit!" He continued: "You watch, when this war is over, everybody will still be demanding a handout from the government! The old work incentive will be like those Japs and Nazis—dead and buried!"

Later in the afternoon, dad had drunk all the liquor in the house. He demanded that mom give him some money to buy another bottle. Mom had no money. Dad frantically searched the house for cash to no avail. Suddenly, his face brightened as he remembered the coin bank on the kitchen counter. He eagerly picked up the bank and smashed it on the kitchen floor. The coins flew everywhere. Without so much as a word, dad gathered the coins and flew out the backdoor intent on satisfying his craving for more alcohol.

I was as crushed as that old coin bank. The dad that I guardedly loved, and was trying to help, callously destroyed my little ritual of caring. My sacred daily ceremony had been abruptly ended by dad for his own selfish needs. I felt betrayed and injured. I learned, in the fourth year of my life, people who love you can, and do, hurt you. Dad never mentioned anything about what he had done that day.

I stopped sorting dad's round circle money when he came home from work. He didn't seem to care, much less notice.

Mom

With Butch off to school, I was mom's companion during the work week. I loved being with her. Mom had beautiful black hair that smelled so good. She wasn't very tall, but with her dark brown eyes, olive skin, petite figure, and pretty face, I always believed she was the most beautiful mom in the world.

Mom wasn't tense like dad. I can't remember her ever harshly criticizing me, telling me to go away or shut up. Butch and I knew that mom adored us. Maybe because she never had a brother, her "boys" were special to her. She certainly was special to us. We worshipped her. I guess we also felt sorry for mom because of the unfair fights with dad.

Mom had many rules to live by for Butch and me. She told us to always be respectful of others, especially people who were "different." We were to never gossip or spread rumors about anyone. Mom stressed not to lie or cheat when playing games. Having a sense of humor was also important. Life, she said, was too short to be sad and grumpy all the time. Treat people like you would want to be treated. Don't be mean and try not to hurt others.

Mom would not punish us for making an error. She was tolerant of our many mistakes and made sure we understood that: "No one is perfect., boys. We all make mistakes. The key is to learn from those mistakes." Mom was so nice. Butch or I would do something stupid, and she would forgive us. It was not in her nature to hold resentments.

Mom did show her temper, and it was not always aimed at dad. If a person had been unjust toward someone else, she got mad.

She witnessed a group of kids from the area abusing our elderly neighbors, the Loomis,' one winter day in early 1944. They rang the doorbell, and when Mr. Loomis opened it, snowballs were thrown into their house. Mom was irate. She reported the incident to the kids' parents. They had them apologize and clean up the mess. Mom said old people should be treated with dignity.

On warm days, when Butch was in school, mom and I played together. She pulled me in our old wooden wagon up and down our street. Often, mom and I sat on a blanket on the front lawn and constructed houses with my log set. In the backyard, mom filled a bucket with water and helped me build mud castles. We played with toy cars on a pile of sand next to our neighbor's garage. On special days, mom set up a table in the backyard and we ate our lunch in the shade. Food always tasted better outside.

On rainy weather when we stayed inside, I often sat on her lap in the living room. She would read to me for hours. We also painted pictures on blank paper in the kitchen. Every "picture" I drew would be called a "gem" by mom. She would hang them on the refrigerator door. Mom made me feel proud of my accomplishments. I cannot recall a moment when she ever truly ignored me. Mom called me "ducky-bumps." My new name was our little secret.

Perhaps my happiest memories with mom were on Saturdays, especially in late spring and early summer 1944. After listening to the Let's Pretend Hour (with its catchy sponsor's song "Cream of Wheat is so good to eat that we have it every day"), and the Billy Burke Show, Butch and I changed out of our pajamas and walked to the Zenith Market on Central Street, just across from the West Theater. Mom's sister, our Aunt Edith, was a clerk at the market. Mom bought some groceries (using her ration stamps), and then Aunt Edith would join us for lunch. We usually ate at Fritz's ice cream shop down the block, next to Strang Jewelers.

Aunt Edith

Fritz, the owner, always greeted us with a smile, and remembered our names. This custom gave the shop its friendly atmosphere. Fritz genuinely appreciated knowing what was happening in your life.

Fritz and his soda jerk sported white paper hats and matching white jackets and trousers. The shop was fitted with a characteristic marble service counter and red-padded stools. A matching back counter topped with a full-length mirror sported Stainless steel canisters and mixers. Assorted glass containers with shiny metal covers adorned the service counter, displaying malted milk balls, jelly beans, black licorice spears, jaw breakers, giant gum balls, sugar cookies, cherries, salted peanuts, cashews, candies, and napkins. The rear portion of the store contained small oval tables with red tablecloths and wire chairs. The shop was spotlessly clean.

The four of us would sit at two of the oval tables. Mom usually ordered hamburgers with fries for at a quarter a plate. Aunt Edith and mom drank chocolate milk shakes (fifteen cents apiece) while Butch enjoyed a root beer float (also fifteen cents). My choice was always a delicious cherry coke or a Mission orange (for a dime).

Aunt Edith and mom would talk about a million different things. No matter what they were discussing, the topic led to laughter. It was good to see mom laugh. My brother and I loved Aunt Edith because she made mom happy. Aunt Edith possessed a loud, bursting laugh that was infectious. We often had no idea what she found amusing. Butch and I giggled at her style of laughing. Aunt Edith was always a joy to be around.

After lunch, my brother and I were given the choice of either spending our nickel allowance on candy at Fritz's or at Brotherton's Confectionary Store, a virtual penny candy emporium. We always chose Fritz's because we knew Aunt Edith would give us a second nickel before returning to her job at the grocery store. Fritz had a large enclosed glass candy case opposite the soda fountain, near the front door of his store. I always chose a Nut Goodie as I loved the taste of maple. My brother opted for a Walnut Hill. Mom would then pay the bill and leave a tip of ten to fifteen cents. The total cost for the four of us was less than two dollars.

On the way home, we visited the confectionary store. Brotherton's sold at least 50 varieties of penny candy. Butch and I were euphoric as we entered the narrow little building. Since most candies were sold at five to ten pieces per penny, my brother and I were each able to fill a mid-size bag of sugar delights. We were diligent in getting the most candy from our treasured nickel. We labored over the countless choices of sweet candied gems like some bride-to-be scanning a dazzling array of wedding rings in a jewelry store.

I loved licorice flavored Sugar Babies. (The candy was commonly called "nigger babies" by most everyone, except the Gran boys. Mom did not allow such language in any form. Mom said saying "nigger" was disrespectful to the "colored people" and made them feel bad).

Other favorites of mine at Brotherton's were button candy sugar-glued to paper, Bit-O-Honey's, Seven-Way bars, Caramel Creams, pipe-shaped licorice, Mary Janes, Root Beer Barrels, Mallo Bars, Charm's Suckers, Yucatan, Black Jack, Clove, Beeman's, and Double Bubble gums, and the wax bottles filled with sugary syrup. I also liked the tingly taste of little black sen-sen squares, packs of candy cigarettes (with their red tipped ends), and bubble gum cigars. A real, but rare, treat would be a pack of chocolate cigarettes. Butch and I made believe we were smoking, our first feeble attempt at imitating grown-ups.

When we arrived home, my brother and I ran upstairs to our room and emptied the candy on our beds. We'd sort the candy by type and slowly begin the process of devouring each piece. It was a delightful way to end a wonderful lunch with our mom and Aunt Edith!

After supper, when dad was at work, mom gave us a warm bath. Putting on our pajamas, Butch and I would go downstairs to the kitchen. Mom tuned in our favorite programs on the little Crosley radio. We would lie down on the kitchen counters and listen to the broadcasts. Coupled with fresh homemade popcorn, a nickel bag of Red Dot potato chips, and a bottle of O So Grape or O So Orange soda pop, we were ready for the night's agenda. A special treat would be a bottle of Nehi soda (any flavor). I think I liked the shape and feel of the bottle more than its contents.

Mom ironed clothes on Saturday night. The ironing warmed the kitchen and left a slightly burnt but comforting smell in the room. Periodically, mom sprinkled water on a clothing item using a Pepsi-Cola bottle with a sprinkler cap. The hissing sound of steam complemented the burnt odor from the ironing. The combination was relaxing to Butch and me.

If she had little ironing to do, mom would repair our socks by pulling the sock over a light bulb. She would sew enough thread to cover the gaping hole that was usually at the heels of our socks. We often wore socks that had been sewn so often they hurt your feet when you walked on the bumpy patches.

We also loved the nightly routine of singing the Marines Hymn and Anchors Away just prior to bedtime. After tucking us into bed, mom led us through a chorus of the patriotic songs. We always prayed for the safety of the American troops. A prayer was then said for our neighbor's two sons, and our Uncle Bob. All three of them were off fighting in the war.

Finally, mom softly serenaded us with the tongue-twister melody, "Mares eat oats and does eat oats and little lambs eat ivy; a kid'll eat ivy too, wouldn't you?" She blew us each a kiss, turned out the lights, and, just before cracking the door, whispered the familiar warning to "sleep tight and don't let the bedbugs bite."

After mom started her serious drinking, such memorable evenings were no longer a priority.

Mom was not a competitive person and disliked arguing. Dad was extremely frustrated by her unwillingness to actively engage in his many battles. She preferred being happy, especially with her children. Mom trusted people. She had a beautiful innocence about her. Mom needed to be loved. She longed for respect from her husband. Mom had so much to give.

Our mother contended that Finlanders were "God's frozen people." Dad rarely hugged or kissed us. I don't think he possessed the emotional makeup necessary for warm communication with his family. He had been reared in a very formal setting. Dad's stepmother never once gave Butch or me a present for our birthday or at Christmas. When we needed a warm touch or kind word, my brother and I always sought out mom. Dad was the disciplinarian of the family. Mom was the source for affection and understanding. As children, my brother and I easily favored our mother.

While I feared dad, I privately and cautiously loved him. Butch despised him.

Butch

Little brother and Butch, 1943

MY BROTHER BUTCH WITNESSED MANY family arguments as a child. Frequently, dad blamed him for the domestic discords.

One summer Sunday in 1943, while mom was away visiting her mother and sister, dad was left with the rare responsibility of taking care of us. While I was sleeping in my bed and Butch was reading, dad proceeded to get drunk. He called a woman on the phone and invited her over for a drink.

When she arrived, dad ordered Butch to go play in the yard. Dad proceeded to lock the outside doors. It began to rain heavily. Butch yelled to get back into the house, but was ignored.

Eventually, our neighbors, Mr. and Mrs. Daniels, took my brother in from the rain. When mom returned home and unlocked the front door, she found dad passed out on the couch. Butch was missing. Mr. Daniels soon returned my "soaked" brother. When dad awoke, he claimed that Butch had gone outside on his own and accused him of locking the doors. Butch fearfully denied it, and told mom that dad had been drinking with another woman and refused to let him back in the house.

All hell broke loose! Dad called Butch "a little fucken liar" and claimed no woman was in the house during mom's absence. Mom saw lipstick on dad's face. Dad eventually confessed that a woman had been present. The lipstick, however, was merely the result of a friendly kiss on the cheek. Butch and mom knew dad's story was bullshit.

Butch was afraid of being alone with dad and tried to keep his distance. He literally would shake in his presence, especially when dad was drinking.

Butch became a scapegoat for dad's anger and insecurity. He was a sensitive and caring boy. His tender temperament was interpreted by dad as a weakness. He asserted Butch was "hiding under mama's apron strings." Dad often called Butch a "mama's boy," treating his allegiance to mom as disloyalty to him.

In my preschool days, dad would often pick on my brother. He rarely hassled me. Perhaps my being the "baby" of the family was somehow a form of protection? Butch and I could say or do the same thing and dad would applaud me and scold my brother. Dad said I had a "promising future." Butch, predicted dad, was "too emotional to go anywhere" in life.

One rainy day in mid-summer 1944, my brother and I were stuck in the house cutting and pasting with construction paper on the dining room table. My brother wanted the only pair of metal scissors we had to cut a pattern. I was using the scissors. He insisted I give them to him at once. I resisted.

Butch reached over and crumbled my paper project with his glue laden hands, in the process exclaiming, "Now you have no need for the scissors, you little asshole."

I got so mad I took the sharply pointed scissors and jammed them into his leg, above the kneecap. Butch screamed in pain! The small pointed ends of the scissors remained stuck in his leg as he fell to the floor. Blood began squirting from his wound onto the dining room rug. He cried for mom.

Mom ran into the room demanding to know what all the noise was about. Quickly assessing the situation, she pulled the scissors from Butch's leg and hurried back to the kitchen to get a wet washrag and dry towel. The light-colored rug my brother was bleeding upon was brand new. The recently installed carpet now had a large blood stain on it.

After mom dressed Butch's wound, she did her best to remove the stain from the rug. Unfortunately, the blood spot was still quite visible.

"I dread what your father will do to you two when he gets home," warned mom. "Prepare yourself for a good spanking!"

We were sent to our room and nervously waited for dad's appearance and inevitable punishment.

My brother vowed that he was going to kill me for stabbing him. I was scared silly. My ass soon faced a whipping by dad and my brother would later murder me. After what seemed like a month's time, dad came home from his day job at the Brass Works. We knew immediately when mom informed him about our spat. Dad loudly cursed his "useless shithead sons!" He was equally livid over the blood stains on the new rug. Dad stomped up the stairs and burst into our bedroom.

"All right, goddamn it," he howled! "What the hell happened?!"

After dramatically telling him different versions of what had transpired earlier in the afternoon, dad reached a verdict. He said Butch should have shown patience and an act of sharing with me. (I, of course, could not have agreed more with this assessment). Butch received a spanking and was not given supper that evening. I ate with my parents. Dad never reprimanded me and apparently approved of my stabbing Butch.

Dad felt the act was justifiable. In fact, he later winked at me that night and predicted I was "going to grow up to be a rugged soldier. You're not afraid to stand up for what is wrong."

Mom eventually got my brother's blood stains out of the rug. But justice was not mine. Butch got his revenge.

A day or two later, Butch and I were playing outdoors, a distance away from our house. Butch grabbed me by the shoulders and kneed me so hard in both cheeks of my ass that I could barely walk. I didn't dare tell my parents what Butch had done. Butch would simply give me more ass kicks for ratting on him.

For days, it was difficult for me to take a number two. I could not rest my bruised cheeks on the toilet seat. I was forced to hover above the rim. It would have been easier for me to crap outdoors. Zeroing in on the restrictive confines of a toilet was far more difficult than dumping out in the expanse of the woods. I was a happy boy the day I could sit on the toilet seat and "grunt" without pain.

Dad liked to drink at the kitchen table. After many "belts," and tired of arguing with mom, he would yell for Butch to come down from his bedroom. Dad wanted Butch to play his game of "who loves whom the most?" Butch hated the ploy. Dad would grab my brother's arm and ask him which parent he loved the most? In tears, Butch always responded, "mommy."

"Why you little son-of-a-bitch," dad would yell! "Get the hell out of here, mama's boy! Go to your room!"

Butch returned to our room and cried for a long time. He was always being cornered by dad into this no-win situation. Dad knew, of course, that my brother would side with mom. The predictable choice only served to fuel and justify dad's anger, and sense of "desertion," resulting in his consumption of yet more alcohol.

When my brother needed new clothes or shoes, it became a challenge for my mom to convince dad of the legitimacy of such purchases. Dad would take Butch and mom to our bedroom to see if a certain shirt, pair of pants, or underwear was worn out. Dad was convinced that most clothing could be patched by mom or Grandma Kier (who was a seamstress). Shoes with holes in the soles could be sent to a nearby cobbler and fixed for a quarter. A winter jacket was to be used one more season. Mittens, scarves, woolen socks, and winter hats could be patched or woven by mom during the summer months.

Dad emphasized the importance of stretching a dollar. The few and exceptional trips to purchase clothing were filled with anxiety on Butch's and mom's part. For dad, there were no bargains available for children's clothing, and any such trip brought on another bout of anger.

I was not subject to such treatment by dad. My clothes were hand-me-downs from my brother and cousin, Sheila. Butch had no one to give him second-hand clothing. I know he detested the demeaning shopping experience. He had no love for dad.

The Jap Zapper

WHEN DAD WAS SOBER, HE sometimes was fun to be around. One Sunday in June 1944, he woke me up and whispered: "C'mon, son, let's get you a toy. We have to go for a walk."

Dad never got me up before. My birthday was two months away. I was stunned and perplexed. I had no idea where we were heading. I dressed in the dark of my bedroom. We tiptoed downstairs and slowly opened the screen door to our backyard. Dad was a fast walker and I struggled to keep up with him.

"We're going to the beach down at the bay," dad confided. "We have to get something to finish your new toy."

I thought to myself: "What toy is he talking about? Is dad surprising me with a raft or something?" I was thrilled he chose to spend a morning with me and planned to give me a toy.

After a long hike, we reached a beach area of the St. Louis Bay. The rocky shoreline was littered with driftwood. Dad scanned the assortment of well-seasoned wood scraps.

Suddenly, he declared: "There! Those are the pieces I want! They're perfect for your toy!"

Dad walked to a pile of driftwood on the beach and picked out three spindly pieces of the white, water-worn wood.

"Let's go home, son," he said. "I have to complete something."

I was disappointed. "Am I just getting smelly driftwood," I asked myself? "My so-called present is dried up old wood?" I knew money was scarce, but how was I supposed to get excited over the junk dad had just retrieved?

The trip back home lacked any of the excitement and pride that typified the earlier trek to the beach. I figured dad was probably going to paint some dumb designs on the stupid beach wood.

After we got home, dad told me to wait on the backdoor steps while he finished my toy in the basement. I sat there, sadly, with my hands on my cheeks.

With the basement door open, I could hear sawing and sanding. I smelled glue and paint. Finally, dad walked up the stairs. He was holding a toy machine gun with tripod legs (made from the sticks he had found at the beach).

Dad laid the toy on the sidewalk and proudly announced: "Here's your toy, Tracy! You now have your own Army issued Jap Zapper!"

My eyes got bigger than saucers! I could not believe what I was seeing! The homemade gun was painted metal grey with two silver colored triggers. It had red lettering inscribed on the outer side of each of the two barrels. On the right barrel was the inscription, "US ARMY." The left barrel had the painted phrase, "JAP ZAPPER."

The gun could swivel in any direction on its tripod base. It even had silver sights mounted between the barrels.

"All you need now is a foxhole, Tracy," dad exclaimed, "and a supply of Japs to mow down."

I hugged my father like I never hugged him before. I was crying happy tears inside. I not only treasured that gun, I also was honored dad had taken the time to make it just for me! The wooden weapon was a perfect toy for a lad living in the shadows of a world war. The "Zapper" just might help America overcome the struggle against the evil Japanese and Nazis.

Like most American children, kids in my neighborhood were inundated with the propaganda that Japanese people were a dangerous foreign race. We believed the Japanese represented America's greatest enemy in the war. The yellow color of the Japs signified they had no backbone. Their slit-eyes implied a conniving and uncivilized character. They had snuck up to a place called Pearl Harbor and killed many American soldiers. Japanese needed to be eradicated.

We were also conditioned to despise the Nazis and their insane leader, Hitler. Dad told Butch and me that while Hitler was white and Protestant (as were we), he was a horrible man who was trying to take over the world. Hitler was killing anyone who disagreed with him. Dad told us to hate the Nazis, and we did, even though none of us had any real idea who the Nazis were other than bad German white people.

The kids I hung around with had no political grasp of the war. We did understand that America was being threatened by many foreign people, whites as well as yellows. During the war years, and soon after, the play in my neighborhood centered around the slaughtering of Japs and Nazis. Our "kill-games" were played on battlegrounds drawn from movies and radio programs. We butchered opponents at those "faraway places with strange sounding names" such as Guadalcanal, Okinawa, Iwo Jima, Pearl Harbor, and Berlin.

My homemade machine gun was put to good use. All the neighborhood kids wanted to play with it. Dad got such joy in seeing the enthusiasm produced by the weapon that he made some wooden rifles, handguns, and grenades and gave them to my friends. He even helped us dig small foxholes around our street so we could protect ourselves while slaying the enemy. Dad became a popular figure with the neighborhood kids. His provision of toy weaponry was much appreciated not only by my buddies, but also their parents.

The positive responses and respect dad received from our neighborhood must have made him feel more involved in the war effort. For the moment, at least, I was proud of my father.

Kindergarten Disaster

My "new" bike, 1944

I CELEBRATED MY FIFTH BIRTHDAY in late August 1944. I was so excited that I forgot entrance into kindergarten would transpire during the first week of September.

Mom baked a large three-layer spice cake, planning to surprise me with the delicacy when I came down to breakfast on the big day. My "surprise" was finding dad's face partially imbedded on the surface of the cake. Apparently, in his drunken state from the previous night, dad had mistaken the cake for a pillow.

One side of his face was smeared with icing, and candles were stuck in his hair. The cake (along with my father), was thrown out of the house. My birthday was a failure. I would not be getting anything for turning five. I went outside, sat down behind our neighbor's garage, and cried.

In early afternoon, dad returned home. He acted like he felt ashamed. To my great surprise, dad brought with him my first two-wheel bike and a fancy cake with my name and birth date on it! My brother was given a scout knife. Even mom got a bouquet of flowers. We ended up in a group hug in the backyard. The day had turned out well. The rarest of events had just taken place.

The bike was a hand-me-down from my cousin, Sheila. It was a girl's bike, but I didn't care. My only transportation had been an old wagon used by dad when he was a child.

Dad put training wheels on the rear of the bike. I remember hopping on the "four-wheeler." I had never been so happy or excited! My glee must have been obvious as my mother started to cry. She gave my father a big kiss.

I was now the first five-year-old kid on our block to have his own bike. I quickly left our house and proudly rode up and down 51st Street. I couldn't believe how fast I could go! The bike even had a working brake! I was in seventh heaven!

That night I had five candles on my "second" cake. I blew them out, but my wish had already come true. I pleaded with my parents to allow me to take my bike up to our bedroom. I wanted it next to me as I tried to get to sleep. Mom and dad consented. Butch and I hauled the bike up the stairs to our room.

Before I got into bed that evening, I polished all the metal parts of the bike and even cleaned the tires. Both of our parents came to kiss us good night, an unusual event for us. I remember telling my father he was the best dad in the whole world.

My happiness was short-lived. A few days after my birthday, my brother began chanting the refrain, "Fun no more in September 44. Lulu's going to get you-you!"

First day of school, 1944

It was time for me to enter kindergarten at Irving Grade School. Unfortunately, starting school was also time for me to meet Miss Carr, the teacher who hated little kids and, on occasion, would eat one. Butch also told me that Miss Carr lived alone in the Prescott House, a haunted mansion on 54th street. He said Miss Carr was a real witch who flew back and forth to school on a broomstick. I did not want to go to school.

I vividly remember that first Monday morning of September 1944. Home had been my safe play retreat. My haven was about to be disrupted and, once more, fear overtook me. I was too nervous to eat breakfast. I felt sick to my stomach. Putting on my "school clothes" felt awkward. My attire consisted of overalls and shoes once worn by my brother. The secondhand outfit I was forced to wear made me feel I was in shackles, dressed for prison. My feet were uncomfortable wearing my "new" shoes. I had spent the entire summer barefooted.

My brother continued talking about the evil Miss Carr. He said that she had a long wooden switch used for slapping a student's hands! Sometimes, Butch claimed, Miss Carr would yank you by your ear into the cloakroom, pull down your pants, and spank you on your bare butt. Butch added that if you failed to correctly answer a question, Miss Carr put a dunce hat on your head and made you sit in a corner facing the wall. Many times, for no reason, students were chained to their desks and not allowed to go to recess.

I believed what Butch was saying. After all, he had recently been in Miss Carr's class. The memories were fresh in his mind. He was trying to forewarn me. His information left me almost to the point of fainting. I was biting my nails right down to the half-moons.

In the previous days leading up to my forced exodus from the safety of home, mom again tried to ease my fears by repeating that kindergarten was a place to have fun. She assured me I would be involved in a lot of exciting games, outdoor recesses, that I would learn to read, and meet many other kids my age.

Being very shy and afraid of meeting new people, the thought of making new friends and playing with them was frightening. Butch and mom were trying to help me prepare for Irving Grade School. To me, what they were saying made me want to run away from home.

On that first day, mom took our picture by the tree in the front of our house. It was time to leave for Irving. (My face in the photograph wore the expression of doom).

I bawled my eyes out as Butch and I walked the four blocks to school with mom. With each step, I was convinced I was shortening the distance to my executioner.

Irving Grade School was an imposing structure. Built at the end of the nineteenth century, the building was a huge, block long, three-story structure constructed from stone, concrete, and wood. The entrance doors were enormous. And inside, the floors were freshly varnished and, because of their age, had become warped. When I walked on them they squeaked. The strange odor and noises of the place scared the living hell out of me!

I had never been in such a large building. If only my parents would let me stay in my bedroom, I would do my best to be the perfect Finlander. I would brush and grunt every hour on the hour!

Mom literally had to drag me up the school steps and down the long hallway to the kindergarten room! When we arrived at Miss Carr's door, I stopped crying. Being so self-conscious, I didn't want other kids to see me bawling and making a spectacle of myself. Miss Carr met us at the door. Mom introduced herself and told Miss Carr that my name was Tracy.

Miss Carr smiled and stated that until today she had never met anyone with the first name of Tracy. She said something like: "I'm sure you are as unique in personality as you are in name." I interpreted her observation to mean that I was going to be punished for having such a stupid name. I began to whimper.

Quickly, Miss Carr saw that I was about to burst into tears. She gently took my hand, leaned down, and gave me a hug.

"You'll love it here, Tracy," she promised. "There is absolutely no reason to be scared."

As she waved goodbye to mom, Miss Carr added: "You are one of my new little friends and I am truly honored to meet and get to know you."

Miss Carr didn't act like a witch. But I thought she was just being nice in front of mom to create a good impression. I felt abandoned. How could mom desert me in my worst moment?

After I entered the strange and very large classroom, my feeling of abandonment was replaced by a sense of awkwardness and stupidity. I was now in a foreign land and everyone was looking at me. I remember being led to a long table where I was placed in a chair between two other boys. The fellow on my left was named Harley Gellatly, and, to my right, Dan Carich. (Ironically, we would become fast friends and eventually graduate together from the same high school).

Our name tags were placed in front of us on the table. Miss Carr went around the room and introduced each student by loudly calling out their first name. As she read my name, titters came from some of the students. It was the beginning of my being called "Dick Tracy" for the next thirteen years. I had been branded with the title of a comic strip character, only reinforcing my shyness.

We spent the morning putting wooden puzzles together (which I enjoyed), drawing a picture of our favorite animal, being shown where the washrooms were, and hearing a story read by Miss Carr. During story reading time, I glanced to the right of Miss Carr. Against the wall, was a large straw broom. I immediately concluded that it was her mode of transportation and my brother was right! Miss Carr was a witch! All my fears came surging back! When would she get me?

It was a tradition at Irving to have lunch at school on the first day of class. Normally, all students walked home for lunch. (With neighborhood schools being the norm, busing was rare.)

We had milk with our lunch. I hated milk. Our mother would always serve it at meals long before we sat down to eat. When I eventually drank the stuff, I'd squeeze my nose to avoid the warm, sour taste. Invariably, I was on the verge of retching trying to gulp the white poison. In my mind (and stomach), the only way to drink milk was to almost freeze it and blend the miserable liquid with Bosco or Ovaltine.

I somehow managed to down the half pint of milk at kindergarten lunch. I knew that if I did not drink the concoction or puked it back up, I would find myself in the cloakroom with Miss Carr and her switch!

After lunch was over, Miss Carr told us to line up. We were having our group picture taken outside on the front steps of the school. Then we were going to the gym for some exercise games.

As we were forming a line, I started to feel "it." In my haste and fear while preparing for school, I neglected a very important morning ritual. I HAD FORGOTTEN TO TAKE A GRUNT! I now had to do a number two! Never had I done a number two in a foreign toilet, much less a large public washroom. I certainly wasn't about to interrupt Miss Carr as we walked down the creaky hallways. I could not run up to an adult that I feared, and didn't know, in front of strange kids, and request halting the picture taking for a while so I could shit!

I was self-conscious about urinating and defecating, which to me was a private, almost embarrassing act. I tried to pee into our toilet without making a sound by avoiding a direct stream into the water. Doing a number two was always performed quickly with assistance from our handy Air-Wick dispenser. Grunting in a public toilet with my teacher and classmates waiting impatiently outside, within hearing range, was unimaginable.

My stomach started to ache as my need to release my bowels increased. When we sat before the camera, I bent forward to relieve some of the pain. Consequently, my face was barely visible as Principal Becker snapped the picture.

As the class headed downstairs to the gym, I knew I had lost the battle of delaying my bowel movement. I took the only available action for a neurotically frightened and abandoned five-year-old boy. I tried to relieve the pressure by farting. I shit in my pants instead. It wasn't a big, juicy production, thank God. My grunt was in agate form, rather like enlarged milk duds. With each step, a fecal pebble dropped into my shorts. Four of them were now confined in my skivvies. None of my classmates seemed to know what I had just done. With no obvious odor to give me away, I guess I had some "shit luck."

My luck continued when the pebbles lodged snugly on the underside of my testicles. If I didn't walk with a long stride, or jump or run, I was confident that the nuggets weren't going anywhere. It did prove difficult, however, to maneuver down the stairs to the gym. The downward stride dislodged one of the pebbles, and it dropped out of my shorts. It proceeded to roll down my right pant leg and ended up on a step. I was mortified and terror-stricken! What if one of the kids step on the little brown orb?! What if they discover it was me who was responsible for the now visible turd!? I would be labeled for the rest of my school years! I could tolerate "Dick Tracy," but epitaphs like "shit-for-brains," "stinky," or "shitty" were beyond acceptance!

My shit luck was extended once again when the pebble rolled to a stop in the corner of a stair. No one saw it, much less step on it. God was on my side. Ultimately, however, I was sure the janitor would be displeased by the anonymous deposit.

I was praying I could avoid dropping the remaining three stools when my luck ran out. Miss Carr joyfully announced we would have a racing contest in the gym. GREAT! I became convinced there was no loving God in Heaven.

I imagined the remaining poop pebbles distributed all over the gym floor. I became pale from anxiety! If Miss Carr discovered that I had shit my pants, I probably would be chained to my chair or forced to wear a dunce hat. For the first time in my life, overcoming my shyness and fear, I meekly approached Miss Carr. I quietly told her that I had a chest cold and was not supposed to run. She accepted my lie and told me to go sit on one of the benches lining the gym walls.

I was saved! My shitting-in-my-pants-on-the-opening-day-of-school act would forever remain a secret! I immediately calmed down and started to breathe normally. I cautiously sat on the edge of the bench so as not to squash the pebbles that were still in my shorts. I even gained enough confidence to scan the gym. The room was unusual in that it had four large padded poles in the middle of the floor. I guess they were support beams but it made it difficult to play a game with those huge structures in the way. Many of the kids ran into them and fell to the floor. I remember feeling a little jealous that I could not show off my skill at running. I was quite fast for my age, or so I thought. But in my present condition, I decided it best to remain seated.

The class stayed in the gym until the final school bell rang at 3:26p.m. My prison sentence was over. We were to leave for home through the basement door of the gym. Miss Carr handed each exiting student their drawing of an animal picture to take home. I made sure I was the last kid to leave. I did not want any of my classmates see me walk as though I had shit in my pants, even though I did have shit in my pants.

Miss Carr gave me my drawing and said she looked forward to seeing me tomorrow. I thought to myself that by tomorrow, I would be hiding somewhere far from Irving Grade School. I was not coming back to this awful place!

Walking cautiously, with my eyes squinted (I reasoned that tightening my eyelids would assist me in holding the pebbles within my shorts), I met my brother. Butch was waiting for me, per mom's command, at the corner of 56th Avenue West and Nicollet Street, next to the school. She had given him strict instructions to always walk me home—a duty I know he despised.

"Well, young brother," Butch arrogantly greeted me. "How was your first day in the witch's class? Any ass whippings yet? It's only a matter of time, ya know, before your rear end gets it." I did not care for his snotty attitude. He hoped I had experienced a bad day!

Butch was acting so superior. "I have Miss Riddle," he boasted. "She is really nice. I'm going to love my class. Today she gave us candy after lunch and we went for a walk down to Irving field. We had our picture taken in front of the warming house. What a fun day it was."

With his cocky grin on his face, Butch took notice of my adjusted gait as I walked with him. Mockingly, he asked, "Why are you walking like you have shit in your pants?"

"Because I have shit in my pants," I responded, on the verge of tears.

Butch's face lit up like a new light bulb. His eyes were as big as baseballs.

"You did ca-ca in your drawers?!" My brother never seemed happier. "I don't believe it! Where did you do it? What did you do with the ca-ca? What did Miss Carr say? How did the students react? I bet they laughed, didn't they?"

Butch couldn't have been more thrilled as he anxiously awaited my answers to his many questions. I had made his day. He was adding to the destruction of mine.

I started crying. I told him how "it" happened, most of the remnants were still in my shorts, a piece was left on the basement stairs leading to the gym, and neither Miss Carr nor any of my classmates knew about my accident.

"I'm never going back to school," I vowed! "I'm running away from home."

"No, you little idiot," Butch responded emphatically! "Just take a crap at home before you leave for school. Anyway, if you run away from home, where will you crap then? Do you want to shit in a dumpster, someone's flower pot or, more likely, again right in your shorts?"

The entire time he was providing me with his "wisdom," Butch was laughing as hard as I had ever seen him laugh. He pissed me off. Worse yet, I pissed myself off. I was doubly pissed off.

I remember beginning to suspect the truth behind my brother's horror stories about Miss Carr and his false concern for my welfare. I think he enjoyed seeing me suffer and was playing me for a dumb ass.

"Come on, shit pants," my brother directed. "I know a place where you can empty your drawers and not be seen."

Butch took me to a bushy area bordering Central Avenue. On a path that wove through the bushes, I took off my shoes and pants, and carefully, removed my shorts. I wrapped the shorts around the shit pebbles. While I wiped my ass with the animal drawing, my fingers poked through the thin paper. Now my right hand smelled like shit. My first drawing at school, solely intended to be brought home so that my parents could brag about it, was lying crumbled on the ground, next to my shorts--both items full of my "pebbles."

At home, after telling my mother what happened to me, she softly advised me not to worry about it as "those things just happen." She made me feel a little better, but I was worried what dad would say.

Dad got home and, before asking his daily question concerning brushing and grunting, my brother rushed to greet him and proudly reported he had brushed his teeth for five minutes that morning and grunted quite well. He then happily informed dad that I crapped in my pants on my first day at school. Butch revealed that I had wrapped my "dump" in my shorts. Furthermore, he related I had cleaned my rear end with my first school drawing and left the shitty mess outdoors in a bushy grove near Irving.

As expected, dad lectured me on the need to be ready so such incidents never happen. He also criticized Butch for being a tattletale. (Butch could never get on dad's good side.)

Turning back to me, he said: "*Sisu*, son. Sisu! Being prepared is being smart. Accidents are the downfall of the weak and the shortsighted. In fact,

I don't believe in accidents. Accidents are just a name for poor planning and bad judgment. Tracy, you stupidly neglected to grunt at home before you left for school. Unless you are a big baby or retarded, there is no excuse for what happened today. At the very least, you should have told your teacher you had to go. That's why they have washrooms in schools."

In a very stern voice, dad added, "Tracy, I am very disappointed in you. A person with *sisu* thinks and plans. You are not some lower form of animal that grunts in public. This will never happen again! Do you understand!? Never again! Do not embarrass yourself and the family! I will not allow it!"

At that moment, I was ashamed of myself.

I was denied supper and had to stay in my room. (It was the only time such punishment ever happened to me). My parents spent the evening arguing about the "incident." Mom ended up being slapped by dad, abruptly ending the argument. I felt lonely and ever so guilty. I had let my parents down and mom was hurt because of me. It was the worst day of my young life.

I never shit in my pants again. But I secretly fantasized about leaving a pebble of crap in my brother's breakfast cereal some future morning while he was busy preparing for school.

Butch began to piss me off. I slowly realized that he wasn't protecting me with his false words of wisdom and artificial acts of selflessness. Rather, Butch was setting me up for unnecessary worry and pain. I began to have a growing distrust of his motives.

Miss Carr turned out to be a wonderful lady. Kindergarten became fun, exciting, and instructive. She was a kind, patient, and extremely understanding teacher. Except for the first tragic day, I treasured every moment of my kindergarten experience.

I loved Miss Lulu Carr.

Barefooted brothers, 1944

Mom's Drinking

AFTER I STARTED SCHOOL AT Irving, mom changed. She began to drink, and drink a lot. I didn't understand why this was happening, but I surely knew Butch and I were being treated differently. Mom didn't play much with us anymore. She was tense like dad. Mom often was critical and intolerant toward Butch and me. My brother said he didn't feel as close to mom as he once did.

Mom's drinking reduced the tension between mom and dad. Dad now had a domestic drinking partner. They drank together when he came home at night. Every Sunday, they were tipsy most of the day. They had fewer arguments, and dad stopped hitting mom. But the change between our parents didn't make Butch and me happy. Mom was now ignoring us like our dad did.

Mom also started drinking with other men at a tavern on Raleigh Street. When she went to the bar (usually on a Saturday afternoon when dad was working), mom brought Butch and me. We drank sodas and ate popcorn while mom flirted and often got drunk. Usually some man would drive us home in the late afternoon and mom would go to bed.

On many Friday nights, mom would take us to the West Theater where dad worked. Butch and I would be seated in the front row of the theater while she sat in the enclosed smoking room with one of our parents' male friends. But the men were more than friends, and their meeting was prearranged. Mom's lipstick was often smeared when she came to our seats after the show was over. I could smell alcohol on her breath. Mom seemed so different. Butch said mom was suffering "because of dad." I didn't understand what Butch was saying. But I knew I was suffering.

Sometimes, Butch had to take charge of our getting ready for school because mom was in bed with a hangover. Mom became impatient. During the week, at lunch breaks, she would often yell at us to "hurry up and eat your food!" Mom was also unpredictable. Her moods changed throughout the day. She would be curt with us in the morning or at lunch. When Butch and I returned home from school in the afternoon, mom would hug us and act just the opposite of her behavior earlier that day. And she usually smelled of alcohol. Following supper, mom changed and seemed to not want to be around us. Butch and I brushed our teeth and went to bed by ourselves. When dad returned home from his night job, our parents would drink and mom became happy again. Sometimes, she would wake us up to give Butch and me a kiss. Always, mom once again smelled of alcohol.

On Sundays, when mom and dad drank the most, they often promised to take us on a fun-filled trip the following Sunday. A walk to the zoo, a picnic at Jay Cooke State Park using a neighbor's car, a bus to Canal Park to watch iron ore boats entering and exiting St. Louis Bay—these pledges were exiting to anticipate throughout the week. When the next Sunday arrived, our parents always had an excuse not to go on the excursion. For a while, we accepted the cancellations. There was always next week, our parents assured us. Eventually, however, Butch and I ignored the alleged plans being guaranteed for the following week. The promises were never fulfilled. They were made and cancelled in an inebriated state. We never went anywhere.

I remember feeling that mom and dad no longer liked Butch and me. They couldn't have fun with us. Butch told me dad was going to pay a person to kill us because we were "in the way." Even though he didn't believe what he was saying, the comment did frighten me. I started to have bad dreams about someone intent on murdering us. I began leaving a hall light on to ward off potential murderers. Each night, before bedtime, I would check to see if the house doors and windows were locked. If I had a scary nightmare about an intruder, I would huddle in the corner of my bed, unable to sleep. Any unexplained sound would panic me. Was the killer in my room?! Was I about to die? I began to have a sense of impending doom—and I was only in kindergarten.

I couldn't explain my fear of being abandoned (and even murdered) to mom or dad. They were the source of my fears! Mom and dad were becoming absentee parents. They enjoyed partying and tavern life, hardly positive domains for rearing children. Butch and I were no longer a high priority on our parents' list of desired activities. We had to tolerate broken promises, cancelled trips, and being alone.

It wasn't fun to be around a drunk mom and dad. So, mom and dad often became "make-believe" parents, real to us only when they were sober and nurturing. My brother and I learned to reinvent our parents through fantasy. We "played out" the fantasies in our bedroom. We not only went to the zoo with mom and dad, and saw the animals, we also fed and petted many of them. Our mythical picnics with our parents lasted for days, camping in a park and sleeping in tents! Our many fantasies were "real" and served as shields against constant disappointment.

The fantasies about mom and dad subsided after a few months. Butch and I escaped into other endeavors. My brother began to read everything he could get his hands on. He took up sculpture and painting. I invented fictional characters who were kind and trusting. I made believe I had a dog named Corky. The two of us helped nice people who were experiencing trouble. I was never lonely or disappointed in the company of my dog and the people we mythically assisted. They were my friends and I never let them down. Corky and I saved a child from drowning, rescued a couple from their burning house, located a man in the woods who was lost, and accomplished countless other good deeds. We were loved by the people we aided and viewed as heroes by our neighbors. My daydreaming served as a treasured coping mechanism in dealing with mom and dad's neglect.

President Roosevelt and Sonny

MISS CARR TOLD MY MOTHER that I was an "extreme" daydreamer and had a habit of talking to myself. I, of course, was merely participating in a skit with my imaginary buddies. At home, mom pleaded with me to begin concentrating on school topics and stop playing with my fictitious friends. She said I must be going through a "stage."

Mom was always placing Butch and me into these supposed stages. To her, the accusation meant we were undisciplined or immature. Often, if we misbehaved, such as doing fart contests, she would explain it away as a ridiculous, but thankfully, short-lived "stage."

On the other hand, when Butch or I did something positive, and mom was sober and not "hung over," she was usually loving in her praise, asserting "good" stages last a lifetime.

Dad always gave us an abbreviated *sisu* sermon when we misbehaved. He rarely bestowed credit for any accomplishment. Dad felt compliments diluted the competitive spirit.

"Work for the sake of self-betterment," he would say. "Don't do something looking for praise! If you do, you'll only lower your standards and become a people pleaser!"

Dad religiously stuck to that credo. Dad felt Roosevelt's New Deal was killing the pride of industry and workmanship. The social welfare handouts being given to the poor people rewarded laziness. Dad predicted if Butch and I followed his dictates, we were destined to succeed. Compliments were for sissies. He'd be damned if he was going to rear his boys as crybabies seeking useless affection for every little thing they did. Dad was adamant that rational, consistent discipline builds character.

Mom loved President Roosevelt. She said he was trying to help the underdog. I think mom looked upon him as the father figure she never had and a hero who guided the country through some very hard times. After all, he had led America out of the Great Depression and through World War II.

Our mother said President Roosevelt spoke plainly and honestly to the public in his "fireside chats."

"His voice is comforting," mom said. "President Roosevelt especially loves the poor people of the United States. He assured us we will get through the tough times because of the American spirit. Before you were born, he gave a wonderful speech in which he said: 'The only thing we have to fear is fear itself.'" (I was confused as to what mom was saying. I feared most everything.)

Mom said President Roosevelt was telling Americans to be courageous in facing the country's problems.

I remember the day, in April 1945, when President Roosevelt died. I was playing alone in the backyard. Mom came out of our house in tears and told me of his death.

Many neighbors put black blankets or cloths in their front windows as a sign of respect and mourning for President Roosevelt. Miss Carr had us say a group prayer for him. The school flag was placed at half-mast. Our kindergarten class sent a sympathy card to Mrs. Roosevelt with our names on it. Miss Carr cried as she signed the card. It seemed everyone was saddened over the President's death, except dad. I remember him saying, "Finally, the king is dead." For some time, I thought Roosevelt was both our President and king.

The passing of President Roosevelt was tempered somewhat because Adolph Hitler's death was reported on the radio a few days later. Our mother told us Germany would soon give in. (The Germans surrendered on May 8, 1945. The date would be called V-E Day, or Victory in Europe). Everyone seemed so happy and relieved.

Dad was more reserved over the news because, as he said: "We still have to wipe out those damn Japs and get your Uncle Bob home in one piece." Uncle

Bob was serving in the Pacific. Butch told me that was where all the Japs were hiding.

There was another unexpected death that shocked everyone in our family and neighborhood. Sonny, the youngest son of the Daniels,' was killed in France during the last days of the war. One Sunday, the Daniels' came to tell our parents about the loss of their youngest boy. Mrs. Daniels clutched a crumbled telegram in her hand, informing them of Sonny's death. I remember hoping if Mrs. Daniels squeezed the telegram harder, Sonny might somehow come home alive.

It was the first time I could "feel" the war. Sonny's death was literally so close to home. I was sad for Mr. and Mrs. Daniels. What could I do to make things better for them? I had no answer. We all stood in our living room, clutched together, crying like babies. I had never witnessed my father cry before that day. Mom and dad got very drunk and wept into the evening.

After that day, Mrs. Daniels disappeared. Butch said she had a nervous breakdown and was confined indoors. On several occasions, through the flimsy common wall of our adjoining duplex, I could hear Mrs. Daniels screaming and sobbing. Sometimes mom turned up the volume on the radio when Mrs. Daniels cried to drown out her sorrow. Mom also attempted to "soften" Sonny's death by telling us of the five Sullivan brothers who had all died in 1942 when their ship, the USS Juneau, was destroyed. But the story made me feel worse.

Sonny was buried in France. My mother said he died for our country and was a hero. Mom said because of Sonny's death, Mrs. Daniels would become a "Gold Star Mother," which was a very great honor in America. A lot of our neighbors already had blue stars in their windows signifying a family member was serving in the Armed Forces. But I had never heard of a gold star. To me, a gold star could never adequately replace the loss of Sonny.

Mother told me that when I was a baby, Sonny would push me in my stroller on the sidewalks of our street. As I got a little older, I vaguely remember having snowball fights with him. He also built a snow fort for my brother and me. Mom said Sonny and his older brother volunteered for the service and felt honored to have the chance to fight for our country. Service was one thing I could understand, but death, and burial, in a foreign land? His parents would never see their youngest son again! I hoped the French people would take good care of his grave. I hated the Nazis for killing Sonny.

But most of all, I hated God. He had ignored my nightly prayers for the safety of the Daniels' boys. Our mother said Sonny had recently been engaged to a girl who had just graduated from nearby Denfeld High School. Sonny was only nineteen years old! How could God be so cruel? And why did He kill all the Sullivan brothers?

I couldn't understand people loving and worshipping God. God let so many people die, and at such a young age. God was mean and uncaring. God was more like the Japs and the Nazis!

Miss Benson in Sickness and Very Little Health

⚭

IN SEPTEMBER L945, I WAS in the first grade. In grades 1 through 6, a student sat at a wooden desk and attached seat. The top of the desk could be opened to provide storage space for books and papers. Each desk top had a rounded slot for pencils and pens. The desks were neatly lined up in rows.

I loved my desk with its fresh varnish smell. It had a glass inkwell with a spring-loaded cover. Once or twice a week, the school janitor would come to our room with a giant pitcher of ink and fill each well. We were only allowed to use our ink wells on certain assignments. Each student had an ink pen embossed with Irving Grade School. We used our pen to write the alphabet and print certain words. We also received a writing tablet with pictures of other schools on its front cover. I enjoyed the smell of the ink and the scratchy sound my pen made on the tablet paper.

World War II had just ended. Something called a nuclear bomb had defeated the Japs. Miss Benson, our teacher, began each day with the Pledge of Allegiance. We stood next to our desk and faced the American flag. Miss Benson reminded us to place our right hand over our hearts. We then had a moment of silence for those who had fought in the war.

During that brief quiet, I was thankful that my Uncle Bob had returned home safely. The Japanese had surrendered on August 14, 1945. The victory became known as V-J Day or V-P Day, Victory in Japan or Victory in the Pacific). I also reflected on Sonny Daniels, buried in a grave across the ocean. I remember the gratitude I felt for each of them. Sonny sacrificed his life so that mine would be safer. At age six, I was proud to be an American.

In kindergarten, we sat on moveable chairs and the floor. We could talk and walk just about when we wanted to. In Miss Benson's class (and the next five grades to come), the wisdom and authority of the teacher was the primary emphasis. Discipline, decorum, and staying in your seat came next. Silence was a virtue, symbolizing respect and good citizenship. I adapted well to this structured environment.

I craved adult discipline. I viewed my teacher as my school parents who controlled me for my own good. Strict and consistent rules and regulations at Irving gave me comfort. These basics were lacking at home where nurturing was often inconsistent. Right could be wrong and wrong could be right depending on parental moods.

My experience in the first grade, sadly, was spotty and unsatisfactory due to a series of illnesses. While Miss Benson was a wonderful teacher and person, I was ill much of the time. In the school year 1945-46, I contracted the chicken pox, mumps, and measles. My brother came down with the same diseases. Our house, and in some cases, our neighborhood, was "quarantined" by the city health department. A quarantine sign was stapled on our front door warning all visitors to stay away. I also had colds, including a bout of pneumonia, as well as the flu.

Initially, dad was impatient with our sicknesses. While he was generally concerned for our health, he told us we were letting our guard down. Butch and I were not adhering to the core principles of *sisu*. Dad's bedside manner was abrupt and rarely sympathetic. "Real men just don't get sick," he'd say. Mom stayed sober while we were sick. She must have wanted to keep a responsible watchful eye on us.

With every cold came the mandatory Vicks Vapor Rub on-the-chest treatment, together with a tablespoon of the greasy medicine. Sometimes, mom would have me suck on a vile tasting medicinal licorice stick for days at a time.

I spent almost as much time in my bedroom as in the classroom. Our family physician, Dr. Bakkila, made numerous house calls. At one point, my weight decreased to around 35 pounds and I was being considered for a stay in the hospital. I was weak from dehydration and had no appetite.

My brother was just as sick. I remember him vomiting every day for what seemed like weeks. As time passed, dad became seriously concerned about our health. He eased off his repeated mention of references to the magical principles of *sisu*. I guess he realized one, or both of us, might die. He had lost his oldest sister, Mildred, to influenza when she was a child, and nearly lost his brother, Robert, to the same disease. Luckily, my brother and I eventually recovered and got through that awful year.

Because I was home for much of the school year, I indulged in my imaginary play. The preoccupation with fantasy again seeped over into my classroom. When I finally returned to school, Miss Benson (like Miss Carr) was concerned about my conversations with myself. I'm sure she thought I was delirious from the illnesses.

Miss Benson was a very caring lady. She would send home class assignments with our neighbor, Jerry Hagberg. She often called me on the phone to see if I had any questions or difficulties with the work. When my brother was quarantined with me, both Miss Benson and Miss Nelson (my brother's fourth grade teacher), drove to our house and left us assignments and graded work in our mailbox. Once or twice a week, they would drop by and pick up our finished papers.

Miss Benson and Miss Nelson were like so many of the grade school teachers of the 1940's. They were dedicated to the mental, physical, and spiritual health of their students. School work and the motivation to learn became easier when you had teachers that loved you and, in turn, you loved back.

On the last day of school, my mother gave my brother and me each a box of chocolates and a thank you card to bring to Miss Benson and Miss Nelson. As I recall, they received a lot of gifts on that day.

Teachers as Parents

After the war was over, many parents divorced. Homes were "broken." Teachers became substitute parents and sacrificed much of their personal life assisting affected children. Their perseverance and wisdom sent a message of hope to kids. To borrow a phrase from a previous world war, they kept "the home fires burning." I doubt such devotion would have been possible without the existence of neighborhood schools.

Nabisco (And The Art of the Fart)

CHERYL LAIRD WAS HER REAL name. Dan Carich, a classmate of mine in Miss Abrahamson's second grade class, nicknamed her Nabisco, because she smelled like stale crackers. He originally called her "Cheryl the barrel," as she was the fattest girl in the class. In fact, Cheryl was the fattest girl at Irving Grade School. She also had large gums and tiny nubs for teeth. Her front teeth were so widely spaced that I often wondered if it would be possible to insert a wooden ruler between the gaps of her little choppers.

Any extremely overweight girl, clearly an exception in postwar America, was subjected to the cruel attitudes of pre-adolescent boys dictating that such females had no right to associate with boys. Simply put, feminine body type determined male acceptability. To be a chubby girl was the subject of male ridicule and avoidance.

Chubby girls had no right to a pleasing personality. They were generally ignored by all the boys in class (and by most of the girls). The only kids who were friends with fat girls were other fat girls. Any boy associating with a fat girl was called a "queer." As a "queer," you became the butt of jokes by your male buddies.

Sadly, I wore the "queer" crown briefly in the second grade, the result of forced interaction with Nabisco.

At Irving Grade School in 1946, the curriculum required a year-long unit of square dancing, which meant talking to and touching girls. I had no girls as friends. I was completely ignorant of the opposite sex. I was okay around my cousin, Sheila, because she was a tomboy. With my Uncle Bob's daughters, Bobbi and Carol, I was a mute. Girls were a mystery. I was afraid of them.

Every Friday morning at 9:00am, we were paraded to a basement room by Miss Abrahamson. I was nervous, in fear of vomiting my breakfast. Boys were lined up at one end of the room, girls at the other. Luck would have it (bad luck in my case), there were ten boys and ten girls. It was impossible to be excluded from having a dance partner.

As an early lesson in gentlemanly decorum, each boy was instructed to walk over to a girl and politely ask if they would be their partners for the dance session. Every boy was trained to say: "May I have the honor of being your partner this morning?" Each girl was instructed to curtsy to their boy partner and reply: "I would be most honored."

Because I was the shyest kid in North America, I always ended up with Nabisco as my partner. (What choice did I have? All the other boys broke indoor speed records running directly to any girl except Nabisco)!

Nabisco would attempt to perform the ritualized curtsy by bending her bulbous knees as she spread the bottom hems of her large skirt. She then would loudly mutter, " I would be most honored, Stacey." Nabisco always called me Stacey. Never once did she get my name right.

Nabisco perspired. Her hands would get clammy. Each time I grabbed them to parade around the room, it felt like I was holding a piece of raw bacon. The only thing we had in common was that we both chewed our fingernails, not exactly a desirable bond of endearment.

The sashay was the worst of the struts. We sidestepped in a circle around each other and then I would move behind Nabisco. It was embarrassing dancing with a girl who was twice my height and certainly triple my weight. I felt (and looked) like a paper kite being pulled by a barge on a windy day.

The hour we spent dutifully following the dance instructions recorded by a whiney cowboy was the most miserable hour of the week. When the charade was finally over, we returned single file to our classroom. On the way, I would desperately rub my hands on the sides of my trousers to eliminate the remnants of Nabisco's cold hand sweat. I knew my buddies were going to be teasing me for smelling like stale crackers.

The myth developed that Cheryl loved Crisco, a shortening used in cooking. Being her reluctant but ever faithful dance partner, my buddies soon labeled me "the Crisco kid." I was now a "queer."

Nabisco missed school on the second to last Friday of the school year in 1947. A male classmate was also absent. I would now have at least one opportunity to ask a "safe" girl to be my dance partner. I gleefully settled on Jeannette Pollard, whose older brother, Virgil, was a close friend of Butch. Jeannette was as light as a feather. She smelled like Ivory soap, and her hands were not clammy. I now had some control as to where I was going on the dance floor. No longer would I be flung around by a girl heavier than my mother!

My happiness was short-lived. Ten minutes into the session the school fire alarm sounded. It was a fire drill! Square dancing was over as we sped out of the building. It was kismet. God was punishing me for my dislike of Him.

God never seemed to come to my aid. During the school year, I prayed He would make me sick on a Friday, or create a record-breaking snowstorm, thus closing the school. I prayed for my dental and doctor appointments to fall on Friday. None of my pleadings was ever met. Zippo. Not once did God make me sick on Friday nor was school ever cancelled that day. All my medical appointments were scheduled for Saturday mornings—the most treasured time of the week!

On the last Friday morning of the second grade, God apparently had compassion for my suffering.

We were all in the dance room and, as usual, I found myself requesting Nabisco to be my dance partner. Complying with custom, Nabisco attempted to curtsy and in the process of bending her legs, she let out a loud fart that sounded "wet." Instantly the room quieted, everyone mesmerized. The stench that soon arose was an odiferous admixture of, and I'm only guessing, something that smelled of burnt cabbage, fried onions, and baked beans. It was a magnificent rectal gem that could simultaneously peel paint off the walls while stinging your eyes. Students instinctively held their noses in the attempt to shield themselves from the rank odor. A few classmates began to wretch.

To make matters worse, a trickle of diarrhea was running down the inside of Nabisco's leg. A pool of watery, brownish stool formed on the dance floor.

Nabisco stood frozen in shock as the fecal stream gained in volume and intensity. Poor Nabisco was soon standing in a small lake of wet shit. She had her eyes closed, tears streaming down her face, and her head was pointed toward the ceiling. Miss Abrahamson began to clear the room. We needed no coaxing to leave, Kids were running over one another to evacuate the smelly scene. As we exited, Miss Abrahamson repeated the apologetic mantra: "Accidents do happen, children. Accidents do happen, children."

The vile vapors trailed off as we nearly galloped to our odor-free classroom. I felt awful for Nabisco. She was not a bad person. But never would she be able to "live down" this crapping episode. A life of ridicule was facing her.

We never saw Nabisco again. She was sent home with the flu, remaining there during the last three days of classes. Miss Abrahamson had the class sign a "hope you are feeling better" card and sent it to her. Dan wanted to write something like "you're a good shit, Cheryl," but thought the better of it.

Nabisco and her family moved to Two Harbors that summer. She was the first girl I ever heard let a fart. It became a historical moment in my young life. Until that event, I had assumed girls never "passed air."

In absentia, Cheryl became a folk heroine. Witnesses to the actual happening claimed they deserved a badge of bravery. Many classmates bragged they were at the square dance room on that fateful morning in 1947. In the ensuing years, when an embarrassing situation would occur, such as a loud burp in the library, or an unintentional fart during class, often, someone would recall Miss Abrahamson's apologetic phrase, and explain away the incident by saying: "Accidents do happen, children. Accidents do happen, children." Poor Nabisco.

THE ART OF THE FART

Most of my male buddies professed that farting was an admirable custom. The challenge was to deliver the methane bomb in a group and successfully escape detection and blame. The ideal place to fart was in a dark movie theater when two actors on the screen were about to kiss. And all my peers participated in impromptu farting contests at recess, at the ball field during the summer, or in the showers at the local Y.

The champ was Ron Hicks. He could fart at will, and his productions were always the loudest and most repulsive. Guys rarely would "let one go" in the presence of girls, but Ron never discriminated. I guess he was an early advocate of equal opportunity. He would even fart in class and then point a finger of accusation at some innocent sucker nearby him.

Early in the second grade, Ron asked Marcia Hinkle (who sat immediately behind him), to use her eraser. Marcia, who was easily the prettiest and most proper girl in our class, obliged by passing the item to Ron. When he was finished using the eraser, Ron turned to give it back to Marcia. In the exchange, Ron told Marcia the best way for him to say thank you was for her to pull his little finger. Marcia, as naive as she was pretty, pulled his pinky and Ron detonated one of the foulest farts in the history of Irving Grade School. Being stunned into embarrassment and consequent tears, Marcia reported to Miss Abrahamson what Ron had done. Miss Abrahamson already was aware of the act. Ron was told to write on the blackboard, fifty times, the phrase, "I will not disrupt class again. I will be a gentleman." We gave him the nickname of "swamp gas." Marcia wanted her seat moved away from Ron. Miss Abrahamson obliged.

Predictably, Ron failed to live up to his promise to be a gentleman (at least when it came to public farting). Just prior to the Christmas break, the class was quietly copying some math homework Miss Abrahamson was writing on the blackboard. Suddenly, the silence was broken by a loud sizzling squeal (like a bicycle tire being purposively deflated).

It was Ron's crown jewel. The subsequent odor from his fart was record-breaking in offensiveness. The class was aghast at Ron's repeat performance! Most of us quickly stood up and ran to the front of the classroom to distance ourselves from Ron.

Miss Abrahamson was livid. "Ronald," she screamed! "Get out of my room and report at once to Principal Becker! You will be whipped for this disgusting act!"

Even though it was a cold December day, Miss Abrahamson opened all the windows of our room.

Ron received a thrashing from Principal Becker and was not allowed in school until after Christmas vacation. When he returned, he apologized to the class. His days of public farting at school were over.

Competitive public farting was beyond my realm. I never passed air at school if I could help it. I was very cautious about not repeating my kindergarten performance in turning a fart into a dump. I did manage to have an attack of diarrhea once on the way home for lunch. I was "pardoned" by my father because I was coming down with the flu. I even vomited on the trip home that day.

If my "accident" ever happened again while I was in school, I would have killed myself to save my father the pleasure.

Irving Grade School

Dead Puppies and Scarface

~

IN SUMMER 1947, I TOOK my imaginary friends outdoors on good days. I built a neighborhood of dirt houses, roads, mountains, and tunnels in the hardscrabble between our house and back alley. At night, we continued to play in my bedroom.

I don't recall having any "real" friends come into our house during those early years. My brother and I never stayed overnight at a buddy's house. Friends yelled out your name at the back door without knocking. Butch and I did the same thing at friends' houses. The outdoors was our playground, even on coldest of winter days.

The area surrounding the nearby Diamond Match Factory was the best place to play. Butch and I, along with our usual playmates Harland Lund, Herbie Anderson, and Jerry Hagberg, hiked to the backside of the factory. The workers let us have all the matches we could carry. We lit matches for hours in a nearby gravel pit, child pyromaniacs keeping secrets from our parents. It was a miracle none of us ever got burned.

Sometimes we would gather for play in Harland's barn behind his house. We loved going there because Mrs. Lund was a such great cook. She always fed us something tasty. Her sugar cookies were my favorite. They were so big I had to use both hands to hold them.

Mr. and Mrs. Lund hosted a Fourth of July party each year for the families in the neighborhood. At sundown, Mr. Lund would set off an unbelievable display of fireworks in the big field behind their garage. Mrs. Lund supplied food as did some of the parents who came to witness the impressive show.

They also held a Halloween party for the kids living on 51st Street. The first time I went to the festival, unbeknownst to me, Mr. Lund was in costume. He dressed as a straw-covered scarecrow, standing motionless in his garden. As I approached the barn for the Halloween fun, Mr. Lund raised his right arm and saluted me. My heart stopped! I was startled and began to cry. I turned to go home, running into a clothes-line pole. My face was cut and bleeding.

Mr. Lund immediately apologized. He hugged me and put a bandage over my cut. He promised to never frighten me ever again. I felt better, but I would always hate garden scarecrows. Butch called me "scarface."

Mrs. Lund organized games in their barn. My favorite was dunking for apples in a tub of Kool-Aid while blindfolded. Dad bought two large pumpkins and carved faces into them. The "1947 editions" we took to the party ended up filled with candy.

A few days later, I saw two dogs stuck together on Mr. Lund's front yard. I had no idea why or how it happened. Mr. Lund told me I was watching a rare two-headed dog called a "push me-pull me." He said it would never leave home. I asked why? Mr. Lund said, "Tracy, just as soon as one end starts going east, the other end starts going west."

I really believed him. I had no idea the two canines were stuck together in the heat of intercourse. I knew nothing about sex.

Weeks later, while I was playing near the Lund's barn, I heard a splat-like sound inside the old building. I peeked through the front window and saw Mr. Lund throwing newborn puppies against the back wall. He was killing the puppies just as soon as they were born. Mr. Lund was pitching them like baseballs. I couldn't believe my eyes! Four or five puppies lay in a bloody clump on the floor of the barn. Mr. Lund was back scaring me again!

I ran home as fast as I could and tearfully told mom what I had just witnessed. Mom tried to console me but I couldn't get over the image of those puppies being flung to their deaths. It seemed so mean of Mr. Lund. Why didn't he just give the puppies away? Kids in my neighborhood would have jumped at the chance to have a dog. Now, the puppies were nothing but a bloody pile.

Later, at dinner, dad explained that killing animals was a common chore on farms. Mr. Lund was only being practical by eliminated the puppies. I refused to accept dad's reasoning. That night, in bed, I made believe the dead puppies awakened, ran away from that evil barn, and lived in my backyard. They became more make-believe friends. I now owned healthy and happy puppies that quickly became buddies with my older dog, Corky.

I never forgave Mr. Lund for his cruelty.

Another place to play was at the housing construction site for postwar veterans. A low cost wooden complex was being developed about two blocks from our house. After the workers left for the weekend, we would gather there.

One Sunday in 1947, I got a huge splinter in my ass sliding down an old board at the site. Dad, who was already mad about something, and a little tipsy, had to come and carry me home. He cussed all the way. I remember him saying that "you fucken kids aren't worth the tits on a boar pig!" When we got home, he quickly pulled out the splinter using a pair of pliers. Blood gushed everywhere, unfortunately including onto his new shirt and dress trousers.

Dad yelled "FUCK!" He went upstairs, changed his clothes and headed for the basement.

In the evening, when he came upstairs, he was drunk.

Early the next morning, dad reminded me that young people with *sisu* rarely get into accidents. He said that sliding down an old board was stupid. Dad commanded Butch and me to start "shaping up or we would face serious consequences." We made sure we took a "grunt" and brushed that day, reporting our eliminations and brushing as soon as dad arrived home from work. The news seemed to satisfy him.

Another favorite outdoor game was throwing pieces of glass at some windows of an abandoned building near the match factory. A small piece, tossed by Herbie Anderson, accidently hit me close to my right eye. I started bleeding. Jerry Hagberg began rushing me home. As we were running, I stepped on a broken bottle and lodged more glass into my left ankle. Now I was bleeding in two places.

Jerry picked me up and carried me the rest of the way. Mom was shocked! Her youngest son was a bloody mess.

Mom did not drive, so a neighbor took us to the hospital. My eye took two stitches and my leg required five. Mom called dad at work and he rushed home early to see how I was doing. His first words were something to the effect: "If you kids live to be fifteen, it will be a Christless miracle." Dad was not very mad. He was relieved I was okay, although very disappointed in my choice of outdoor games. Invariably, I received the "*Sisu* son, *sisu*" lecture. Every neighborhood kid now called me "scarface." I thought the nickname was cool. It certainly was better than "Crisco kid."

Another great place to play was at the New Duluth Laundry. (The employees at the cleaners never knew my dad was the man who had gone into a tirade over my bloody shirt a few years earlier.) We got to ride in the back of the truck on deliveries throughout West Duluth. I decided I wanted to be a laundry truck driver when I grew up.

We also had fun walking with our mailman, who made deliveries twice a day. Our mailman had suffered from shell shock in the first World War. He talked to himself while he was talking to you. We never made fun of his injury. Mom and dad told us to respect him for his sacrifice. He liked kids and it was fun to follow along with him as he delivered the mail. Sometimes he let us put mail in the boxes.

Everyone was so friendly to him, and he was always in a good mood. In the winter, he frequently was given hot chocolate or coffee, along with some sort of goodie during his rounds. He also received many envelopes containing money at Christmas as a form of "thank you." Even though he suffered from mental problems, our mailman must have loved his job and was treated accordingly. I also wanted to be a mailman when I grew up.

Playing in Mr. Daniels' 1936 Ford was a favorite place to spend time. Adults who owned a car rarely drove them. Walking or taking a bus was cheaper. Riding in a car was a special treat. Almost every car was black. The Daniels' car was special as it was a light blue, four-door, sedan. Mr. Daniels said it was alright to play in their car so long as we didn't touch the starter button or get the insides dirty. We would pretend that we were on long trips. Herbie, Harland, Jerry, Butch and I would take turns driving to mythical destinations. The interior of the car was immaculate and very "comfortable." Its seats were so soft. I once went to sleep while sitting in the backseat.

Very few people in the neighborhood had new cars. Cars were not made during the war years because steel was needed for the war machines. After the war, most people simply could not afford them.

In Spring 1947, dad bought his first car. It was a black 1936 Buick. The first day he brought the car home, I washed its wheels. I thought it was the most beautiful car in the neighborhood. I felt proud our father was its owner. Even though it was nearly eleven years old, the car smelled "new" inside. I quickly became convinced that Buicks were the best cars in the world. When I grew up, I would only drive Buicks.

Relatives

~⟋~

MOM AND DAD RARELY HAD visitors at home. With dad working long hours, and mom preoccupied with drinking, when we did have guests, they were relatives, the consequence of celebrating Christmas, a birthday, or going out to eat.

We would often go to the Peking Café. These outings were memorable events. It was an adventure to scan the menu with its foreign food names. I wasn't much of a reader so Butch read the menu to me. He pronounced words that made us laugh. (Dad did not share in our laughter.) Butch was so funny with his wording of "who flung dung," "flied lice" and "gum poop" soup. Something called a "poo poo" platter was renamed a "ca-ca" platter. Butch said he was going to get bugs and cat crap for dinner.

Butch wasn't making light of Chinese people. When the waiter asked him for his order, Butch never made fun of the food items on the menu.

Dad would down three or four drinks at the restaurant. (Mom no longer drank alcohol when Butch and I were present. She didn't drink in front of any of our relatives. It was the beginning of hiding her "indulgence.") Dad mocked the Chinese waiters. He was quite loud. Mom always got angry and reprimanded him for his rude behavior. The atmosphere at the table would become tense. Butch and I knew a "walking home" argument was developing. Every time we went to the Peking Cafe, the gathering started out fun-filled, ending with mom and dad fighting. Dad was jealous of Butch making us laugh. He wanted to be the center of attention.

One time in the summer 1947, we met Aunt Edith and her husband (our Uncle Ralph), at the Peking. Dad was already drunk when we got there. He became very loud and offensive. Dad took two chopsticks and inserted them in his mouth. The chopsticks served as his eye teeth. He began to talk gibberish Chinese.

When the waiter came to take our orders, dad continued to talk "Chinese" with the sticks in his mouth. Mom and Uncle Ralph told dad to stop. Dad responded by saying, "I only flucking around. Chink know he stupid." The waiter happened to be the owner of the Peking. We were told to leave. Everyone, except dad, was mortified.

Dad yelled that he was insulted to be mistreated by a "fucken Chink!" He wanted to punch the owner. Fortunately, Uncle Ralph talked him out of his drunken plan. Dad angrily took off in the direction of a nearby bar. After that incident, it was a rare for the family to dine out.

Grandma Kier was my favorite relative on mom's side of the family. She was a funny lady and reminded me of the actress, Spring Byington. Grandma Kier always announced her presence by opening our backdoor and yelling a phrase from a contemporary song: "It's just us chickens!"

Grandma Kier

Grandma had experienced a series of failed male "relationships" in her younger years. Perhaps because of that, she exhibited a wonderful perspective on living.

"I've led a life of lunacy," Grandma would say. "But I've had one helluva lot of fun in my mental illness!"

Grandma Kier treated us as loving grandchildren, not as devious "brats." There were always lots of hugs and inquiries about what "we were up to." Grandma said: "You 'chillens' will make mistakes, but they are tests. Mistakes make you wiser and stronger." In time, she said, you'll see them as humorous.

"Butch and Tracy, maybe I'm going to hell-in-a-handbasket for how I have lived," grandma declared, "but life should be enjoyed. Remember, have some fun while you're alive, because you are going to be dead for a very long time."

Each time, as she was leaving the house, Grandma Kier would grab us and secretly insert a Morgan silver dollar in the palm of one of our hands. Butch and I accumulated quite a collection of the heavy coins.

Grandma Kier often brought her father to our house. Great-Grandpa Reid was a crusty old retired railroad man in his mid-seventies. His principal preoccupation was now gardening, and he had become quite expert at growing vegetables and flowers.

Great-Grandpa Reid constantly drooled, and insisted on kissing Butch and me square on the lips when he greeted us. I remember cringing at this act of affection on his part. But he was an interesting man and mesmerized us with tales of his adventures.

Great-Grandpa Reid had met many famous people during his railroad days. We loved hearing his stories. He had talked to Buffalo Bill and Annie Oakley. He had met Harry Houdini, Al Jolson, John Barrymore, and Knute Rockne. In the late twenties, inside a railroad station washroom in Elmira, New York, great-grandpa encountered Babe Ruth at the urinal trough! They exchanged hello's and he was fortunate enough to get the Babe's autograph. He said Babe Ruth was on something called a "barnstorming tour" and that his real name was George Herman Ruth. I was now the only kid my age who knew the Babe's real name! Regrettably, the signature of the "Sultan of Swat," was lost.

Dad's only brother, Uncle Bob, was my most popular relative. His visits were special and memorable. Uncle Bob always brought much needed laughter to our house. He regularly played the role of an ignorant Finnish immigrant.

His accent and misuse of words was hilarious. When Uncle Bob came for dinner, he invariably imitated his father's eating habits. He would stuff a table napkin into his neck, roll up his sleeves, hold his knife and fork upright on the table, and, in broken English, demand to be fed.

Uncle Bob

Uncle Bob would loudly slurp his food as he ate and stuff three or four pieces of bread in his mouth. Then, in mocking Finnish, he would ask mom to pass the mash potatoes. Mom would not have any idea what he wanted. Uncle Bob then pretended to get angry and spit the saliva soaked bread all over his chest napkin and onto his plate. My brother and I would laugh so hard that our stomachs ached. Our parents would be in hysterics. Uncle Bob brought joy to our house.

Uncle Bob wasn't enamored with his father and stepmother. In high school, he had run away from home and somehow got himself to California. He couldn't stand his father's dictatorial style of discipline (nor the snobbishness of his stepmother). He eventually was found by a detective grandfather had hired and, begrudgingly, escorted back to Duluth.

Butch said mom should have married Uncle Bob instead of dad. Both were loving, carefree, and enjoyed a good laugh.

I was proud of my middle name, Robert, given to me in honor of Uncle Bob. I wished he lived in our neighborhood. He was a hero in my eyes. I know dad was very proud of his brother. Uncle Bob was wounded in battle against the Japs and received a Purple Heart. He brought the medal to our house once, and it was passed around the kitchen table for everyone to see. The service award was precious to all of us. So was Uncle Bob.

Grandpa and Grandma Gran's presence, however, brought out other emotions.

It was an unusual event when the elder Grans came to see us. Mom dreaded their arrival. She would barely say boo in their presence. Even after fifteen years, Grandpa and Grandma Gran still did not condone their son's marriage to mom.

Grandpa Gran

We had to dress up for their visit. Dad warned everyone to be on their best behavior. Surprisingly, dad would act like a juvenile around Grandpa Gran. He continually tried to impress his father while showing false concern about the health and welfare of his stepmother. I think he never lost hope that Grandpa Gran would somehow change his mind and support him through law school, but it never happened.

Dad's parents would arrive in a chauffeur driven white Packard (Grandpa Gran never learned to drive). The chauffeur's name was Ballister. I was always impressed with Ballister's black leather hat, matching outfit, and high buttoned boots. He never came into our house. While Grandpa and Grandma

Gran were inside, Ballister spent the entire time buffing the interior and exterior of the Packard. It was the most beautiful automobile I had ever seen.

Butch and I disliked Grandma Gran. She was very cold and distant. Mom felt judged by the woman. She was critical of all of us and not impressed in the way we lived. To her, our home was on the wrong side of town. Neither of our parents were college graduates, they had no status as professionals, and obviously lacked "class."

During one dismal visit, Grandma Gran asked mom where she had gotten the matching sweaters Butch and I were wearing? In all innocence, mom said she bought them on sale at "Penney's."

"Oh, good gracious, my lady," Grandma Gran abruptly remarked. "We never shop at that store! The type of people they attract and the lack of quality in their inventory is appalling!" Mom was embarrassed and angered by the rude remark. I know she wanted to visit the basement for a long drink.

My brother said he wanted to shit in grandma's hat and squash it on her fat, blue-haired head. The image of Grandma Gran crowned with a hat full of shit was branded on my brain. Thereafter, every time she put on one of her stupid-looking hats, I would titter. I'm sure she thought I was retarded. My brother began complementing her hat selection solely to make fun of her. I could see what he was doing and it made me giggle more.

Grandma Gran wore fur pelts draped around her neck during the winter. She used a silver cigarette holder when she smoked and carried a gold case for her cigarettes. Her clothing was expensive and conservatively stylish.

Grandpa Gran always wore a striped suit, white shirt, tie, and expensive straw hat. He was a large man who smoked big cigars, and wore his pocket watch at the end of a long gold chain connected to his belt. Grandpa Gran's belly was as heavy as his Finnish accent. His speech was very hard to understand. Every time he talked, I thought of Uncle Bob's comical Finnish imitation and had to hold back my laughter. Grandpa was uncomfortable around Butch and me. And we were equally uncomfortable around him.

Dad told us stories of what it was like to have dinner at his house when he was our age. Our grandparents employed a cook who also served their meals. Uncle Bob and father (and their young sister, Rhea) would have to dress formally and were not allowed to speak during the meal. It was common to have dinner with well-known guests. Dad remembers having supper with "Uncle" Charlie. For years, he believed that "Uncle" Charlie was a blood relative. Charlie's full name was Charles Mayo, the co-founder of the famous Mayo Clinic in Rochester, Minnesota. At other times, Govenors of Minnesota Burnquist, Preus, and Christiansen would stop by and share an evening meal.

Grandpa and Grandma Gran were on a first name basis with other luminaries such Marshall H. Alworth, the Congdons, and countless numbers of lawyers, politicians, speculators, educators, doctors, and business people.

Being "connected," was a status that dad admired and Uncle Bob despised. Grandpa Gran emphasized the importance of associating with individuals who were advantaged and powerful. "You help them, they help you," he said. Uncle Bob couldn't tolerate that formula for success. He loathed what he felt was his parents' exploitation of other people.

When the elder Grans dined with us (and mom served a bone-in meat entree), grandpa would gnaw on the bone and eat the marrow. He regularly enjoyed eating fish head soup, calves tongue, blood sausage, head cheese (made from cow brains), lutefisk (white fish soaked in lye), raw hamburger on crackers, and even something called prairie oysters. He seemed to have no awareness that ordinary people rarely, if ever, ate those items.

He was also insensitive to nakedness. During a very cold day in late winter of 1947, dad, grandpa and I took a trip to my great uncle Frank's farm in Bovey, Minnesota. My grandpa wanted to visit his older brother. When we arrived at the farm, I was amazed at the size of the place. The main barn must have been 300 feet long and other smaller barns dotted the expansive acreage. My great uncle was the strongest man I had ever seen. He was very muscular and his hands were the size of catchers' mitts. When he hugged me, I disappeared in his tree-trunk arms. Not long after we arrived, my great uncle announced that the sauna (Finnish steam bath) was ready.

All of us, included my great aunt, walked to the large barn. A sauna was in one corner of the barn. I looked through a small window on the door of the sauna and saw wooden tiers and a miniature stove. When I turned back to tell my father what I had seen, I discovered that all my relatives were stark naked!

I almost fainted! I had never seen a naked grownup before, much less a gigantic, fat-bellied grandpa, an aged great aunt (with enormous sagging breasts), a great uncle with the largest penis in the world, and my skinny alabaster father. I was mortified!

Dad told me to strip. I started to cry. I couldn't do it. I didn't want anyone to see my button penis. Thankfully, dad relented and let me keep my underpants on. We all went into the sauna and found a seat, the higher the tier the hotter the temperature. I sat on the bottom row and all the adults took seats on the top tier. They remained subjected to the intense heat for what seemed an hour and drank a liquid that smelled of alcohol. Finally, my relatives rose from their seats, exited the sauna, and ran outside into the freezing temperatures screaming in Finnish. They then dove into some big snow banks next to the barn. My relatives had all gone crazy!

I will never forget the scene of watching these huge, naked, flabby, sweaty, super-white skinned people frolicking in the snow in below freezing weather. I began to appreciate mom's statement that *sisu* makes people do strange things.

That day also taught me that jumping naked into a snowbank makes every male—no matter their original dimension---have a button penis. I felt better for having gained this new knowledge.

Palmer Method, "Morning Papers," Birth, and Helen's Panties

~⌒~

As I ENTERED THE THIRD grade in the fall 1947, I was especially excited because Miss Riddle, my new teacher, was going to teach me cursive writing.

The instructional tool was called the Palmer Method. The introductory lessons required making repetitive circular motions with my fingers only, and my forearm resting lightly on the desk. Then, using a pencil, Miss Riddle had me draw elongated, circular tunnels between two horizontal lines. This was the beginning of the Palmer Method. Once I had mastered the circle drawings, cursive letters of the alphabet were introduced, using the same methodology. The Palmer Method also taught me to hold my pencil in a precise manner.

Miss Riddle directed that all her students learn cursive writing using their right- hand. She said writing with your left-hand was abnormal. Joe LeDoux (pronounced "La Do"), was the only "southpaw" in our class. He could barely print letters, even using his left-hand, his natural side. Joe's attempt to write using his right-hand was a disaster! His circles looked like tangled spaghetti. Every morning, Joe tried to hold his graphite pencil with his right-hand, and every day, his pencil would fly across the room. Joe would start crying. Some kids began calling him Joe LeDon't because he could not master the required right-hand style. Poor Joe was frustrated. I know he felt stupid. Eventually, Miss Riddle relented, and allowed him to learn cursive with his natural hand. His pencils stopped flying across the room.

Miss Riddle's had allergies and her nose was constantly stuffed up. She always had a tissue in each hand to wipe away her drip. (She also continually pulled at her bra straps. Miss Riddle was a large lady as were her breasts. I remember thinking that it had to be a chore carrying those things around all day. Her bra must have been gigantic, like a backpack worn backwards!) One day, I was practicing my Palmer circles on the cheap paper issued to school kids during and after the war. Miss Riddle bent over my desk to observe how I was doing.

When she leaned, her nose discharged and a blob of mucous landed on my paper in the middle of the largest circle. Miss Riddle was very embarrassed. She tried to mop up the snot with one of her handy tissues, but her attempt only made the graphite smear. My paper was a mess. When I later told my friend, Dan Carich, what had happened, he quipped that I should have said: "Nice shot, Riddle—a direct hit! The Air Corps could have used you during the war!"

We also were introduced to music in the third grade, specifically voice and instrumental units.

Miss Riddle' daily music lesson began with a note she played on a pitch pipe. She had the whole class first hum the note, and then each individual student was expected to sing the phrase "morning papers," matching the tone of that same note.

I would rather square dance with Nabisco than sing in front of my classmates. I had trouble talking, much less singing, in public.

When my turn came, I choked up. My "morning papers" came out like I was having an asthma attack.

All the girls sang the phrase like song birds. It was my bad fortune to be seated between two of the more skilled singers, Barbara Billsley and Jeannette Pollard. The contrast in our musical output couldn't have been more different, or embarrassing--the belabored breathing of a dying crow seated between the perfect cadences of two beautifully melodious loons.

One morning, when it was Stinky Malone's turn to sing the phrase, he inadvertently sang "morning fucken papers." The room instantly went still.

Miss Riddle was horrified. (Stinky's real name was Eddie, his family was poor, and his home life was rough. He was called Stinky because he always smelled like a horse barn. He swore like a dockworker). Miss Riddle escorted him by the ear to Principal Becker's office where he received a spanking and was expelled for a week.

I thought the punishment was unfair. Stinky didn't mean to swear or be disrespectful. He just wasn't concentrating and let his guard down. Swearing was a common occurrence in his family, and he simply forgot where he was. To me, Stinky was a great kid. He even liked his nickname.

Stinky added to his legend from another slip-of-the-tongue in the fifth grade. The class was talking about their pets when Stinky piped up that his male dog was "one frisky son-of-a-bitch." The teacher, Mrs. Shields, didn't find that statement funny, even though it was factual. Stinky got spanked again by the principal.

Besides learning how to write and sing, the third grade also introduced us to the recorder instrument. Two styles were offered: "potato" and "clarinet." Both had a small mouthpiece and various openings for your fingers to cover or leave alone, depending on the desired note. I chose the potato style because of its shape. It appeared to be easier to play. My choice really didn't matter. Like my attempts at singing, the sounds emanating from my potato were awful.

The educational reasoning behind this unit of music was to discover who had talent for instrumental music. Any student demonstrating musical ability with the recorder was encouraged to "graduate" to a traditional instrument, such as a trumpet, saxophone, or flute.

Miss Riddle passed out music sheets for the song, "Old Black Joe." (In the forties, racial prejudice was not in the minds of most all-white school districts like ours. "Old Black Joe" contained lyrics such as, "I hear the darkies' voices singing..." No one felt we were playing a racist song). Our class was expected to perform the song on stage during the Fall recital.

Helen Johnson had the best singing voice in our room. Helen had received formal training in the field. She was chosen to sing "Old Black Joe" at the recital while the rest of the class played the background music on our recorders.

In November, a lady come to class to help us play the song on recorders. She gave us hour-long lessons each Monday and Friday. She described my playing style as "random." If I hit the correct note, it was purely accidental, as was my hitting the incorrect note. My finger dexterity was almost nonexistent. Trying to remember what holes to cover, when to blow into the mouthpiece, and how to hold the potato, was a serious challenge for me. A monkey could have easily replicated my performance. After a while, I faked playing by "pretend" blowing into the mouthpiece. I was not a budding musician. I was a prop.

The lady teaching us to play appeared to be gaining weight as the weeks passed. Her belly was growing. Sometime around Easter, Miss Riddle announced that the lady was in a "family way." She would be with us for only one more month.

The phrase "family way" was something new to me. Luckily, Ron Hicks (of fart fame) told me that "family way" was just a polite phrase for being "knocked up." This added little to my understanding. By way of explanation, he said that one of his older sisters told him that a kid grows in a woman's stomach after she swallows a baby pill. A woman who wants a kid can buy the pill at a drugstore. Eventually, the baby comes out through the woman's mouth,

Ron's information was scary. I vowed that in the future, if I happened to see a pregnant woman open her mouth as wide as a yawn, I'd instantly run away.

In early October 1947, Irving Grade School had its Fall Recital. Helen Johnson performed a lovely solo to a packed audience of proud parents, all of whom seemed to enjoy her singing. I was fake-playing as usual. During Helen's performance, however, something very unexpected happened. Helen's panties dropped to her ankles. There was a momentary gasp, but Helen merely kicked them off her feet and didn't break stride.

The audience began clapping for her and when she finished singing, they all stood and cheered.

Not only did Helen have a fine singing voice, she also had style and class. Because of her vocal artistry and dignified panty dispersal, our third grade was the hit of the recital.

I never "played" the recorder again, much less graduate to a more sophisticated musical instrument.

A New Neighborhood and Betsy

My House

In late October 1947, when I was in the third grade, we moved to a new West Duluth neighborhood. Dad bought a house at 5714 Wadena Street. He quit working at the Duluth Brass Works and was hired to sell World Book Encyclopedias. He held on to his nightly employment as a movie projectionist. Prior to our moving, dad traded his briefly owned 1936 car for a pristine 1939 Buick. The car was a black, heavily chromed, "cherry." Dad apparently was making a good income.

Butch and I received permission from Principal Becker to remain at Irving Grade School. Our Wadena Street house was in a different school district. All the youngsters in our new neighborhood either went to Longfellow Grade School or St. James Catholic School.

I quickly wound up with no after school play friends. My Irving buddies were not in our residential area. Being the shyest kid in Minnesota didn't help matters in seeking out new friends surrounding Wadena Street.

My new neighborhood was populated primarily by Scandinavians (Swedes, Norwegians, and "Finlanders"). Smaller numbers of Serbians, Italians, Greeks, and Germans also resided there. Most of our neighbors owned their homes. It was a community of hard working, "blue-collar" people who enjoyed hunting, fishing, and camping. Many of the adult males worked at the local steel plant in Morgan Park. Dad said the steel plant paid very good wages. The plant had three rotating eight-hour shifts.

Dad soon learned our neighbors shared many of his views. They had a basic mistrust of big government and banks and paid for everything with cash. Frugality and industry were common values. Working hard, saving money, paying one's bills, and "going without" was a common practice. Living above your means on credit was considered irresponsible.

We occupied the first floor of our new residence and rented the second floor. Butch and I still shared a bedroom. The yards surrounding the house were shoddy and poorly maintained. A better playground a child of eight could never find.

About fifteen feet to the right of our bedroom was the house of Mr. and Mrs. Peterson. Their teenage daughter, Patti Ann, was a high school dropout, unmarried, toothless, and very pregnant. She wasn't old enough to buy a "family way" pill, so someone obviously had helped her get one. Mr. Peterson was out of work, spending a large part of the day listening to country music and playing guitar in his kitchen. Patti Ann and her mother spent most of the day arguing.

The Peterson's partied late into the night three or four times a week. Since our houses were so close together, Butch and I often could not sleep because of the music and clamor. Dad often went to the Peterson's house and asked them to "tone it down," but usually joined the party, (sometimes with mom), and got drunk with them.

I think Butch had a crush on Patti Ann. She always teased him and tousled his hair with her hands. My brother would watch Patti Ann from our bedroom window when she was outside. I kept my distance from her in fear of a slime-soaked baby erupting from Patti Ann's mouth at any moment. I remember asking Butch if he was going to marry Patti Ann after she vomited her baby? My question got me another kick in the ass for an answer.

After Patti Ann coughed up her baby, the Peterson house became even noisier. The baby was always crying, Patti Ann and her mother increased their arguing, and the parties became more raucous. I never did go into their house. It smelled like rotten wood.

Another house, diagonally behind us, was occupied by the Center family on the first floor and George Phillipovich, the owner-landlord, lived alone on the top floor.

Mr. Phillipovich was a gruff Serbian immigrant who recently retired as a crane operator at the steel plant. He had cancer in one of his legs and no longer could work. Mr. Phillipovich was always alone, rarely having visitors. He spoke in loud broken English and apparently was impatient with people who could not understand him, especially children. While his large yard, adjoining ours, was an ideal place to play, I soon avoided it. He scared me.

Mr. Center was born in Greece and immigrated to the United States as a young man. He owned a butcher shop on 57th Street. Mr. Center insisted that adult men could feed babies by producing milk from their breasts. He stated it was a common practice in his native Greece. Ernie, Mr. Center's teenage son, thought his father's efforts to produce milk from his own breasts was inane. Mr. Center said someday he was going to get a "breast pump" and attach it to his nipple. I vowed on that day I would be absent from the presence of Mr. Center.

Mrs. Center was a large woman who suffered from asthma. She spent most of each day sitting on her enclosed back porch hooked up to a respirator. She had trouble sleeping and, at night, sat in the cool evening air rocking back and forth. The floor boards of her porch squeaked in a methodical rhythm as she rocked. The sound produced was peaceful. I would get up in the night to go to the bathroom and see Mrs. Center asleep in her chair. I felt bad for her.

She suffered so much just trying to breathe. I never once heard her complain about her ailment. Mrs. Center seemed to be more concerned about the welfare of others. I don't think she had a self-centered bone in her body. Even as shy as I was, I felt comfortable talking with her. Mrs. Center was a gentle lady.

Mrs. Center was also a wonderful cook. Their house often smelled of lamb and mint sauce. She gave our family baklava and spanakopita. I never tasted food so delicious. The Centers' parties featured traditional foods and dances. Our family was often invited to share in the festivities. I like watching the men dance with one another, each holding an end of a handkerchief, which I had never seen before. The music was different but entertaining, everyone had a good time, and they were respectful of their Greek culture. And, to my delight, nobody got drunk.

We were three homes, close to each other yet worlds apart. The Centers were welcoming and happy, hosting an occasional party honoring their heritage. The Petersons, were loud and argumentative, frequently partying to a drunken stupor. The Grans, in the middle, were quiet and tense, increasingly isolated from one another.

I grew to appreciate the relaxing cadence of Mrs. Center's old rocking chair, much gentler on my nerves than the drunken binges of the Petersons or the strained atmosphere of our house. I longed for the day I could have a bedroom on the other side of the house. It never happened.

BETSY

Dad called his new car "Betsy." Because there were no kids to play with in the neighborhood, dad began taking me with him when he gassed up Betsy. Every Sunday, he drove to a Texaco station in the West End of Duluth. Pulling up to one of the pumps, Dad honked the car horn twice and, within a few seconds, three station employees came running out of the small service building. The attendants were dressed in Texaco hats and uniforms, with bow ties. Big, enthusiastic smiles were on their faces and each man carried a spotless wiping rag.

One familiar attendant asked, "How may we serve the two Mr. Grans today?" Dad would respond, "Hi, Charlie! Betsy's thirsty. Fill her up, please."

While Charlie pumped gas, a second attendant cleaned all the windows and the head and taillights. The third raised the mammoth hood and checked the oil, belts, and water. He asked dad to examine the dip stick and agree if oil needed to be added. One of the attendants checked the air pressure of the tires, including the spare in the trunk.

Dad recorded everything in a booklet kept in the glove compartment, including dates, miles between fill ups, average miles per gallon, and the cost of gas and oil. The price of gas at that time was about 20 cents per gallon.

Charlie gave me a candy bar as a treat and said something like, "Here's some energy for you too, son. You'll need it riding shotgun." After we left the station, I made believe that I had a steering wheel and helped guide Betsy home.

I cherished the moments when my father asked me to go with him to the Texaco Station. I loved the smell and sound of the car, as well as the rare time alone with dad. To me, Buicks were the best cars in the world because dad owned one.

Butch never came with us on these excursions. He kept his distance from dad.

Swanee

Swanee's House

ONE DAY IN APRIL 1948, I was sitting on our front porch. Suddenly, this kid appeared at the foot of the steps. I had seen him at his home across the street at 5715 Wadena, shoveling snow, helping to push cars that were stuck, or working with his dad in their garage. He was older than me, and I wanted to get to know him, but I was too shy to introduce myself.

"Hi! I'm Swanee," he said. "You're the new kid on the block, aren't you? And your name is Tracy." He had a very confident air about him. He seemed nice.

Swanee (his real name was Paul Swanson), was a fifth grader at Longfellow, a school high on a hill in West Duluth. He was husky and tall for his age. A full-blooded Swede with thick blond hair, and light skin, Swanee lived with his parents and a brother, Wayne, who was in high school.

Swanee said the neighborhood kids were afraid of my neighbor, Mr. Phillipovich. They avoided him as he hated all young people. The kids called him "Mr. P." because they couldn't pronounce his name. Swanee said Mr. P. had murdered a child about ten years back and buried him in his yard. He warned me to stay away from Mr. P.'s property as I could fall into the grave. Now, I was really scared of Mr. Phillipovich. He just might kill me one day.

Swanee was not afraid of Mr. Phillipovich. He called the feared man: "Mr. Son-of-a-Bitch." Swanee related that a few years ago, the old man had caught a retarded boy pissing on his front porch. Swanee said the handicapped kid just had to let his "lizard spit." Every kid in the neighborhood regularly pissed outdoors. Apparently, the boy was never seen again. A rumor developed among the neighborhood kids that Mr.P. had killed the boy and buried him near our house! Mr.P. soon became a fearful figure because of his reputation of being a child killer.

Most kids liked Swanee. He was also appreciated by adults in the neighborhood. Swanee would go out of his way to help someone or a needy family.

Swanee mowed the lawns of older neighbors, shoveled their walks and driveways in the winter, and even painted a house for an elderly neighbor. Swanee selflessly volunteered to push Mr. Harrison, a wheelchair-bound invalid, to and from his appointments at a local clinic. He refused to accept offers of payment for any of his deeds. While Swanee never cared for organized religion (he was forced to attend church by his mother), he was a kind and devoted servant to a multitude of his neighbors. Many people thought of him as a son or grandson. But Swanee could be vindictive.

Swanee told me that one of his teachers was mean. All the kids in his class hated her. One day, as "an act of kindness," he baked chocolate cookies with shit in them (a contribution from his dog, Ruff) and brought them to school for the teacher. She apparently "dunked" three or four into her coffee at lunchtime and devoured them! Swanee said that she must have liked the shit cookies. She asked him for the recipe!

Actually, Swanee was quite mature for an eleven-year-old. He was the youngest member of a household where playtime was rare. His parents were both high school dropouts, and his older brother was about to do the same. They believed in hard work and earning your own way. If Swanee wanted something, he had to work for it. And he did. When we met, he had a part-time job at a local "mom and pop" grocery store, washed storefront windows for three area businesses, mowed the lawns of a funeral home and car dealership, scrapped and painted the trim of his parent's garage, house, and summer camp, and washed the cars of several of our neighbors.

Swanee had little time for make-believe games such as re-fighting World War II, or playing cars, or games such as hide-and-go-seek, building snow forts, or bicycle riding. Swanee's spent most of his time with adults. Swanee reserved his imagination for real life situations.

I, on the other hand, was an eight-year-old who principally lived in dreamland. Playing with my fictional characters and plots, I had little interaction with adults or my brother. Swanee soon became a second older brother and my best friend. I learned to tell Swanee about any problem or question I found confusing. As we grew closer, he provided sound advice and helped me understand many things.

But he was not beyond playing tricks on his new pal.

A few weeks after we met, Swanee and I were walking along an alley near our houses in search of discarded empty Lucky Strike cigarette packs. Whoever saw one would step on it with one foot and, pivoting, slug the competing kid in the arm, saying: "Lucky Strike pack, no strike back." Swanee was successful three straight times, nearly breaking my shoulder.

We found a lost balloon. Swanee thought it would be fun to fill the balloon with water and toss it at some innocent stooge. His idea was to climb a nearby railroad trestle and drop it on an unsuspecting kid riding by on their bike.

"Finlander," (Swanee's new name for me), "go home and have your mom fill the balloon and meet me at the trestle. We'll have fun bombing a moron."

I ran home with the balloon. I couldn't wait to see it bulging with water! I told mom that I had found a balloon and asked her to fill it.

"Jesus, Mary, and Joseph," mom gasped! "Tracy, this is a filthy condom! And it's been used!"

She immediately threw it into the trash and, after washing her hands, scrubbed me down. I was in shock at how mom reacted to a simple play balloon.

I rushed back to the trestle and told Swanee what had happened. I said my mother called the balloon a "common" and it was "used" and filthy. I didn't understand.

Swanee had a hard time catching his breath as he was laughing so hard. When he recovered, Swanee informed me that the "balloon" was a condom or rubber. He said a man slides it over his penis when having sex to prevent a woman from getting pregnant. His story was hard to believe.

Women had babies from pills, and rubbers were what you wore when it rained. Either Ron Hicks' knowledge about sex was wrong or, more likely, Swanee was playing me for a fool. After all, he had just tricked me in going home and being a dope in front of mom.

I decided not to tell Swanee, or mom for that matter, that on my way home with the balloon, I lost my breath a couple of times trying to blow the damn thing up.

Porky, "Dant-Da-Daah," and Saturday Matinee

⸺ᦄ⸺

A FEW DAYS AFTER THE "balloon" fiasco, I was watching a man delivering ice blocks to a woman who lived on the second floor of a nearby house. The man worked for Pekkala's Ice Company. He pulled out a huge block of ice and positioned it on his rubberized back. Then he carried the load up a long and steep set of wooden stairs, to the lady's ice box refrigerator, a not uncommon appliance in the forties.

Standing next to me was a kid dressed like a cowboy. He had a set of cap guns strapped to his waist and wore chaps, cowboy boots, and western style hat.

"That's my house," he said to me. "My mom's getting her ice. It's fun to watch."

"Yeah," I responded, surprised a kid I didn't know was talking to me.

"Do you like my outfit," the boy uttered? "I'm pretending to be Gene Autry. Do you know who he is?"

"He's a cowboy in the movies," I said knowingly. "I've seen him at the Doric Theater. He's good."

"Do you want to play cowboys," the kid asked excitedly? "We can ride our horses and kill Indians!"

I jumped at his invitation! "Sure," I said! "Come and I'll get my stuff," We began walking up the alley to my house.

"My name is Jerry, he said. "It's actually Gerald, but everyone calls me Porky." We shook hands. "What's your name?"

"Tracy," I said, knowing what was coming next.

"Dick Tracy," Porky predictably responded! He paused and said: "I bet you get that a lot, hey?"

"Yeah," I said. "Everyone who hears my name for the first time comes up with Dick Tracy. It happens almost every day. It gets tiring."

"I'll never call you Dick Tracy again, Tracy." Porky had a grin on his face. "But you do have a square chin. And what about your secret wristwatch? Can I see it?"

We laughed.

Like Swanee, Porky became another fast friend.

Unlike Swanee, Porky was about my size. He had a freckled face, turned up nose, and light red hair. He was ten years old. Porky's parents were divorced. (I later discovered that his father was dead.) He lived with his mother and older sister. Porky's mom was a waitress at Teve's Bar and Grill in West Duluth. They lived at the other end of the same alley that paralleled our house, a one block separation.

I now had met two kids who would end up as my closest friends through high school and early college. Swanee was soon to be in the sixth grade, Porky in the fifth, and I in the fourth. Swanee and Porky were already friends.

Our age and grade differences didn't seem to matter. There was a compatibility among the three of us.

Swanee was the mature leader of the group. He was a thinker and analyzer. He welcomed challenges. Swanee provided words of wisdom, strategies for behavior, and keen insights about girls, religion, and puberty. He was too serious for imaginary endeavors. But Swanee was an excellent athlete. We would play a lot of catch and basketball in the ensuing years.

Porky was an impulsive, imaginative companion for any proposed adventure. He rarely thought through the repercussions of his (or our) actions. Porky was truly my number one "play" mate. His imagination made him fun to be around. And Porky's carefree personality helped me release some of the anger and tension that I had developed from my home life.

I was the young naïve kid desiring to be accepted as an equal. I was open to learn everything I could from my new buddies.

"Dant-Da-Daah"

A typical Sunday in late spring of 1948 was spent playing outdoors from eight in the morning until four in the afternoon. I then listened to all my favorite "kid radio shows" prior to suppertime.

Arising early, I gulped down my breakfast and rushed out to the back-yard. The early morning sun was so bright that I had to squint my eyes to see. The air smelled like fresh soil. Playing outdoors was wonderful!

Porky would arrive at my house and we'd "set the scene." (Swanee was forced to attend church and rarely with us on Sundays.)

Setting the scene involved pre-play in two parts.

Part one was to determine what make-believe characters we were going to mimic or invent, at least initially, that morning. We decided and began part two with the phrase "dant-da-daaah." The phrase signified that play was about to begin. World War II play games were fading by 1948. Most games we played were based on heroes from the movies and serialized radio programs.

Porky might say, "Let's play The Lone Ranger for a while. You'll be Tonto and I'll be the Ranger. Okay?" I agreed and we would say: "dant-da-daaah." Playtime was underway! We'd play until our moms yelled to us to come home for supper. (Lunch was usually skipped.)

In the late 1940's, television was still a rumor and personal computers were science fiction. Everyone, young and old, would gather around radios and listen to their favorite programs. My parents had a mammoth console in our living room. Every night after supper, I would lay on the rug and tune to L, A, V, A, L, A, V, A, The FBI in Peace and War, Gangbusters, Amos and Andy, The Shadow, Lux Presents Hollywood, Milton Berle, Red

Skelton, Bob Hope, The Great Gildersleeve, Fibber McGee and Molly, The Lemac Show, Mr. Keene, Tracer of Lost Persons, George Burns and Gracie Allen, The Green Hornet, Inner Sanctum, The Whistler, and so many others. Lucky Strikes cigarettes was the major sponsor of one program, and the letters L.S.M.F.T. were a prominent feature of the commercial.

The initials stood for "Lucky Strikes Means Fine Tobacco." Swanee convinced me they meant "Loose Straps Mean Floppy Tits." I naively believed him. I was intent on sharing this new knowledge with my parents one evening at supper. I wanted to ask them what are "tits?" Thankfully, the "correct" version was broadcast on the radio just prior to my question. Swanee later told me tits were women's "chest bumps." I then recalled my teacher, Miss Riddle. She had enormous bumps. My cousin Sheila had pretty bumps. Nabisco had balloon bumps. Most girls my age had no bumps. Patti Ann Petersen always scratched her bumps. I began to stare at females' bumps. There were so many different kinds.

My favorite comedy show was The Jack Benny Program. It would air at 6pm on Sunday while we were having dinner. I liked Rochester and Dennis Day and all the other characters. During the school week, when we came home for lunch, I always tuned in Ma Perkins. When I was home ill, I listened to all the soaps! I loved them.

There were countless programs that invited the listener to "project" themselves into the plot and actively use their imaginations. One had to envision the segments of each plot—the characters, the scenes, the background sounds, and the prior events in the never-ending serial. Each kid (and adult) came up with their own interpretation. It was a wonderful exercise in the "theater of the mind."

And, for some kid's programs, it was also exciting to "send away" for something from a place called Battle Creek, Michigan. A secret ring or magic whistle could be purchased for a just a few coins and a correct number of cereal box tops. It was a joy to check the mailbox every day in anticipation of a package arriving with your very own name on it.

In my youth, children were comfortable playing by themselves, with few external props, utilizing the strengths of their imagination. Playing indoors was okay, especially on rainy days or when the temperature hovered at extremely low temperatures. Then most kids would usually play cars, board games, or read funny books.

On occasion, when we were forced to stay inside, we would set up dad's Lionel model train set on the living room rug. Uncle Bob gave the set to dad in 1935. The electric-powered 700e locomotive with attached tender pulled four multicolored box cars and a caboose on a three-rail, oval track. The cars were labeled New York Central.

I would spend hours playing "railroad" on our living room rug. I was amazed at the beauty and precision of workmanship of the train set. When I was done playing, I carefully rewrapped each car in its original paper and put it in its own special box. The train was my favorite toy, and I was always careful with it. At least twice a year, I would polish the locomotive, tender, cars, and caboose. I then oiled the prongs on the track system and wiped down the rails. I truly loved that train. Somehow, it made me feel closer to dad and Uncle Bob. When dad was home, he enjoyed watching me play on the rug with his train. Perhaps the train also brought back pleasant memories for him?

But it was always more fun to play outdoors. You could hear kids "dant-da-daahing" all over the neighborhood. Only kids who were sick or quarantined stayed indoors in good weather. We played for the pure sake of play. None of us were ever bored. All outside play was organized by the kids themselves. Parental input was limited to a cautionary reminder about not poking our eyes out, and coming home to supper.

We would invent our own plots and characters and play them one after another, or over and over, all day long. Everyone also engaged in pickup games of softball, baseball, tag, hide and go seek, inny-inny-eye-over (pig's tail!), dodge ball, blind man's bluff, follow the leader and Simon Sezs. I could stand in my backyard and yell for Porky, Larry, Jim, David, Mary, Darla, Kenny, Joe, and John, and within minutes, they would be in my yard, usually bringing some of their other friends along.

Those early years of outdoor play taught me how to get along with other people and control my selfishness. I also learned to be comfortable when I chose to be alone. I didn't need my parents to "plan" my pursuits and watch over me.

SATURDAY MATINEE

Saturdays were special days. We were out of school, and it was time for a trip to the matinee! The Doric Theater would show a comedic "short" subject, cartoon, one segment of a "good guy-bad guy" serial, and a feature action movie every Saturday afternoon.

Kids from the neighborhood stood in line down Grand Avenue all the way to the Ben Franklin's Five and Ten Store, anxiously waiting for the doors of the Doric to open for the noontime start. The quarter mom gave me covered the costs of the afternoon's entertainment. My ticket was nine cents, leaving me with sixteen cents to buy a dime box of fresh popcorn and six cents for penny candy.

I would always go to the movies with Porky. Swanee's mom barred him from joining us, claiming movies were sinful. Even "Lassie" was not suitable for impressionable minds, she said.

At least twice a month, Swanee figured out a way to attend despite his mom's ban. He would tell Porky and me to save him a seat. He knew his mom always checked the line of waiting kids, in the process handing out religious tracts. After she left, he would pay his nine cents and come in before the feature movie started.

When the matinee was over, Swanee left by a rear exit in case his mom might be watching at the front entrance. He never got caught, and explained away his afternoon absence with stories about running errands for some older neighborhood people (which he did on certain Saturdays) or reading the Bible in the nearby library (which he never did on any day).

Swanee respected his mother and understood her concern for his moral welfare. But being together and having innocent fun with friends was important and justified. Swanee believed his mother's restriction was archaic. He contended his deception was merely a trivial untruth, a "white lie." Fibbing was not sinful.

Normally, during an evening "adult" show, an usher accompanied you down the aisle, with a flashlight, and determined your seating. You were not allowed to talk during the movie nor could you put your feet up on the seat in front of you. Ushers had the right to remove you from the theater if you were misbehaving.

The "house" rules about talking were never enforced at Saturday matinees. We booed the villains, cheered on the heroes, and laughed raucously at the slapstick comedians. We could sit where we wanted and moved around the theater during the matinee.

My favorite matinee combination was a Bugs Bunny cartoon, Laurel and Hardy or Three Stooges short, Buck Rogers or Captain Marvel serial, and Roy Rogers feature. Just about every Roy Rogers picture began with Roy, Dale Evans, Roy's sidekick, Gabby Hayes, and the Sons of the Pioneers, riding their horses along a dusty trail while singing a song. As the song came to an end, shots would be heard in the distance and the plot of good versus evil began (with good always winning out). When the shots rang out, some of the kids would yell "Dant-Da-Daah." The stage was set. The good guys would wear white clothes and bad guys would be attired in black. (Roy was clean shaven, never drank alcohol, swore, chewed tobacco, or killed, unlike the villains he faced). And there was little, if any, embarrassing romance, especially kissing, in his movies. Near the end of the adventure, Roy would ride off singing, "Happy trails to you, until we meet again."

The theme was much the same for other popular western stars such as Gene Autry, Hopalong Cassidy (played by William Boyd), Smiley Burnett, Lash LaRue, Bob Steele, Randolph Scott, Hoot Gibson, The Lone Ranger and Tonto, The Cisco Kid with Poncho, and Tex Ritter. I also loved Andy Devine who played a raspy sidekick in "oater" movies.

On occasion, a Tarzan movie would be double-featured with Nyoka, The Jungle Woman. Leo Gorcey and Huntz Hall were also two of my comedic favorites. The one short we collectively despised was "Follow the Bouncing Ball." It involved stupid singing and was corny. The matinee never included global news such as "The March of Time." Any serious topic that deviated from the topics of comedy, action thrills, and simple western or jungle plots would be booed loudly by the young audience.

Porky insisted on an aisle seat so he could quickly escape to the lobby during a scary scene. He said he was going to the bathroom, but we knew otherwise. We caught him peeking in the exit door to see if the frightening part of the movie had ended.

Swanee and I never said anything about his escaping. We had our own private fears. I remember during one Frankenstein movie Porky went to the "bathroom" eight times. He said he had the flu, but we knew he was simply afraid of the monster on the screen played by Boris Karloff.

After the matinee, we would rush home and re-enact the plots. This was almost as fun as watching the actual movie. I would be Roy Rogers or Gene Autry. My cousin Sheila loved Nyoka and played her character for weeks on end. Porky did a good imitation of Curley of the Three Stoogies.

On rare occasions, when his mother wasn't home, and we pressured him, Swanee would play a villain. With him as the bad guy, many of our scenarios ended up backward with evil winning out over good. Swanee was a tough kid.

Make-believe with Porky was a way to soften the hard edges in both of our lives. Porky had a great imagination and developed fictional scenarios that became unexpectedly therapeutic.

Porky's parents were divorced and he wanted desperately for them to get back together. Unfortunately, when Porky was nine, his father died from a heart attack in his early forties. His father's sudden death destroyed any hope of Porky's parents remarrying. Porky found it very hard to accept his dad's death. He began to make-believe that his father was still alive and merely away on business.

I would pose I had seen Porky's father in downtown Duluth. His dad reported he would be home soon. Such pretending seemed to help ease Porky's sadness. We also bluffed my parents were sober, happily married, and did everything for their children. Our creative world was a great relief for us.

Porky felt better that his father was just "away" for a while, and I was glad that my parents were not drinking and enjoyed being with each other. We knew much of our reality was mythical, but we didn't care.

A Big Hurt

In July 1948, just before my ninth birthday, dad attempted to kill mom and himself with a gun. The weapon was the one he used hunting down our former 51st Street milkman (and alleged adulterer), Mr. Anderson.

Dad had apparently reached a dead end. His marriage was failing. His night job as a projectionist paid little and the hours were tiring. During the day, he was trying to sell encyclopedias with very little success. Earlier, in the summer, mom told us money for the new house and "Betsy" was loaned to him by Grandpa Gran. Dad had little means to meet family needs, much less pay Grandpa Gran back. Contributing to his lack of success was his sullen demeanor and heavy daily drinking. Dad was fearful of failure, and unable to accept defeat.

The day dad attempted to commit murder/suicide was earlier spent at a conference in Duluth, sponsored by the encyclopedia company. Dad arrived home by cab, drunk. The cabbie had to help him get out of the taxi and into our house.

Dad was staggering from room to room. In his underwear, I remember dad knocking over a lamp in the dining room. He was sobbing loudly and yelling about all his failures. Dad screamed he was sick of his life and tired of having no support from his wife. He had a pint of alcohol in his hand and was swigging from it. Mom looked frantic. She told my brother and me to go outside and play. Butch thought that dad had finally flipped his wig. I was scared. Mom was trying to console dad but he wanted no part of it.

A short while later, as Butch and I were making mud pies in the backyard, we heard a crackling sound within our house. I first thought our father broke another piece of furniture. Mom came running out the back door with an alarmed look on her face. "You kids! You must stay out of the house!" She screamed at us in a voice I had never heard from her before.

Our nearest neighbor, Mr. Peterson, was in his yard and yelled to our mother, "Mary, what's wrong? What happened?" Mom had both of her hands up to the sides of her face. "Please," she pleaded, "go check on Russ! He's pretty drunk and he's got a gun!"

As Mr. Peterson cautiously entered our house, mom ran to the Centers, and pounded on their screen door for help. Mr. Center came out and went into our house. Mr. Center's son, Ernie, approached us and told Butch and me to come with him to his father's nearby meat market. I was dazed. The commotion around our house and the look on my mother's face—in fact, the look on everyone's face---made me nervous. Ernie gave us some candy bars. He said our father might have hurt himself.

We heard a siren and looked out the store's front window. A police car was racing up 57th Street toward our house. About thirty minutes later, it sped back by, the siren now off.

I remember Ernie saying: "If anything bad happened, the police car would have its siren on. Everything is going to be okay."

Ernie's attempt at consoling us didn't help me from feeling that dad had seriously hurt himself. Mom, Butch, and I spent the night at Aunt Edith's house, surrounded by a lot of hushed conversations. Our relatives were concerned for our welfare. Butch said we were being handled with "kid gloves." I guess he meant we were being treated in some special way.

After the shooting, Uncle Bob came to our house and stayed the night with dad. Prior to our returning home, mom was visited by the police at our aunt's house. Butch said that mom probably would not press charges. I had no idea what that meant. No one would tell me anything. I think they felt I was too young to hear bad news.

Later, mom told us a rather sketchy story how dad accidentally shot in her direction as he "cleaned his pistol." The gun had then jammed. She said dad's "nerves were on end" and he needed lots of rest. Dr. Bakkila came to the house and gave dad some medicine that relaxed him. Dr. Bakkila said we had to be very quiet and make an extra effort to not upset our father. Butch and I had been trying not to upset dad for most of our lives.

My brother said mom's "accident" story was bullshit.

"Why would dad be cleaning his pistol when he was drunk and enraged? It makes no sense. He shot at mom," Butch said adamantly. "The bullet went through the door while mom was running out of the bedroom. The shot was no accident. The second bullet was meant for dad, but the gun jammed! He tried to kill mom and himself."

I wanted to believe mom's story. People with *sisu* never try to kill themselves or their loved ones. *Sisu* people confront the hurdles they have and don't run away from life. Dad was not a killer. He was a fighter.

But deep down, I knew Butch was right. Dad had tried to murder mom and then himself. Butch said dad showed his true colors. I think he wished the gun hadn't jammed on the second shot. He had a smirk on his face whenever the topic of the "accident" was brought up. The botched attempt at murder and suicide was easy proof to Butch that "big perfect daddy" was a weak man.

Butch claimed dad couldn't handle the pressures of family life. He sincerely believed that on the day of the "accident," the "old man was planning to kill all of us." Since dad had failed in this drunken pursuit, soon he would butcher us at night when we were asleep.

"It makes sense, blockhead," my brother declared. "Mom and dad drink too much, and cheat on one another. They're not happy. Mom and dad were not meant for each other. Dad screams about money problems and how much it costs to raise us. And he has a short fuse. He's already tried to kill Mr. Anderson, beat the shit out of a guy at work, got in a scuffle at the New Duluth Laundry, and wanted to punch out the owner of The Peking Café. You know dad doesn't like me and he's often impatient with your lack of following the *sisu* bullshit."

Butch paused and then concluded: "It all adds up. We're going to get it some night, mom included."

Night Fears

I BEGAN TO BELIEVE WHAT Butch was warning. (A few years earlier, Dad viewed Butch and me as economic burdens. I was convinced at the time, thanks to Butch's fabled commentary, dad had hired a person to kill us.) Now, Butch's serious prediction persuaded me that dad was going to kill all of us. Since he had surrendered his gun to the police, Butch said dad would slit our throats as we slept.

I tried to stay awake until our father came home from his projectionist job at around 11pm. If he was going to attack me, I wanted to be able to fight back, so sleep was out of the question. Every night, I waited in my bed to hear dad's house key being inserted into the front door. Dad routinely went down to the basement to add coals to the furnace. I would hear him shut the furnace's heavy door.

His next step was to check on us. Would this be the night? I clenched my fists and waited for him to creak open our bedroom door. With one eye shut, and the other slightly open, I prepared myself to deflect the blade of a knife. Every night, he would peek in and then quietly shut our door.

A sense of relief would overcome me. Dad had decided not to kill us tonight. His presence now made me feel sheltered. I could now sleep. An unusual mindset developed toward dad. I was fearful that he might kill us. Yet, I coveted his protection. My emotional relationship with dad was neurotic. When sunlight appeared and our mom came to wake us, my tense experience of the night before was gone. I had control over my destiny in daylight. No one, much less dad, dared to harm us while the sun was up.

I eventually lessened my anxiety of dad killing us. But I replaced that terror with a generalized death fear —someone, sometime, regardless of dad, would break into our house and kill us. Once again, I developed a schedule of "securing" before I went to bed.

Every night, I examined all closets for a murderer. Entrance doors were locked. The windows were shut and fastened. With flashlight in hand, and trepidation in my heart, the next area of coverage was the basement. There were many dark corners in our cellar. Those spots had to be checked out. The storeroom behind the furnace was a frightening area to enter, even during daylight hours. I would quickly open the wooden door to the room and flash my light into every corner, realizing this could be my last act as a living human being. Seeing no intruder, my feet barely touched the cold concrete basement floor as I scampered back upstairs.

To not account for potential killers would be irresponsible. I had to safeguard the night. No one in the family knew of my "securing." When I made my rounds, mom and Butch were sleeping, and dad was at work. I never told Swanee. I wish I had. Swanee was always a help in explaining my fear and anxiety.

I looked underneath my bed. I never found anyone hiding, but continued to sleep in a fetal position, fearing that someone would cut my legs off. Then, I waited for dad to come home. Since I never found a killer in the house, I came to believe my inspections were warding off murderers.

I wasn't so fortunate with my nightmares. Consistently, one of two terrifying dreams would occur. Less often, I dreamt that the backdoor to our house would not lock. The hole accommodating the deadbolt was too shallow and when I attempted to lock the door, it popped open. I would run down the stairs to our basement for an ice pick to deepen the hole. As I returned to fix the problem, a hand would rip through the outer screen door, grab me by the neck, and pull me into the backyard! The intruder was dressed in a black cloak and he had no face! He took the pick from my hand and jammed it into the side of my face! I would wake up, with my heart was coming out of my chest!

Another nightmare repeated itself for years. I left the Doric Theater one night and a man began to chase me. I started to run. My legs became numb and I could barely move. The man caught up with me. He grabbed me by my neck and slit my throat with a long sharp knife! After he slashed me, I would wake up. My whole body was shaking! I'd turn on the night light and feel my neck for blood.

Soon, my nightly chore of securing the house included a knife inventory. A specific kitchen drawer was checked to count our knives (there were fourteen of them). If a knife was in the sink or on a counter, it would be placed back in the drawer. If a knife was missing, I would search until I found it. If all the knives were in their "proper" place, I deduced they couldn't be used to hurt me. If a knife remained unaccounted for, I would take one to bed with me to "even the score" against my potential killer.

Going to bed at night was a meticulous set of physical and mental procedures. I stuck to them religiously. If I heard strange sounds, my neurotic 'cleansing' was often repeated.

One could never be too cautious at night.

First Love

_&_

In September 1948, I fell in love. She had strawberry blonde hair and smelled like fresh vanilla. Her light brown freckles surrounded the most beautiful eyes in the world. She was wearing a brightly colored sundress. When she walked, her every move was poetic. Her teeth sparkled as she spoke, and in those treasured moments when she addressed me, I was putty in her hands. She was my fourth-grade teacher, Miss Nelson.

The moment I walked into the classroom, I thought I was looking at Doris Day. And when she first spoke, I heard the soft, raspy voice of the popular songstress.

My new teacher softly shook my hand and said: "Hi, Tracy. Welcome to the fourth grade. My name is Miss Nelson."

She was so pretty! Miss Nelson wasn't "old" like my other teachers. They were nice people and very caring, but unlike them, Miss Nelson did not remind me of my Grandma Kier.

Miss Nelson was young and petite. She dressed like a high school student. I was thrilled being in her class. I vowed instantly, on first look, I would love Miss Nelson until my dying day.

I hated myself for being so young and insanely shy. If only I were older, I could ask Miss Nelson to marry me, or at least date her. But I had just turned nine and Miss Nelson told us she was 24. I was disheartened.

My fantasies about Miss Nelson really took flight at home when I went to bed. I invented that Miss Nelson would ask me to stay after school. She reminded me I needed help with my writing skills. With only two of us in the room, she came to my desk and, in her soft, husky voice, asked me to "scoot over."

When she sat next to me, I nearly fainted from being in such proximity to this angel. She gently placed her hand on mine and guided me through a practice sequence of cursive writing. Her other arm was placed around my back to "comfort" me. After appraising the circles and letters, Miss Nelson tilted my chin up to her face with a scented finger. She assured me that I was improving. I was also her favorite student! She then kissed me tenderly on my cheek. The warmth of her lips on my face set every nerve in my scrawny body on fire. I was so in love with Miss Nelson. I prayed my fantasy would become real.

One unit in Miss Nelson's class was proper teeth brushing. Every month, a puppet would appear in the window of our classroom door, signaling it was time for the lesson. The puppet was attached to the arm of our school nurse. She would demonstrate, with the assistance of Miss Nelson, how to brush stroke our teeth. Since most of us had lost several "baby teeth," the nurse emphasized how important it was to maintain our new adult teeth (fluoride was yet to be used as a cavity fighter). I stared in awe as the puppet dry brushed Miss Nelson's porcelain front teeth in her perfectly proportioned mouth.

At the end of the demonstration, each student was given a new toothbrush and small container of tooth powder. I imagined trading brushes with Miss Nelson. I knew her spit would be as sweet as the best of candy.

One Saturday, I saw Miss Nelson leave a bank building in West Duluth and walk into the arms of a tall man who kissed her on the lips. They skipped hand-in-hand to the man's nearby convertible and, shoulders-touching-shoulders, drove away. I was crushed. The love of my life was with someone else, and he had a convertible to boot!

My used Western Flyer bike was lovingly polished and equipped with a shiny chromed rearview mirror, light, and bell, highlighted by grips with long, beautiful red and white streamers. It purred from the baseball cards vibrating against the rear spokes. But a fancy secondhand bike could never compete with a beautiful automobile. Even if I had managed to date Miss Nelson, it would have been impossible to balance her on my handlebars.

I still adored Miss Nelson and forgave her for loving someone else.

My first unrequited love did have a positive outcome. I began to take interest in girls, even if only observational. I was too shy and naive for direct contact with a female schoolmate. I went to Swanee for his wisdom concerning girls. It was a smart move.

Swanee introduced me to the "mysteries" of the female. I learned about "falsies," cup sizes, nipples, degrees of breast bounce, behinds, panties, public hair, colors of hair and consequent behaviors, and vaginas.

Initially, I heard the word vagina as Virginia. I could not understand why a parent would name their baby after a female body part. I thought, what if mom and dad had named me penis! Penis Gran! I'd kill myself while still in diapers! When I asked Swanee why two of the states were named after "that area," he quickly corrected my sexual lexicon. For quite a while, I also assumed Swanee was saying "public hair" when referring to the growth between one's legs. Since "down there" was normally hidden, why wasn't it called private hair? And why was I still bald?

Grade school did not provide any formal unit on sex education. Parents were responsible for discussions about the "birds and bees." It was believed that teaching sex in school would encourage early indulgence. (Even the secondary schools avoided the topic). The only movies shown at Irving, with even a hint of sexual intercourse, were short, dreary film clips on bee pollination. I guess we were supposed to infer there was a relationship between these science flicks and human reproduction? In my mind, bugs and flowers had nothing to do with sex.

Swanee was only two years older than me, but he seemed to know a lot about the opposite sex. It turned out Wayne, his older brother, was his teacher. Wayne was in high school and had his own car (a rare possession for a teenager in the late 1940s). He had a lot of dates with a variety of girls.

Throughout the fourth grade, Swanee and I would often observe females from the privacy of his enclosed, heated front porch. As the "fairer sex" strolled by, Swanee described each female with a profile.

Shirley Hortzer lived on 59th Street and frequently walked past Swanee's house She was a tall, bleached blond woman in her twenties. Swanee noted that Shirley was wearing fake breasts. He told me they were "falsies."

"You can always spot falsies," Swanee noted. "Falsies never bounce, they're overly large, and look like steel cones."

Swanee professed that females like Shirley, who dyed their hair, applied too much makeup, and wore girdles to hide their fat, sloppy asses, were to be avoided. These "types," warned Swanee, were as phony as their falsies.

"What would your impression be," Swanee asked, "of a male who colored his hair, wore gobs of makeup, and stuck a tennis ball in his undershorts to appear to be hung?"

Swanee, as always, answered his own question. "Such a guy is going to be labeled as weird and laughed at. The same is true for women like Shirley. Her type is desperate for attention and pretends to be someone they're not."

I thought Swanee's logic was brilliant.

Aline, a dark-haired 13-year-old, often ambled past on Wadena Street. Swanee drooled as he commented.

"Hubba Bubba! It's Aline, my dream! Now there is a girl worth keeping, Finlander!" Swanee's desire for her was obvious as he described her profile. "Her breasts bounce naturally because she's wearing a light, simple bra. Aline's dark skin is beautiful, just like her natural flowing hair. She will never need or use much makeup. Aline has a great behind, slim legs, and flat stomach. I'll bet Aline is satisfied with what she looks like, and what she's going to look like." (Aline became a local beauty queen in her late teens). Swanee concluded: "There are no disguised features or false fronts with that sweet girl."

Every time he liked what he saw in a female, Swanee would quip, "I bet it would be fun to dress her in the morning." Swanee had countless dreams of "clothing" Aline as they arose together from a night's sleep.

Swanee had many pearls of wisdom about females. For example, he said women with hairy arms and thick heads of hair had lots of "public hair" (the latter being an asset). Females who fold their arms under their breasts while they walk lack self-confidence. Girls with fat legs and pretty faces will eventually have fatter legs and fat faces (not an asset). Women with small breasts have high intelligence. (Swanee deduced that with the emergence of falsies, there were a lot of hidden geniuses roaming the streets). Women with quiet voices and soft eyes make the best moms as they rarely panic and can handle pressure. Loud females with frantic eyes make lousy mothers (and spouses) as such types are impulsive and poor decision makers. Girls with big noses have large, tight vaginas (which I assumed, once again, was a virtue). Flat-chested women have the nicest nipples. Slightly pigeon-toed females have more "style and character" than their flat-footed counterparts. The latter walk and think like penguins. Women who display a pleasant smile also smell great. Redheads are the best kissers as they have fuller lips and longer tongues.

I never questioned the authenticity of Swanee's axioms. Although I did not understand most of what he was telling me, I respected his wisdom. I was lucky to be the recipient of such knowledge. I kept what I learned to myself, foreign as it was, as I wanted to have an edge on my other buddies. Maybe, having gained this storehouse of female facts, my chances of dating the right girl (or any girl) might increase.

Thanks to Swanee, I was now equipped to fall in love with girls of my age. I pledged to avoid making stupid mistakes in the company of potential girlfriends. I didn't want to scare them away. Predictably, even with my newfound knowledge, I scared myself away.

I'm Given Religion

~~

AROUND THE TIME THAT I was falling in love with Miss Nelson, dad unexpectedly decided to require his sons to attend church. The only time Butch and I had been inside a church was in infancy, when we were baptized. Our family was not religious in thought or ritual. Prayer before bedtime ended after the war was over. Grace was never said before a meal. I cannot ever recall the love or wrath of God being used for good or bad behavior. God was irrelevant to mom or dad in disciplining us.

Dad was strict and exact in his discipline. If you failed to act as an adult, and not do your best, you were made to feel guilty. We never let God down, only dad. God entered our life only through dad's cursing. He regularly "goddamned" something or somebody. Mom was plainly not religious. Sin and salvation were not her guideposts for behavior. If mom was "tipsy," there was no discipline. When she was sober, her "rules" were enforced by the reminder to "be good."

My parents confused me. They talked about the importance of moral values, but behaved just the opposite. Mom and dad stressed the need for Butch and me to act "correctly," yet their lives were filled with adultery, alcohol abuse, and endless arguments. How could my brother and I be satisfied using mom and dad as the role models they professed to be??

I lived in the present, satisfied with my little world of imaginary characters and scenarios. As much as possible, I avoided wishful projections (except for one day marrying, or at least dating, Miss Nelson). I had little trust in the people a young kid was supposed to trust, his parents. But I did trust my buddies. And grade school teachers were my saviors, kind and attentive, with a positive outlook on life. My teachers gave me hope and inspiration. I was motivated by their example.

While dad's murder/suicide attempt left me with a lingering fear of being murdered, it was a wakeup call for dad. He stopped drinking, although Butch said he suspected dad continued "socializing" with other women. Butch seemed to enjoy holding that against dad.

With no longer a domestic drinking partner, mom regularly drank "underground" in our basement. In my nightly search for killers, I occasionally found one of her empty vodka bottles. Mom's hidden secret was no longer that hidden.

Dad's sales of encyclopedias improved. He worked only part-time as a projectionist. Dad became active in the Masonry and Shrine, two organizations that his brother and father regularly attended. I think the fellowship in these groups helped alleviate some of the depression and anger that had troubled him for so long. Dad was also paying back his loan to Grandpa Gran.

Dad was still very strict and demanding with us, but his outbursts were practically nonexistent. Perhaps he wanted Butch and me to go to church to share in what he was experiencing in his new group alliances?

With dad's insistence, my brother and I "agreed" to become members of the West Duluth Evangelical Church at the corner of Wadena and 57th Street. Every Sunday morning, commencing in early September 1948, we put on our best clothes and meandered to the old wooden building that smelled of mildew and cheap perfume.

Church services were led by Reverend Noble Scrotters. He spoke with a strange Southern accent. The reverend sported a wig and wore white socks and cheap shoes that squeaked when he walked. He greeted each parishioner with a put-on, artificial smile. I hated shaking hands with him. His hands reminded me of Nabisco's cold and clammy grip in the second grade. With his southern drawl, Reverand Scrotters would greet each person as they arrived by repeating the phrase, "be one with Geeee-sussss."

The Church I Left

I wanted to be one with Porky or Swanee, or anyone outside of that smelly building. I was not meant for church. I felt uncomfortable from day one.

Why did I have to "dress up" and travel to a church? Why couldn't I stay home, in regular clothes, and respect God there? Saying a quick prayer at night, prior to bed, made more sense to me than enduring in fancy clothes for an hour every Sunday. Getting on my knees, clasping my hands with strangers, and praying as a group left me very self-conscious. God rarely answered my prayers anyway. Did God save me from the agony of square dancing with Nabisco?

Reverend Scrotters always opened with the same prayer or blessing, the choir sang a repetitive set of hymns, the 23rd Psalm was voiced in monotonous unison, and Scrotters' sermons were filled with unintelligible words. Only a Quaker or Mennonite could understand him. Who expressed themselves using words like thee, thou, verily, or beseech, in their daily speech? And why did Reverend Scrotters yell when he delivered his messages!

What the reverend preached was ghastly! The vengeance of God, fear of the powers of the Lord, dying unsaved, going to Hell, and the imperfection of human beings—these were just some of the themes in his Christian messages. How could you love someone who had the power to send you to Hell? Reverend Scrotters' sermons were too long (Butch initially referred to the pastor as Reverend Scrotums), and always emphasized the evil misdeeds of everyone. He exhorted that it was good to suffer as pain was God's test of one's faith in Him. Well, I was suffering every Sunday and flunking the exam. Going to Scrotters' church made me feel anything but Christian.

One time, after services, I innocently asked Reverend Scrotters a "poser" about the afterlife. I wanted to know if a good Christian's husband dies and goes to Heaven, and his widowed wife remarries and eventually she and her second husband also go to Heaven, does the second marriage cancel with the wife returning to her first husband?

Reverend Scrotters berating me for even asking such a question. I was mortified! I was innocently trying to solve a riddle, but received only criticism that made me feel ashamed. I never spoke to Reverand Scrotters again.

The music within that building wasn't the stuff of Glen Miller or Harry James. Reverend Scrotters' teenage daughter, Hope, who was uglier than a mud fence, would play a few hymns out-of-tune on her alto saxophone. Only the old people in the pews sang and, like the accompanying cacophonous saxophone, they were equally out of tune.

Reverend Scrotters' choir sounded like an assembly of mourners at a wailing wall. The choir had no male tenor or bass voices. The choir consisted of female ultra-sopranos who cackled like a nest of hens.

And I really struggled with the Bible. Instructed by Reverend Scrotters to learn and repeat an assigned passage each week, I continually failed. None of the verses stuck with me. Most of the sentences used ancient English and were foreign in meaning. It was hard to understand a time that was so long ago.

Lastly, I could not trust a man who simultaneously spoke about the evils of vanity while wearing a wig. I remember thinking if Jesus were to return to West Duluth and happen upon the services of Reverend Scrotters, He would be shocked at what was transpiring!

I left the "sacred walls" every Sunday with a headache. I couldn't tolerate "organized" religion. My attendance waned and ceased after about a month. I faithfully left the house with my brother each Sunday but never made it to the church. I typically prearranged to meet Porky, a preteen heathen like myself, and played outdoors until the service was over. Swanee would never be with us on these diversions. His mother forced him to go to the Gospel Tabernacle. He'd be gone for the whole day! I felt sorry for the poor bastard.

My only fond memory of the church occurred just prior to my abandoning the place. Hope Scrotters was destroying the hymn, "Jesus loves me, this I know," when she suddenly took the saxophone away from her ugly mouth. Hope proceeded to vomit on Mr. and Mrs. Vanaker, a lovely old couple sitting in the front row. While I felt compassion for their unexpected plight of being showered in puke, I surprisingly experienced a sort of exaltation that God had just made an apt commentary on Hope's musical ability.

My absence from the church went unnoticed by mom and dad. Mom really didn't care what I had supposedly learned each Sunday. She would methodically ask the unchanging question: "How was church today?" All I needed to say was: "Okay," and she was satisfied. Mom asked the identical question about school, and I gave the same answer. Dad never inquired about our church experiences. He was now preoccupied with his sales job.

The Revival Meeting

JUST BEFORE THANKSGIVING 1948, MY brother decided to be "saved." Apparently Reverend Scrotters had "reached" Butch.

I asked Swanee what "saved" meant. He said it was a delivery from sin by giving yourself completely to God. I had no real understanding what Swanee was saying, but I did know my brother was acting differently.

Butch became extremely serious and, one day, at age thirteen, he announced he was "turning his will and life over to God." Butch wanted to become a Christian missionary. (Swanee said Butch was becoming a crazy "church monkey.") Butch said he felt chosen to save the "ignorant and misinformed brethren" from something called "paganism." He told mom and dad that his goal was to banish the world of sin. My brother wanted to "transform mankind." I was trying to decide which was better, Coke or Pepsi?

One night at supper, Butch announced he was joining a different congregation, the Alliance Missionary Church in the West End of Duluth. He began to go to this gathering three or four times a week. When he was not in church, Butch would hang out with other "monkeys." He carried a Bible to school and prayed during study halls.

Butch began to distance himself from me and our friends. He stopped playing back alley baseball and other street games. Butch stayed in our bedroom to pray. He subscribed to a religious magazine called the "Moody Monthly." I told him he was going "gaga" over religion and, to piss him off, saying the most frightening words in the English language were "Bible camp."

My joking didn't seem to bother him. He possessed an air of confidence about his new church affiliation and mission.

Butch asked me to go to a religious meeting with him. The "Very Reverend" William White, a Baptist preacher from the South, was coming to town and going to lead a "revival meeting" on Friday and Saturday. Surprisingly, Butch said he would buy me a new Rawlings baseball, the best hardball made, if I attended the revival with him on Friday. (My baseballs were string wrapped in black electric tape). I consented to go. I would do most anything for a new Rawlings baseball.

On a Friday evening in December 1948, Butch and I took a city bus to Wade Stadium. When we arrived, I was amazed. The place was packed! Everyone there had a smile on their face. I saw a few people I knew (including Reverend Scrotters with his hideous daughter), and one of the teachers from Irving Grade School.

Suddenly, behind me, I heard a familiar, hated greeting: "Hello and be one with Geeesusss, Russell and Tracy!" It was Reverend Scrotters.

"Boys," he exclaimed, "we've missed you at church. I am so thrilled to see you at the revival! Praise Jesus for your presence! The Very Reverend White is a spiritual magician! You'll be a lot closer to the Almighty after this session is over."

"Oh yes," chimed in Hope. "You'll never regret what you are about to experience tonight. Get ready for a complete transformation of your body and soul!"

Reverend Scrotters abruptly grabbed my arm.

"Come sit with the congregation," invited Reverend Scrotters. "I have reserved seats for our flock. And Russell, I must say I am delighted you have committed yourself to missionary endeavors. There are so many poor souls needed to be saved. Your unselfish efforts will help in this heavenly process. Bless you, my son. Bless you. Come sit."

We entered the tent. Reverend's Scrotters' church members sat just to the left of the stage. I was squeezed in between Butch and Reverend Scrotters. Hope, the wicked witch of West Duluth, sat next to Butch. As I looked furtively at her, Swanee's lines came to mind.

"She has such buckteeth," asserted Swanee, "she could eat a sandwich through Venetian blinds!"

Hope gave me the willies. She was so self-assured. Someone as homely as her should never be allowed in public. Her strong faith had given Hope a personal confidence that pissed me off.

"What I won't do for a baseball," I thought. "I should get at least two for my attendance."

Everything within the tent was dressed in white--the chairs, carpeting, lectern, even the large curtain. Prior to entering the tent, I noticed the reverend's bus was a bright white and had the inscription: "The Very Reverend William White, World Renowned Evangelist and Faith Healer," in bold letters on its sides.

I asked Butch why the revival atmosphere was all white?

"Because it symbolizes purity," he responded.

"What is purity," I asked?

"Purity represents the state of perfection," he replied. "In Christianity, the goal is to strive for the perfection of the soul, as did our Lord, Jesus Christ, Son of God. A start on the road to purity is to redeem your sins and surrender to God. Purity is never fully reached by mortals, and we are true mortals. Purity is only gained through the reward of being chosen to go to Heaven upon one's death."

God, I thought, why did I even ask? What a frustrating way to live your life. You strive for perfection, knowing full well that such a goal can never be reached. You must die to get the promised reward! This religious stuff was an enormous commitment. What if the whole thing was a desperate, man-made charade? What if you just die, rot, and no part of you goes anywhere?

The revival started with testimonials. People on the stage related how they had terminal cancer, were blind, or couldn't hear—and all of them were sinners. The speakers claimed through the realm of renewed faith in God, and the glorified assistance of the Very Reverend White, their afflictions were banished and they became reborn. As the testimonials were going on, money plates were being passed throughout the crowd. Luckily, mom had given me a roll of pennies. Every time the plate passed my way, I dropped in a cent or two.

Periodically, a choir would sing a hymn. All the members of the choir were dressed in white. I had to admit they were damn good singers. As the evening progressed, the crowd also seemed to energize into a higher and higher fever pitch. People were standing up in loud prayer, with their arms extended, and shaking their hands toward the roof of the tent. Many were crying during the testimonials. The atmosphere became frenzied. A few in the audience passed out on the floor or were rolling and writhing on the white carpet. Other people were talking gibberish as they walked up and down the aisles. Butch said they were talking in "tongues."

Then it was time for Reverend White!

The white curtain behind the stage was back-lit with a bright light. Slowly, the curtain opened to reveal the Very Reverend White. The attendees went mad!

"Ladies and gentlemen of Christ," an announcer boldly bellowed. "I am honored to introduce the faith healer of faith healers, the Savior's esteemed representative in assisting sinners, the curer of afflictions through God's will, the Very Reverend William White!"

Everyone stood up and screamed! Part of the crowd ran to the edge of the stage and tried to touch Reverend White!

Reverend White was dressed in a white suit, tie, shirt, and shoes. His Bible was pure white. His shaded eyeglasses were adorned with white frames. Judging him by his costume alone, you might conclude he was the embodiment of purity. As the crowd screamed in his presence, Reverend White bowed humbly. After what seemed a half an hour, he extended his hand to calm the crowd and asked them to be seated.

With a microphone in hand, Reverend White began sermonizing. He didn't yell like Reverend Scrotters.

"Tonight, my friends, I am going to talk on the topic of investment. Specifically, why we all require the need for investment. To be saved and healed," the reverend emphasized, "you must commit to our Lord Jesus Christ! Invest in Him! Invest in Him! Invest in Him spiritually, bodily, culturally, and monetarily! Your investment in Christ only accrues in value! It will never depreciate! Promise me tonight you will give your all for the sake of Christianity and your souls!" The crowd roared!

The collection plates were once more being passed around the tent. Many people were throwing in ten and twenty dollars!

"You must have faith in the power of God," continued Reverend White. "If you have faith, you will be able to alter your moral state, your spiritual well-being, and yes, I believe, your physical afflictions. We must, in our everyday transactions, commit totally to the investment of the Holy One who died on the cross so long ago and gave His life so we may live. Invest in Jesus as He invested in you! Sacrifice for Jesus as He sacrificed for you! Jesus heals my friends! Jesus heals!"

Reverend White paused and turned toward the curtain behind him.

"Tonight, fellow Christians," lamented Reverend White, "I want you to meet a woman who has been crippled for years."

From behind the curtain, a woman appeared, lamely walking with the aid of crutches. Gasps of sympathy emanated throughout the tent.

The woman slowly, and painstakingly, approached Reverend White.

Reverend White spoke in a quiet, compassionate tone.

"As you can well see, this creature of God can only walk with crutches, and barely at that. She has the affliction of polio. She suffers in pain. This evening, with your prayerful assistance, I will attempt to assist in the healing powers of God. Tonight, I am going to request that you pray for this child of God. Please, find it in your hearts to mercifully ask for a cure so she may walk again without the aid of crutches! We, as Christians, must help our sister in her time of need. Let us appeal to Jesus to heal this precious soul. Invest in the Lord."

Reverend White wrapped his hands on the woman's head, faced the audience, and raised his voice.

"DO YOU BELIEVE I HAVE THE POWER OF JESUS CHRIST IN MY HANDS TO CURE THIS CREATURE OF GOD!?"

The attendees screamed in unison, "WE BELIEVE! WE BELIEVE! WE BELIEVE!"

The reverend continued, "DO YOU HAVE FAITH IN THE LORD THAT HE CAN PERFECT MIRACLES?"

The audience yelled out, "WE HAVE THE FAITH! WE HAVE THE FAITH!"

The Reverend closed his eyes, raised his head toward the ceiling of the tent, and prayed:

"JESUS CHRIST IN HEAVEN, THE SUPREME SAVIOR OF ALL WHO ARE SICK, ASSIST THIS SUFFERING MORTAL BY ALLOWING HER TO WALK ONCE MORE!"

Reverend White turned to the lady and quietly commanded, "Now drop those crutches and walk for Jesus. Yes, walk for Jesus, yes, walk for Jesus."

The crippled woman momentarily hung on to her crutches. Cautiously, she pushed them aside and began to awkwardly walk toward the reverend. The crowd went wild!

On stage, as the woman limped to Reverend White, he would back up, forcing her to struggle further toward him. Soon, the initial awkwardness in her gait disappeared and she confidently strutted around the stage at Reverend White's lead. The audience was screaming in ecstasy.

"LET US PRAY AND THANK THE LORD," commanded Reverend White!

Reverend Scrotters, Butch, and Hope quickly dropped to the floor to pray and, with our arms clasped, they abruptly took me with them. My kneecaps felt broken!

Reverend White loudly proclaimed: "IT IS A MIRACLE! IT IS A MIRACLE! WE HAVE JUST WITNESSED A MIRACLE! THANK YOU, JESUS! THANK YOU, JESUS! THANK YOU, JESUS!"

The woman on stage embraced Reverend White and both commenced in sobbing. The choir began signing: "Glory, Glory, Hallelujah."

"THESE ARE TEARS OF JOY, MY FRIENDS," cried the reverend, "TEARS OF JOY! HALLELUJAH, JESUS SAVES! JESUS SAVES! THANK YOU, DISCIPLES OF CHRIST, FOR YOUR POWER OF PRAYER! GOD ANSWERS PRAYERS AND HE HAS ANSWERED YOURS TONIGHT! THANK YOU, THANK YOU, GOD IN HEAVEN, THANK YOU!

GOOD NIGHT, MY FRIENDS, MY CHRISTIAN BRETHREN, AND MAY GOD BLESS YOU!"

Very Reverend White then quietly instructed the crowd: "Please witness God's power again tomorrow night. Praise Jesus. He is truly our Savior. Invest, my friends. Invest. You will reap the rewards of your investments.

Slowly, Reverend White proceeded to back off the stage, escorting the "healed" woman. The audience was standing and wildly applauding. The chorus now broke out into the hymn, "Jesus loves me, this I know" and, very slowly, the exhausted but thoroughly beaming audience began to leave the tent.

When we got outside, my brother had the grin of the happiest person in the world.

"What a heavenly night! Do you see what faith in God can do, Tracy," he asked? "Are you now glad that you attended this miraculous event? I am all tuckered out. How about you? How do you feel? You must have felt the power of the Lord?"

I had to admit to Butch that my heart was beating fast and the meeting was very emotional. "Butch," I said, "that was the loudest group of people I have ever been with."

My comments seemed to satisfy him as he enthusiastically suggested, "Let's go tomorrow night! Okay?" I hesitated a bit in responding.

Butch was so happy, but, I finally had to say, "I don't think I want to go again. The meeting was scary to me."

"Scary?" My brother's impatience with me was evident and he screamed, "You have just witnessed the power of Jesus! We'll go again tomorrow night. I guarantee you will no longer be scared."

"Let me think about going," I meekly responded.

We walked toward the bus that would take us home.

"Tracy, if you don't go with me tomorrow night," said Butch, "I'm not going to buy you a baseball." Butch had a stubborn look on his face,

"That's not fair, Butch," I cried! "The promise was that if I attended tonight, you would get me a new Rawlings. Are you going back on your promise?" I now wanted to give him an ass kick.

"Yes, I am!" Butch was mad. "You have a chance to enrich your soul and all you worry about is getting a dumb baseball!"

We rode home silently.

That night, in our bedroom, Butch whispered to me, "Tracy, I am going to pray for you. Without God in your life, sin will destroy you. I am committed to make every effort to convert you to the Christian way of life. Things are going to change around here."

"Things" did change.

Butch began by attempting to fine me for saying bad words! He declared his "mission bottle" would receive a nickel from me if he heard me use the name of the Lord in vain (or if I gave him the middle finger). Furthermore, if I failed to attend church on Sunday, he was going to rat on me. And he wanted me to begin reading the Bible prior going to bed at night. Butch was becoming a "dick head." I vowed to myself, with all the *sisu* I could muster, I would resist his conversion efforts. He lied to me and now, he was trying to control me.

During the following week, I confessed to mom that I didn't want to go to services anymore. I told her I believed in God, (and I did), but I couldn't stomach the way He was being presented at church. Besides, I said, what good is going if you only hate it when you get there? Mom seemed sympathetic to my logic, but she said, "The decision is up to your father."

Dad was disappointed in me. He talked about obligation. "Life is made up of all sorts of things you don't want to do," he said. "But duty requires you to carry through to the end. Every project must be completed, Tracy. I don't feel you gave church your best effort."

Dad was "*sisuing*" again. But, his speech notwithstanding, he relented. Since dad had the final say, I was happily released from church attendance obligations (even though I had already stopped listening to Scrotters' verbal manure weeks before).

Dad most likely consented to my wishes because he himself was not raised in a religious household. He understood my anguish. Contributing to his decision was his dislike of Butch's religious conversion and sermonizing, calling it a waste of time and talent. "Butch's preoccupation with religion, at such an early age, is foolish," said dad.

Butch was surprised and hurt that dad had supported my wishes. Butch vowed to never forgive dad for his insulting decision.

I never got a Rawlings baseball from Butch. It didn't matter. Freedom from organized religion was more important to me. Reverend Scrotters and his coyote ugly daughter were out of my life.

In my own way, I now felt "saved," even defiantly victorious.

And I never gave a nickel to Butch's missionary bottle.

My brother and I were growing apart.

Another Love

〜⌒〜

PEOPLES MARKET WAS A SMALL "mom and pop" store, diagonally across from our house on 58th Street. Similar grocery stores existed on almost every street corner in my neighborhood in the forties. Peoples Market employed two butchers, a checkout clerk, a delivery truck person, and a part-time "assembly" clerk.

A popular and convenient service of the market was home delivery. After the order was called in, the part-time clerk would assemble the items and place them into boxes. The delivery person would dispatch the groceries to the homes of the call-in customers. receiving payment on arrival. People's was predominately a "cash and carry" store. But credit was made available.

The owners of People's Market, George and Helen Bengston, lived next door to their store. Mr. Bengston had competed against the Harlem Globetrotters in the late 1930s and played in an exhibition game versus the Minneapolis Lakers. Mr. Bengston boasted that he personally knew such Laker greats as George Mikan, Vern Mikkelson, Slater Martin, Jim Pollard, Whitey Skoog, and the Lakers new coach, Johnny Kundla. Because of his athletic feats and professional acquaintances, he was a hero to almost every kid in the neighborhood.

Porky, Swanee, and I loved to listen to Mr. Bengston's stories about sports. While he was cutting meat, just inside by the screened side entrance to the butcher shop, we would gather outside and talk to Mr. Bengston about sports for hours. He often gave us a free popsicle or a fudgesicle. One hot day we had only a nickel among the three of us. Instead of sharing a nickel coke, Mr.

Bengston treated us with three large cokes (they cost a dime apiece). He said we could pay him back after we became millionaires. I think it was his way of rewarding us for talking with him. We needed no reward.

Mr. Bengston took me to a Duluth Dukes minor league baseball game at Wade Stadium in Spring 1949. Walking into the stadium for the first time, I was mesmerized by the sounds and savored smells of the place. My interest in professional baseball was sparked.

I was thrilled by the bright lights, the aromas of popcorn, hot dogs, and cigars, the contagious excitement of the crowd, the precise manicuring of the field with its finely mowed grass and perfectly raked infield! The people at the park were fans faithful to their team and the game, quick to criticize any bad play and loudly applaud a good one—by either team. Mr. Bengston said true baseball fans were "students of the game." They jeered, booed, and analyzed. Just being part of the crowd was almost as exciting as watching the game. I took in every moment of it. I fell in love again.

The players wore such sharp looking uniforms with fancy leggings and spiked shoes. I couldn't wait to get older and be just like those guys on the field.

Mr. Bengston even introduced me to Frank "Rip" Wade, for whom the stadium was named. He was at my initial game sitting immediately in front of us! I was so excited!

Mr. Wade once played in the major leagues. Mr. Bengston said that he was the only player from Duluth to make it to the big leagues. He also told me that Mr. Wade lived one block from my house in a home bordering Highway 61. My heart was bursting out of my chest! And I had an occasion to pitch to Mr. Wade soon thereafter!

A few days after my first trip watching a professional baseball game, Swanee, Porky and I were playing catch in the alley next to the Peterson's house. Mr. Wade happened along and showed us how to throw a curve and fast ball. Using Swanee's catcher's mitt, he had us each pitch five curve balls to him and five fast balls. For a man of his age, Mr. Wade was still adept at catching and throwing a hardball. When we were done, he said I had the most potential as a pitcher! I was now in heaven! A former major leaguer had complimented my abilities! Wow! Double wow!

After we pitched, Mr. Wade sat down on an old chair next to one of the garages. He told us some stories about his short stint in the major leagues. He played part of the 1923 season with the Washington Senators. He was in the same league with Babe Ruth! (Ruth had recently died in August 1948). Mr. Wade revealed Babe was a very funny and talented man. He said Ruth used a heavy bat. He was very strong and early in his career hit more homers than many entire teams!

Mr. Wade autographed the scrubby baseballs we were using. I think he got a bigger thrill than we did in signed the balls. He obviously liked kids. I was so proud that I got a chance to not only meet and talk to him—I pitched to him! A major leaguer caught my throws!

In Spring 1949, my mind became preoccupied with the love of Miss Nelson and Dukes baseball. I fantasized that soon I would take Miss Nelson to a Dukes baseball game! What a date that would be! My fantasy remained a fantasy.

My Uncle Ralph was an avid Dukes fan. When I told him about my trip to the stadium and meeting Mr. Wade, he suggested I go with him to the games. My parents gave me money for each admission. Soon, my Aunt Edith, Grandma Kier, and mom said they would like to attend the games. The five of us began going to the Duluth Dukes' home contests in 1949.

Uncle Ralph was a true sports fanatic and had, in his youth, participated in many semi-professional leagues. He also was a former player for the once popular Duluth Hornets, a semi-pro hockey team. He still participated in fast pitch softball and was quite a hitter and fielder.

The "ladies" (my grandma, aunt, and mom) discovered they also loved baseball. They went to most of the home games. I also played organized ball for the Irving Cadets, a Little League team representing West Duluth. I was becoming a baseball "nut."

The Duluth Dukes were part of the Northern League, a Class C league organization that served as an eventual "feeder" of players for the majors. The league comprised the Dukes, Superior Blues, Aberdeen Pheasants, St. Cloud Rox, Sioux Falls Canaries, Grand Forks Chiefs, Eau Claire Bears, and Fargo-Moorhead Twins.

The Dukes' dugout was situated on the third base side of the field. We always sat in the bleachers just to the left of their dugout. The stadium was built in the 1930's as a WPA (Works Progress Administration) project. It was an impressive brick structure. Each home game (the season started in late April and finished in early September), we would gather in Uncle Ralph's 1937 Plymouth and travel to the stadium. When Uncle Ralph was working as a bartender at the Kom On Inn in West Duluth, and couldn't attend, we rode the city bus.

It was an interesting time to watch professional baseball as the sport was just beginning to break the color barrier, thanks to Jackie Robinson and the Brooklyn Dodgers in 1947. (One of the first black players for the Dukes was a second baseman, Dick Newberry.)

In those days, there were many fans who didn't accept integration on the athletic field (or any place else). Many black players were incessantly derided. The prejudiced assumption was that "coloreds" were taking away positions from qualified white athletes. Thankfully, that attitude began to ebb (or at least was hidden), and group sports became the leader in "public" racial integration in the late forties. The realization that interdependence is crucial in a team sport served to hinder discrimination on the field. Prejudicial attitudes still existed in the dugouts and stands (and even longer in hotels, busses, and eateries).

Most teams had at least three or four blacks on their rosters. Some of the black players that I remember best were Billy Bruton, Wes Covington, Joe Caffie, and a guy named Henry Aaron. Bruton, Covington, and Aaron played for Eau Claire and rose to the major leagues. They eventually played for a World Series champion, the Milwaukee Braves. Joe Caffie played for the Dukes and made it to the "big" leagues.

I saw future big leaguers Roger Maris playing for Aberdeen and Don Mincher starring for the Dukes. The oddest names I recall were players "Ducky" Quack, Gideon "no hit" Applegate, and Bruno Casanova. Probably the most feared ball player at that time was the slugger, Frank Gravino. In one year, he hit more than 50 home runs, but he never made it to the majors.

Managers of the ball clubs would coach at third base, right near our seats. Former major leaguer Zeke Bonura was our favorite. He would play a "walking game" with the fans. As Bonura strutted from the visitors' dugout to the third base coaching box, the fans yelled in timely unison, "hep," as he took each step. Sometimes Bonura froze his strut in mid-stride to mess up the verbal cadence from the fans. He would also run halfway and then slowly walk. Thus, "hepping" was more difficult. An older gentleman in the crowd near us leaned over the railing one night and yelled, "Hey Zeke, I saw you play for the White Sox in the middle 1930s." Bonura came over to the aged man and shook his hand and they conversed for a few minutes. He was the first former major leaguer (besides Frank Wade) that I had ever seen in person. An intense yearning invaded my heart and soul. I wanted to be a professional baseball player.

Another thrill was to see Eddie Feigner, the King and His Court, come to Wade Stadium. Feigner was a pitcher who could throw a softball ball faster than 100 miles an hour. He would pitch blindfolded, throw behind his back, between his legs, and all the way from second base! No one on the Dukes team hit him, which was a good thing as his "court" consisted of only three other players—catcher, first baseman, and shortstop. The guy was superhuman. I never saw a person who had such mastery over a ball like Feigner.

Northern League away games were broadcast using a phone system. The broadcaster for the Dukes was in a Duluth radio studio. He listened to a "live" broadcaster, by phone, from the "road" town. The Duluth broadcaster would have one ear to the phone and, speaking into his microphone, relay the plays via radio to the listening audience. To add a sense of realism, false crowd noises were added to the play-by-play as the Duluth broadcaster announced a game, sight unseen. A team broadcaster rarely traveled to an away stadium to broadcast games. I heard all the road games and simulated the batting in my bedroom with my trusty 28-inch bat. I knew every player's batting average, runs-batted-in, and number of home runs— for all eight teams! I methodically updated them in a notebook.

In a later year (1953), I managed to collect the autographs of every player for all eight teams in the league. Hanging out at the dugout tunnel as the players went by, I would ask them to sign my book. I never received one refusal.

It was the year Hank Aaron played for Eau Claire (as a shortstop). I treasured his autograph. A few years later, mom, inadvertently, destroyed my book of autographs as she cleaned our bedroom.

Admission to a ball game was 40 cents for kids under 16. Popcorn was 25 cents a box, a soda was 15 cents, hot dogs cost 35 cents, and a program was priced at 15 cents. So, for the price of $1.30, a youngster could enjoy a full game and a meal, with a scorecard to boot.

There were many doubleheaders in those days. Games were typically seven innings apiece, although occasionally the first game would be seven innings and the second a full nine innings. At the completion of each half inning, the players coming off the field left their gloves on the playing ground. Protective helmets, batting gloves, and pine tar rags were yet to be introduced to the game. Pitchers used a full wind up (unless, of course, a player was on base). Pitch counts were unknown and managers could make as many visits to the mound as they wanted. Instant replay was, of course, unknown (it would be introduced sixty years later). The absence of electronic validation of a "call" led to numerous arguments with the umpires. "Kill the ump" was a common chant at every game.

Sometimes my grandma would bake a cake or some pies and literally walk down into the dugout to give the treats to the players. She was known as "grandma" by the team and received hugs from the guys. Such generosity was a common occurrence by many fans in those days. Players would receive all sorts of gifts. Many spectators had players over for Sunday dinner when they were in town.

Beer was served at the ball games but I don't remember any of "the ladies" indulging. They were caught up in the action of the game. I so enjoyed being with them. Each knew as much about the strategies and rules of the game as any person in those stands.

I can still hear my grandmother yell, "goddamn it!" at the top of her voice when an opposing player hit a home run or got a key hit. When the Dukes played well, she applauded by yelling, "How do you like them apples!?" She never booed a player on any side of the field, whether the athlete be white or black. (Racial prejudice and discrimination were not part of "the ladies" makeup}. Grandma Kier just admired a good performance and couldn't stand losing, and with her high-pitched voice, let everyone around her know it. What a free spirit she was!

Miss Nelson was no longer the only love of my young life. I now had baseball.

Mom and The Others

A Lonely Mom

GRANDMA'S CONSISTENT SUPPORT OF THE Dukes, even when they were losing, taught me an important lesson: never give up when competing in sports. Even though she wasn't Finnish, she had more "good *sisu*" than most full-bloodied Finlanders. I admired her tenacity, sense of fair play, and honest competitiveness. She made me happy.

Mom, on other hand, was making me increasingly angry with her drinking. The smell of liquor was on mom's breath almost every day, beginning in Summer 1949. Instantly, I could tell if she had been drinking. The "give away" was her repeating herself (on just about every topic), or humming the same song, over and over. She also kept her distance for fear of my smelling alcohol on her breath, but it didn't matter. Her change in behavior was the giveaway.

I never confronted mom about her drinking habit. After finding her bottle stashed in a basket of laundry, tucked behind the coal bin, or even hidden inside the washing machine, I would take it to the kitchen, angrily, and put it on the table. I was hoping I could embarrass her back to sobriety. When I checked, later, the bottle was always gone. Never once did mom admit to me that she had been drinking.

I could not accept mom abusing alcohol. I didn't know what to do about it. It was embarrassing to think our neighbors might call her a drunk. For a while, I pretended her drinking was just a secret between the two of us. This failed attempt at coping did not improve matters. Sadly, remaining silent was a mistake. If only I had talked to others about mom, something might have been done to help her.

I didn't understand the need to drink so much. I equated excessive drinking as a weakness, not a symptom of disease. Mom was an alcoholic.

Mom also secretly drank with other men. Unlike her dalliances when I was younger, by the end of the fourth grade, I knew the identities of most of her drinking buddies.

Probably the most obvious "consort" was "Uncle Mac," an engineer on the iron ore boats. When in town, he would stay at our house, and in my youthful innocence, I thought he was my uncle. I looked forward to his visits and presents for Butch and me. Uncle Mac told funny stories about his seagoing adventures on the Great Lakes. He took us out to nice restaurants for dinner and was fun to be around.

Uncle Mac was a heavy drinker. For some reason, dad had no problem allowing mom and "Uncle Mac" to drink openly at our house. The three of them would stay up until early in the morning, and talk and laugh. Later, after learning that Mac was not a relative, I still accepted him as a member of the family.

One summer night in 1949, when dad was working and Mac staying at our house, Swanee and I returned home from playing basketball at the West Duluth YMCA. We stopped at his house across the street to have a Coke. Enjoying our sodas on his front porch, we looked at the front room of my house and saw mom kissing Mac on the mouth! And he had one hand on her bare breast!

I was flabbergasted! Mac was "making out" with my mother in our living room! I started to cry. I couldn't help it. I was crushed! Swanee grabbed me by an arm and took me for a long walk. He tried his best to soothe my hurt in saying: "Sometimes, bad things happen when people drink too much." He assured me that he still respected mom. Swanee said mom had always been kind to him and that everyone adored her. His comments made me feel better. Swanee was such a consoling friend. But I was still all numb inside. I had just seen something that a son should never have to see.

When I went home, I headed straight to bed. I couldn't bear looking at either Mac or mom. I didn't sleep very well that night, or for a long time afterward. I felt betrayed.

The seduction remained secret. Swanee would never gossip about mom. Mac was no longer funny to me. I couldn't stand being in his presence. He was not a friend to my father or to any of us. Mac was a liar and a sneak. He was exploiting my mother and her need for affection. My parents' relationship was more of a father-daughter bond. Consequently, mom felt unloved as a mature adult. She sought "love" elsewhere, with the assistance of booze.

I was discovering that alcohol had a way of softening inhibition. Mom was acting the opposite of her true character. That was not my "real" mother being fondled by Mac. As in the past, I tried to envision the scene as fictional in my mind. I simply could not accept what I had observed.

The mom I loved and respected was the baseball game mom, the mom who softly sang while ironing clothes in the kitchen, and the mom who kissed my brother and me at night before we turned the lights out for bed. The mom I treasured was the one who had me clean the clothes lines in the backyard on a sunny day and hugged me after I helped her hang the heavy wash. Later, as we folded the dry bed sheets together, our hands would meet and she would give me a kiss on my forehead and say, "There's another love tap, Ducky Bumps." Although I acted embarrassed, I enjoyed being called the affectionate nickname.

But most of all, the mom I loved listened to the radio at night with her family. She would always dance with us when the "live" big band shows came on from numerous hotel ballrooms across America. I was not much of a dancer but I adored being escorted around the living room, trying my best to not step on her feet, as we kept pace with the likes of Kay Keyser, Artie Shaw, Glen Miller, or Russ Morgan.

On rare Saturday evenings when dad was home, our parents danced together. Everything I worried about, denied, or feared seemed to go away in those moments. Such music-filled Saturday nights were times of joy and laughter. Mom and dad loved Tommy and Jimmy Dorsey, Glen Gray (and his Casa Loma Orchestra), Ralph Flanagan, the Ink Spots, and Benny Goodman. Mom's favorite singers were the King Sisters, Anita O'Day, Dick Haymes, Frankie Lane, and the Andrews Sisters. Dad was a fan of Fran Warren, Dinah Shore, Peggy Lee, Jo Stafford, and, especially, Margaret Whiting. Regrettably, such dance nights were infrequent.

Dad suspected something was amiss with mom. He began to distrust her. Almost every morning, dad would quiz mom about her previous daily events. Where had she been, what had she done, and was she feeling all right? He would inquire about the specifics of how her "weekly allowance" was being spent.

During the week, when dad was "on the road" for days selling encyclopedias, mom usually went out at night. Mom claimed she was going to the library, but Butch and I knew that was a lie. Typically, mom returned home late in the evening very drunk. The next morning, as Butch and I got ready for school or to go outside to play, mom was "hung over," grumpy and impatient, and not looking very well.

One night, I attempted to identify the driver of the car that dropped mom off after a night out. I saw the car was a rare, green, two door Hudson, and I instantly knew who the driver was, George Lunder, a cohort of my father in the book selling business. Another "so-called" friend of dad turned out to be a scumbag cavorting with our vulnerable mother.

I never told dad about mom's "excursions" for fear what he might do to her. After all, dad had tried to murder mom a year earlier. I had so many secrets. After a while, it got tiring and burdensome.

I'm confident my brother held onto some "hush-hushes" that I knew nothing about. He was under more pressure than me, no less confused and unhappy. I really had little true understanding of the severity of his agony. At that time of my young life, I believed Butch was simply a full-blooded prick.

Our mother spent a lot of time with our neighbor, Mr. Center. Mom would go for a preplanned daytime walk. Mr. Center would pick her up to go drinking. I think Mr. Center was a lonely person. His marriage also lacked spousal affection. Mom shared in his loneliness. They would go to bars, usually across the bay in Superior, Wisconsin, where few people knew them.

It was tough to hate Mr. Center. He was not an exploitive person. I had no proof, or belief, that Mr. Center and mom did anything but drink together. Their relationship as "drinking pals," however, was still very embarrassing.

One day in summer 1949, I was playing basketball with my buddies in our alley. Slowly, up the alley, came Mr. Center's car. It stopped about 30 yards from where we were playing. The passenger door swung open. Out stepped mom. She was staggering. Mom slammed the car door and zigzagged her way by us into the back door of our house. It wasn't a pretty sight. I was mortified. My buddies said nothing about what they had just seen. They respected what I was going through, as many lived with horror stories involving their own parents.

Mr. Center knew I loved baseball. A few days after the "alley scene," he took me to a game between the Dukes and Superior Blues at the Superior field in Wisconsin. It was the first road game to a "foreign" stadium that I had experienced. Mr. Center bought me hot dogs, soda, and candy, and the Dukes won!

On the way home, he pulled over in front of a small bar in Superior.

"Tracy," he said, "I've got to go into this "restaurant" for a few minutes to attend to some business. I'll be right out."

About 45 minutes later, Mr. Center came out of the bar with a man who was very fat and wore a loud bowling shirt. Both men smelled of alcohol.

"This is one of Mary's sons," the portly man questioned? "Glad to meet you, Stacey!" He shook my hand and commented, "Ya know your mother is one hell of a great lady! We all love her here at the club! She's just peachy!"

A strange man from a strange club in a strange city loved my mother. I didn't think it was "just peachy."

Alcohol temporarily soothed mom's sense of loneliness. Her drinking provided affection, albeit exploitive, from other men. But at my age, I failed to understand how much she suffered. I know she loved my brother and me. We loved her. But our love could never substitute for the absence of love she received from her husband, our dad.

I hated alcohol.

I vowed I would never drink when I grew up.

To The Hills......

$\backsim$

CAMPING WAS A FUN ADVENTURE for nearly all my neighborhood buddies. At first, in our "blending with nature," outings were in a tent at a buddy's backyard where we slept outdoors overnight. Actual sleep rarely occurred, marred by lumpy sleeping bags, rain and wind, hungry mosquitoes, and continuous farting. When someone walked by, breathing as though they had asthma, we were convinced it was Mr. P. coming to kill us. We immediately abandoned our tent and escaped to the safety of a buddy's bedroom.

One memorable outing a garden snake was discovered amid our sleeping bags. When we jumped to our feet, the tent collapsed on our heads. Our escape from that "snake pit" turned into a scene from a Three Stoogies movie. There was much yelling and disentangling, and once outside, I stumbled over my bike and chipped a front tooth. It was an adult tooth, but luckily, only a small piece was broken off. Dad was pissed, especially after he spent $10 for a visit to the dentist.

Porky, Swanee, and I often hiked to the Skyline Drive, a winding picturesque road through the upper hills of Duluth. The road stretched almost the length of the city. The hills were heavily forested with choice campsites. During the summer, we always started our camping adventure on a Friday. (Saturdays were out because Swanee had to go to early church services on Sundays).

Swanee had a nice tent, just large enough for us and our equipment. All of us had sleeping bags, Porky supplied the utensils for cooking, and we purchased our camping food from People's Market. Mr. Bengston enjoyed hearing the stories of our camping adventures. He said that we'd remember those times for the rest of our lives.

Mr. Bengston knew what he was talking about. A most memorable campout took place in late August 1949, just after my tenth birthday.

The three of us were planning to hike to the Skyline again. The weather was forecasted to be warm, with no rain. We decided to splurge and bought three good-sized porterhouse steaks at People's. They were around .75 cents apiece, paid for with money from Porky's and Swanee's paper routes and my now 50 cents weekly allowance. Mr. Bengston always cut the steaks thicker than normal and charged us less for the meat. He had no son and I think he felt like an adopted father to the three of us.

My mother gave me some potatoes, a bag of "pre-squeezed" margarine, and tin foil for wrapping. (We buried the foil-covered potatoes in the coals of the fire for an hour before we fried our meat.) Porky's mother had contributed some deviled egg sandwiches. Mrs. Swanson provided three large pieces of her exquisite chocolate cake. Of course, consistent with Swanee's mother, the pieces had a religious tract tucked between them.

We also bought a mammoth bag of Red Dot Potato Chips for 29 cents. Red Dots were saltier and crisper than its competitor, Old Dutch Chips. We had Army canteens on our belts filled with water and backpacks to haul the food and equipment.

After the war, every young American boy wanted to be identified with the armed services. Possessing infantry equipment was the cat's meow. In our neighborhood, most birthday and Christmas gifts came from the local army/navy store. Playing "war" was a popular game. I alone killed thousands of "Japs" and "Krauts" in the three or four years after World War II. Such imaginary enemies were all gunned down in my neighborhood using my "Jap-Zapper" machine gun, snowballs, and cap gun. I was wounded a thousand times but miraculously healed after every battle.

We met in the early morning at Swanee's house. The food and equipment were laid on Swanee's front lawn to make sure nothing was forgotten. We had a box of stick matches, a flashlight, ten boxes of Snaps licorice (my favorite candy), a small army surplus shovel, and every kid's favorite, a few boxes of Milk Duds.

We loaded our backpacks and were on our way. I felt like a brave adventurer, a combination of John Wayne, Richard Conte, and Daniel Boone. I had my canteen strapped to one leg, and a short length of rope looped through my belt. Swanee carried the tent and sleeping bags. He had a canteen and a flashlight strapped to his legs. Porky had pots and pans hanging from his backpack, and tied to his legs were a canteen and a large Bowie knife—a gift from his now deceased father. Porky treasured the item. We all were wearing fatigue hats and "pacs" (rubber-soled boots).

As we strutted by the screened side entrance to People's Market, Mr. Bengston came to the door and yelled: "Give 'em hell, boys, there's danger in them thar hills!" We all gave him the two-finger "V" for victory sign as we proudly marched up Wadena Street. We felt like young heroes on a mission.

"You don't have to be with an adult to spend the night in the deep woods," I remember boasting to myself. "You just need guts and savvy." (And a few buddies to accompany you certainly helped. It was amazing how the addition of sidekicks instilled courage in your veins. There was safety in numbers, or so I thought.)

We turned onto 59th Street, crossed Highway 61, and began the long uphill trek to the edge of the Skyline woods. We planned to camp just beyond the DM@IR railroad tracks, where there was a small station house manned by a lone railroad worker. The trail led to an abandoned, monstrous gravel pit. I prided myself in knowing the details of every trail around the rim of that pit, how long they were and where they led.

We agreed to take the trail that followed the left edges of the pit. It was the most crooked and hardest to walk, but it would get us to the Skyline Drive. Our destination was just short of that roadway.

We found a dead dog lying in the entry trail, about 40 yards past the railroad tracks. It was a male collie. His tongue was hanging out of the side of his mouth. We all knelt around the still animal. Swanee felt the dog's neck and said it was still warm. When he took his hand away, his fingers were bloody.

"This dog was shot by someone," he exclaimed. "Look. You can see the wound in the back of his head."

"Why would someone shoot a dog," I said, "especially a collie?"

"He might have been sick," Porky guessed. "He's a pretty old looking fellow. Maybe someone just ended his misery?"

"Hopefully, he died quickly," I added. "It doesn't seem right to leave him out here in the open. Why don't we bury him in the sand pit?"

We all agreed that the dog deserved a decent grave. Soldiers buried their dead during the war. So, it seemed the right thing to do. We took off our gear for an easier burial.

Swanee grabbed the front legs of the dog while Porky and I each took a hind leg. The dog didn't weigh much. We had no trouble lifting and carrying the animal to the sand pit. We took him to a shady spot where evergreens were sprouting up in the sand.

"This is a good spot," declared Swanee. "He'll be in the shade and I don't think anyone will dig for sand here."

I took out my small spade and began to dig. While I shoveled, Porky and Swanee pulled young evergreen trees out of the sand near the grave hole. We took turns digging. The day was starting to warm up and all of us were really sweating.

"Let's cover the pooch with something," Swanee suggested. "Ya know, to give it some honor."

We found an old tarp and some used tar paper near the station house. With the tar paper at the bottom of the hole, and the collie wrapped in the tarp, Swanee gently lowered the dog into the makeshift grave.

"Here, little fella," said Porky, "take this to play with in doggie heaven." He placed an old tennis ball from his backpack into the hole.

"And I'll throw in a box of Snaps so he won't go hungry," I added, contributing the candy from my backpack.

As I picked up the spade to begin covering the dead animal, the religious influence of Swanee's mother moved him to say: "Wait. Before we bury him, let's each throw a spade of sand on the dog, and I'll say a short prayer."

After tossing in one shovelful each, Swanee bowed his head and prayed.

"Dear God, welcome this collie dog into Heaven and allow him an eternal life of happiness. In your name, we ask you this blessing. Amen."

As we were refilling the hole, Porky said to Swanee, "Jesus Christ, Swanee. That was nice. You sounded like a minister. Maybe that's your calling?"

"Ya," I added. "You pray better than the Noble Scrotums guy. You and my brother have something in common. And your mom would be proud of you if she was here."

Swanee had a big grin on his face.

"First, Finlander, I like Butch, but I'm no match for his sermonizing. Second, if my mother were with us, we would be burying her next to the dog. She can barely walk up the front stairs of our house!"

We broke into guarded laughter remembering that Mrs. Swanson, less than five feet tall, was seriously overweight.

"Plus," Swanee added, "how the hell could we have lifted her!? She's quite chunky. My dad says you know your overweight when the clothes you're wearing weigh more than you do!"

Swanee's humor at his mother's expense wasn't meant to be demeaning. He loved his mother and we all respected her. His joking helped hide the fact that the three of us had lumps in our throats over the burial of the dead collie. We all felt like we were honorable Marines burying a fallen comrade, albeit in this case, a canine.

"We should put a cross on his grave," Swanee suggested. "But we don't have any hammer or nails to make one." Swanee paused for a moment and then said: "Shit! Maybe he wasn't even a Christian dog. Maybe he was Jewish?"

"My cat's a Lutheran." I interjected. "Even he can't stand Scrotum's preaching."

We all laughed. The idea of an animal having a religion seemed absurd.

"Let's get moving," said Porky. "We want to make camp before it really gets hot. Today's going to be a scorcher. Even now I'm warmer than a nun's ass in full habit."

Putting our backpacks back on, we silently walked the half mile to our campsite. We were all thinking about the dead dog.

I vowed to plant a cross at the collie's grave on our next trip. In some undefinable way, I did believe in God. But my hazy belief could never be based on the terms given to me by Reverend Scrotters, or my brother, much less that scary revival meeting. I never feared God, but sometimes I hated Him.

I wanted to believe in Heaven, but the dead don't talk. I identified more with Joe DiMaggio than I did Jesus Christ. It was difficult for me to devote my life to a person who lived almost two thousand years ago.

How could Jesus solve problems of a young Finn living in Northern Minnesota? Did He even know I existed?

Was Butch right in warning me that I was leading a life of sin? I tried not to lie (except white lies) and had yet to steal. I never attempted to hurt anyone. In increasing order of intensity: public speaking, violence, drunks, and girls scared me. I was competitive, but I never jeered any opponent. Imagination and fantasy occupied many of my days. I loved to play. And most certainly, I would adore Miss Nelson for the rest of my life. Such was my life at ten. Was I being sinful?

Thinking to myself made the time walking to the campsite pass quickly. It was a familiar spot. The setting was in a grove of birch trees that formed an umbrella-like covering. The ground was generally flat for a hilly area. Nearby, there was a small babbling brook where we washed our utensils, faces, and hands and refilled our canteens. Swanee said running water was safe to drink.

I scouted for dry sticks and birch logs to start the fire pit. Later, in the afternoon, I would get a fire going. On would go the tinfoil wrapped potatoes, and eventually, with charcoal briquettes added to increase the heat, the steaks.

Porky and Swanee began to set up the tent. They were meticulous in making an orderly placement of our equipment. Sleeping bags were laid out in the tent along with our tools and food.

"The key to good camping is neatness," declared Swanee, "and knowing where everything is when you need it."

"Oh ya," I quickly responded sarcastically. "I've seen your bedroom. It's a shit hole with blankets." Swanee instantly grabbed my hand and tightly squeezed it.

"Shut up, Finlander," he ordered. "At least I don't have to share a hell hole with Reverend Russell."

"Let go of my hand, you faggot," I painfully dictated, "or I won't let you cuddle up with Porky in his sleeping bag tonight!"

"Well," responded Swanee in an extremely feminine voice. "You don't have to be so bitchy!"

"Come on, girls," chimed in Porky in an equally falsetto feminine voice. "I'll not tolerate any messing of your hair and makeup, so stop the cat fighting and let's go for a prance. We'll leave our treasures here. They'll be safe."

(Making "humorous" homosexual innuendos among young boys was common practice in the forties. A great deal of homophobia existed. World War II media emphasized manliness and heterosexual erotica. An "ideal man" was the masculine warrior, a fighter who didn't mince words, always victorious, and a conqueror of his women. John Wayne epitomized this admired stereotype. Seriously labeling a male a "queer," "faggot" or worse yet, "cocksucker," was an insult. Boys with lisps and/or high-pitched voices were always "suspect" and generally not included as legitimate buddies. Lesbians were not a topic of conversation. Kids didn't know of their existence).

"Going for a prance" from camp usually meant a walk up to the paved roadway. The Skyline Drive had the best views of the hilly city of Duluth. Some people called Duluth the San Francisco of the upper Midwest. I always felt the "air-conditioned city" was a more apt name because it was so damn cold along the shores of Lake Superior. Separating Lake Superior (and the adjoining St. Louis Bay) was a ten-mile long sandy strip called Park Point. A canal lift bridge on Park Point allowed passage into the bay by giant lake carriers, or, "ore boats" as they were called. The ore boats sailed the Great Lakes, shipping ore to smelting plants in Michigan, Ohio, Pennsylvania, and other states where steel was manufactured. The iron ore was mined in Northern Minnesota, principally from the Cayuna and Mesabi Ranges.

From Skyline Drive, you could see the neighboring city of Superior, Wisconsin, and much of the land beyond. We were lucky to live in such a beautiful area, despite being cold for most of the year. The topography and climate reminded many Norwegians, Swedes and Finns of their native homeland.

We walked the Drive for about a mile and then took a side trail that led back to our campsite. We were tired, hungry, and hot. As we approached our campsite, we saw a man leaning up against a tree near out tent.

"Hello, boys," the man said. "Is this your campsite?"

"Yes, it is," Swanee responded. "Can we help you?"

"Oh, I been taking a long hike and I just stopped here because I saw your tent," the man said. "Ya know, just to rest a bit."

He had an all too familiar smell of liquor on his breath. He appeared to be about forty years old, tall, with bright red hair. He slowly walked over to the Bowie knife that Porky had left stuck in a tree. "Nice knife," the man said as he grabbed the handle.

"It's mine," Porky said, possessively.

The man yanked the knife from the tree and stroked the blade.

"You know, son," the man said, "it is not good for a knife to be left stuck in a tree. It dulls the blade."

He then pulled a pint bottle of whiskey from his back pocket. "I'd offer ya some, boys," he said with a smirk, "but yer a little young for this hard stuff." After a deep gulp, the man threw the now empty bottle on the ground. "Christ, it's hot out," he exclaimed. "Any of you guys in the mood to go for a swim?"

We all said no. We just wanted the man to leave. He was creepy. Still holding the knife in one hand, the man undid his belt, unzipped his fly, and let his pants fall to the ground. He was naked from the waist down and his dick was stiff!

"You know," the man said as we looked on, wide-eyed, "all of you are the right age for this kind of hard stuff." The man began stroking his erect penis with his free hand. I had never seen a hard-on before. It was frightening.

His stiff penis was surrounded by a thick bush of curly red hair at its base. In a threatening voice, the man sternly inquired, "Are any of you gentlemen in the mood to suck me off?" His waved his huge prick in our direction.

"Come on," he said, "you suck me off and then I'll suck you off. It'll be enjoyable for the all of us."

Still stroking his swollen prick, the man turned to Swanee and said, "C'mon, kid, you'll enjoy it. It'll taste good in your mouth,"

I froze in fear. This guy was drunk, had Porky's knife in one hand, and wanted us to suck his penis! And he wanted to suck our penises!

Porky started to cry.

"Stop your bawling you little asshole or I'll slit your fucken throat," the man yelled! "Now one of you get over here on yer knees and suck my cock! And if you try anything funny, I swear I'll slash ya!"

"I'll do it," said Swanee. "I'll do what you want."

Porky and I couldn't believe it. Was my best friend queer, or what!?

"Good boy," said the man. "What's yer name son?"

"Paul," Swanee calmly said. "My name is Paul."

"Well come here, Paul," the man directed, "and let's have some fun."

As Swanee walked to the stranger, the man quietly told him to get on his knees.

"Now I'm going to spread my legs," he said, "and you're going to gently grab my cock and slide it slowly into your mouth back and forth. Just make believe you're sucking a big delicious popsicle."

Swanee fell to his knees in front of the man and carefully grabbed the man's erect penis with his left hand.

"That a boy," said the man in nervous anticipation. "That's a good boy. Let me slide it in for ya."

Then, in one smooth motion, Swanee revealed his flashlight he was holding behind his back and jammed it into the man's balls! The man instantly dropped the Bowie knife and fell to his knees, writhing in pain, with his hands cupping his balls.

"You son-of-a-fucken bitch," groaned the man! "I'm going to kill ya all!"

Swanee sprung up and slammed the flashlight to the back of the man's neck. The man then fell on his side in a fetal position and began to moan. Turning to Porky and me, Swanee screamed, "LET'S GET THE FUCK OUT OF HERE!"

We didn't hesitate. We ran!

I don't remember running down the trail. I was numbed from fear. I thought the man was going to catch and butcher us! He was drunk, mad, and inflicted with pain by a kid who had smashed his "family jewels." I know we ran the distance to the railroad tracks and station house not only in record time, but without ever inhaling air. I expected the man would murder us on the small deck of the station house. Our throats would be slit and that would be that—the gruesome ending for three young campers! All I could hear and feel was the torrential beating of my heart! My life was coming to an end! And it was during the safety of daylight, not in the darkness of night!

When we reached the station house, the railroad worker was sitting on the deck smoking his pipe.

"Hurry," Porky yelled breathlessly, "there's a man coming down the hill to kill us! Put us in the building and lock the door!

"What the hell's going on here," questioned the railroad man? "Who's trying to hurt you boys? Is this some sort of prank? If it is, I'll personally kick your asses!"

In between sobs, Porky explained what had just happened and why we were so scared. The railroad man seemed to believe Porky and let us in the small station house. He even locked the door.

"I don't see any man coming down that trail, boys," said the railroad man as he peered out the small window. "It seems he might be too sore to chase ya, if ya did what ya said ya did?"

Swanee asked the man if he could use the phone to call his brother, Wayne, and ask him to come and pick us up. The old man agreed. Luckily, Wayne was home to answer the phone.

"I'll be right up with Dad," Wayne assured us, "and we'll bring our deer rifles with us. Maybe we'll shoot the fucken pervert?"

In about fifteen minutes, Swanee's brother and father pulled up to the station house in Wayne's truck. They were each carrying a rifle. They were anxious to stalk the child molester.

(In those days, police often weren't called to handle certain "personal" infractions. Justice was more private. Kids had their biological parents, but also were governed and protected by "neighborhood parents." Neighbors often rectified wrong doings).

"Come on, boys," said Mr. Swanson, "let's go find the rascal. We'll make a citizen's arrest and perhaps give him a good licking of a different sort, if you know what I mean."

Wayne, Swanee, and their father began walking up the trail leading to our campsite. With some reluctance, Porky and I followed them. Since two of them carried loaded rifles, and there were, after all, five of us, our fears began to ebb as we got closer to the camp. When we arrived at the site, the man was nowhere to be seen.

"He ran off," Wayne said. "He probably is searching to find something that will soothe his crushed nuts!"

"Well at least that something was not one of you boys," declared Mr. Swanson. "I'd have shot his dick off if he were still here! Goddamn perverted son-of-a-bitch!"

"Holy crap," shouted Swanee! "Look what the faggot did to my tent!"

Swanee's tent had been slashed. The canvass was now in shreds. Porky's Bowie knife was stuck back into a nearby tree.

"It took me a year to save the money to buy that tent, and now it's useless!" Swanee was angry and on the verge of tears.

Swanee's father put his arm around his youngest son and, in the process of consoling him, reminded us that the tent could be replaced.

"And son," comforted Mr. Swanson, "you may have just saved the lives of three young West Duluthians. I'm proud of you. Don't worry about the tent. You've got a birthday coming up."

Everyone laughed when I naively commented to Swanee, "It took balls to do what you did."

"Now let's get this place packed up," said Mr. Swanson. "Seems the sick bastard has not touched anything else. He's probably soaking his oysters somewhere upstream. Maybe a brook trout will bite his dick off!"

That was Swanee's father. He always made you feel special and concerned for your welfare. Instead of scolding Swanee and laying some guilt on him, Mr. Swanson declared him a hero, and rightly so. When a father considers his son to be a hero, and treats his son's friends like his friends, how could you not help but respect the man? Porky and I truly loved Mr. Swanson.

I was relieved Mr. Swanson never told my family (especially dad and Butch) about the ordeal. Dad would have criticized me for being unprepared, and yelled "Use the brains that I gave you, Tracy! Think things through! You're lucky to be alive! *Sisu*, son, *sisu*! Learn to stay away from sick people, Goddamn it!"

And Butch would have snidely lectured me about being introduced to the devil (a red-headed devil at that) because of my sinful ways. (Because of her ever increasing "glow," mom's verbal "discipline" would have been a harmless: "Please be careful, Ducky Bumps; I worry so.")

That night, we slept in Swanee's backyard. We cooked our steaks and potatoes on a clean grill and settled into our sleeping bags in the open air. It never rained and the bugs left us alone! The next morning, we told Mr. Bengston about our ordeal, including burying the dog. I think he was more excited about the story than we were and agitated that some creep tried to molest us. He also promised to keep our "adventure" a secret. In addition, he guaranteed he would take us to his camp and have an overnight. He kept his promise.

In September, Swanee got a new and bigger tent for his birthday. We never went camping up in the hills again that summer. In future years, the three of us camped with an adult, usually Swanee's brother. He always carried a loaded rifle or pistol with him.

The experience with the red-haired pervert was the ultimate fright of our young lives. This was one story I could not relate to my new fifth grade class in September when my teacher inquired: "What was the most exciting thing that happened to you this past summer?"

I can't imagine myself saying: "Well, I went on a camping trip and was nearly forced to give a suck job to a child molester." Such a story would get back to my parents (and likely I'd be sent to Principal Becker's office for an ass thrashing).

My fear of having my throat slashed, however, increased. After all, I was nearly murdered by that method. I was extra precise in accounting for our knives during my nightly securing of the household. And being murdered during the daytime was now just one more thing I had to worry about.

Great-Grandpa Reid

Great-Grandpa Reid

GREAT-GRANDPA REID WAS AN AVID gardener. He raised every vegetable known to man, and kept his gardens in meticulous condition. Great-grandpa would weed every day, although the ideal time to weed, he quipped, was during and following a steady light rain. He joked that rain relaxes weeds and, because "the little varmints are half asleep," they were simpler to pull out. Great-grandpa's vegetable beds were prettier than all the neighborhood flower gardens. Many gardening clubs took tours of his pristine plots, thoroughly impressed by their neatness, productivity, and beauty.

My cousin Sheila and I spent many hours on Saturdays weeding Great-Grandpa Reid's perfectly spaced rows. We were rewarded for our efforts with a lunch of homemade strawberry jam and peanut butter sandwiches, Red Dot potato chips, and the world's best apple pie—hot from Grandma Kier's oven. Her lemonade was so cold it would give you brain freeze.

We always ate our lunch in Sheila's playhouse that great-grandpa had built for her in their backyard. The playhouse had two rooms downstairs and one small upstairs loft with two dormers. I was jealous of Sheila having such a wonderful playhouse. I secretly wished that great-grandpa could build me such a structure in my backyard. He probably would have done so, but I was too shy to ask him.

After lunch, Sheila and I would gather all our weeds and dump them into compost piles at the edge of the gardens. Using an old wheelbarrow, horse manure was added to the compost from a small barn near his home. Cow manure contained a lot of urine, great-grandpa stated, and was too salty and acidic. Plants were "burned" and often died from the excess acid.

Great-grandpa maintained two gardens. The smaller plot was 20' x 40', situated alongside his house on 54th Avenue West, where my Uncle Ralph, Aunt Edith, their daughter Sheila, Grandma Kier and Great-Grandpa Reid lived.

The second garden, twice as large, was in a vacant corner lot a block away. Sheila and I called this plot the "candy garden" because it was located right behind Brotherton's Confectionary Store.

Great-grandpa did everything manually. He was in his late 70's and no stranger to hard work. He had labored on the railroad for more than 40 years. His productive and well-managed gardens were the result of old fashion hard work, diligence, and pride. Soil was overturned, composted, spread by hand, and planted using a shovel, hoe, and dibble. Aged wood chips from a local ice factory lined the spaces between his rows of vegetables. His gardens were bordered by a variety of flowers, enhancing the beauty of his vegetable plants.

When I first helped with his gardening, I whined that the work was too hard and never ending. Great-grandpa decided it was time for a lesson. He put his well-worn hands on my little shoulders.

"Tracy, if you don't like to work, all work will be hard and never-ending. Work is about attitude and approach. The two go together like your grandma's coffee and doughnuts."

At that moment, I had little appreciation for what he was saying. I only knew that I was tired and sweaty. I wanted to go home and play. After all, it was Saturday.

Great-grandpa led me to a bench and sat me down next to him. In his typically soft-spoken manner, he patiently explained the meaning of work.

"Son, there is joy in all work. The joy is in the legs of the journey. Each leg, or task, if appreciated, will be a labor of love. And appreciation is to have a sense of pride in what you are doing—a feeling of self-worth."

I was still a little hazy on grasping what great-grandpa was saying. I usually was when talking with adults. Reading the confusion expressed on my face, great-grandpa continued.

"If you are proud of your work, you'll do a much better job. Do only small legs, no matter the endeavor. The legs add up after a short while as will your sense of accomplishment."

"But gramps," I interrupted, "your gardens are so big."

"My boy," great-grandpa now had a smile on his wise old face. "Never think about the size of a work project. Such thoughts will overwhelm you and lead to not doing anything. For example, do not say that today I must weed the entire garden. That attitude will create panic, sloppy and hurried weeding, and dissatisfaction with the work effort. You'll think of yourself as a failure."

"How should I weed," I asked?

"Begin one plant at a time, again, a small leg in the journey," great-grandpa advised. "Do your utmost in weeding that plant, taking your time, and then move to the next plant. Stop when you are tired and rest. I'll bet you'll begin to enjoy the work process and have at least some sense of accomplishment. Plus, you'll do a better job and want to continue the journey after you have rested. Such a work ethic applies to waxing a car, lawn mowing, painting–you name the endeavor. And remember, you will make mistakes. No one is perfect except for the good Lord Almighty. Sometimes frustration will overtake you. Don't give up! Learn from your mistakes and move forward. That movement takes wisdom and courage. Tracy," great-grandpa assured, " you have both of those virtues."

Great-grandpa paused, raised his head to the sun-filled sky, and then very slowly reflected:

"It's how much you accomplish in a small bit of space and time. That approach makes for a fulfilling life."

I sensed my great-grandpa was now looking back on his life.

Abruptly, great-grandpa slapped his two knees with his hands and, much to my regret, planted one of his classically sloppy kisses on my face.

"Let's get back to work, kiddo," he yelled, "and attack a small leg of the journey! Maybe then we can walk up the street to get candy at Brotherton's!"

No more motivation was needed to go back to work. Candy was my carrot.

One day, great-grandpa suggested that I should plant a garden at my house.

"Start small," he advised, "and in the process of developing the plot, you'll soon be motivated to expand it."

He knew that I would love gardening. In summer 1949, prior to my entering the fifth grade, I began planting a garden in our backyard at Wadena Street. I no longer used the yard for play.

Great-grandpa helped me dig up that original plot. Since he owned no car or truck, we wheelbarrowed compost the four-blocks from his house to mine. We must have made twenty round trips in a week's time. We took turns with the wheelbarrow, moving it along a block at a time. Along the way, great-grandpa would sing songs that were new to me, such as "Onward Christian soldiers, marching off to war" and "Over here, over there…the yanks are coming, the yanks are coming." As time passed, my shyness ebbed, and I sang along with him. The wheelbarrow trips became fun.

After the small plot was ready for planting, great-grandpa gave me a variety of seeds. He then taught me the how, what, and where of planting. He provided me with an old hoe and a rake, and I started my first garden. I enjoyed every minute and was soon addicted. What had been "dirt" was now called soil. When some of the seeds began to sprout, I called great-grandpa on the phone to tell him of my discovery. I was so excited! I had planted those seeds!

Great-grandpa laughed, telling me how proud he was of my achievement.

"Tracy," he said, "the fun is just beginning! Just wait until your plants bloom and bear fruit! You'll treat those plants like they were your precious children! And you'll want more!"

True to Great-Grandpa Reid's prediction, I soon expanded the garden's reach. I did reserve a small area of hardscrabble for mom's clothesline, but everything else became garden. Soon, I was planting beds of flowers on the other three sides of our house. I had fallen in love with Miss Nelson, baseball, and now gardening!

Porky said that growing gardens was "women's work" and people would think I was a queer. He said men don't plant flowers. That claim bothered me. I didn't want to be called a queer. But both men and women in the neighborhood were complimenting me on my garden and flower beds. Did they think I was a queer? I went to Swanee for his opinion.

Swanee said that Porky was just jealous. "Besides," added Swanee, "my father is a flower gardener and he certainly is not queer. Porky's full of shit."

Swanee's made me feel better. Porky was a good friend, but he was a little narrow-minded. Porky always thought if someone was different, they were a potential queer (except Mr. P., who we all knew was a murderer).

Ironically, a few days after Porky's warning, he began helping in my garden. He said he would tell people who saw us together that we were doing a Boy Scout project. Porky stated he was only there to "save my reputation." I think he just realized that gardening could be fun.

His mother gave me some flowers to plant around the vegetable borders. Soon, Porky started his own garden. He even planted flowers and vegetables at his grandparents' house in nearby Proctor. We were both becoming "zealots" of the soil.

Great-Grandpa Reid had taught me the "why" of gardening, each sequence of preparation, planting, and tending to be taken as a joyous, inspiring adventure. I grew to appreciate the rituals he passed on to me.

Great-grandpa never sold his vegetables. Instead, he found joy giving them away to his family and neighbors. Having such "customers" eased his feelings of loneliness and disengagement as most of his close friends had died. He wanted to feel wanted.

Grandma said her father's gardens were his summer loves. While I could identify with what she was saying, for the moment, I still loved my teacher, Miss Nelson (and baseball), just a little more than I did gardening. The aroma of fresh horse manure was no comparison to my love of Miss Nelson's scent, looks, and personality.

In mid-summer 1949, great-grandpa died. He had come home from gardening and told my grandma that he wasn't feeling well, and he was going to take an afternoon nap. Within an hour, he passed away in his bed from heart failure. Grandma said he died peacefully in his sleep. Great-grandpa was the first relative in my life to die. Grandma Kier arranged for great-grandpa to be buried in Grand Forks, North Dakota, next to his long ago deceased wife. There was no funeral service, and I had no opportunity to say goodbye to him. I wanted to thank him for the love and patience he showed me and the skills he taught me. He brought me joy. I missed him. I truly loved my great-grandfather.

There were now two wonderful people lost to me during my childhood: Sonny Daniels and great-grandpa. My grandma said I would one day meet great-grandpa and Sonny in Heaven—most likely at the entrance gate with smiles on their faces.

"You know, Tracy," consoled my grandmother, "your great-grandpa will love his new home. I'm told gardens in Heaven have no weeds."

Butch said that people who never go to church do not go to Heaven. They go straight to Hell.

Great-grandpa rarely went to church. But he was a kind and gentle man. He never harmed anyone. Everyone loved him. Could he be in Hell?

Great-grandpa's death got me thinking that my brother might be wrong about how a person gets to Heaven. Why couldn't living a good life qualify? Can't a church be something other than a building? Is the Word of God only found in church? Isn't God's presence found in a trusting and admirable relationship among people? Great-grandpa gave me more guidance for living a decent life than Reverend Scrotters ever did. And what about all the American soldiers who died during the war? Did they go to Hell because they missed church, even after sacrificing themselves for the USA? Was Sonny Daniels now with the Devil?

A few weekends after great-grandpa's death, I went to Grandma Kier's house. Mom felt that grandma needed some company and suggested the visit.

On my way, a warm rain began to fall. I loved the smell and sound of rain and the freshness that followed. I was never lonely when it rained. Rain at night produced my best sleep. And during a steady rain, I also felt that God or Mother Nature or something bigger than me was saying, "timeout" to all the bullshit in the world. Rain was cleansing in so many ways.

As I passed great-grandpa's garden behind Brotherton's, I saw a small bull-dozer skimming off the topsoil, preparing the ground for some type of building construction.

Great-grandpa had never owned the property, but was given permission to till it into a garden. Now that great-grandpa was gone, the owners apparently decided to make another use of the space.

I stopped to watch the dozer collect the soil great-grandpa had so lovingly enriched and nurtured for over ten years. During the war, it was his "victory garden," his prideful contribution to the nation.

It didn't seem right. This reminder of my great-grandpa's diligence and dedication to the soil was disappearing before my eyes. I felt like crying.

I was about to leave for my grandma's house when I spotted a familiar object lying on the sidewalk near a large pile of loam. It was great-grandpa's dibble! The old hand tool he had used for decades to make holes in the soil for plants, seeds, and bulbs. I picked up the little wooden object, a tangible reminder of his efforts, and spoke to it as though it was animated.

"Thanks, great-grandpa," I said. "I'll keep this and remember you always."

When I arrived at Grandma Kier's house, I showed her the dibble. Grandma's eyes got misty, as were mine. I sat on the living room couch wrapped in my grandma's arms.

We cried for a while.

Every spring, for the past 65 plus years, while I am planting my garden, I use that old wooden dibble for seeding. During that "leg of my journey," I always think of great-grandpa and the importance he still has in my life. He gave me the fundamentals of a work ethic that I practice to this day.

He also taught me to love weeding during a soft, warm rain.

Mr. P.

⟳

IN EARLY SEPTEMBER 1949, I was riding my bike down Mr. P.'s gravel driveway that led to my new backyard garden. Suddenly, Mr. P. appeared out of some bordering bushes and grabbed my handlebars. His hands were the size of baseball mitts! I fell forward into the handlebars as Mr. P.'s grip instantly stopped my bike.

I thought, Mr. P. is going to hurt me! I knew this would happen one day! God help me!

"Teelaycee," Mr. P. said. "Um sorry to scared you. You hurted at all?"

"No," I lied. My heart hurt, my breathing hurt, and even my bulging eyes were in pain!

"Dat's goot." Mr. P. let go of my handlebars. I sat back down on my bicycle seat. My ass hurt too.

"Teelaycee," Mr. P. said. "You do goot vork on your garten. You helped me vid mine? I vant to grow nice tings. I vant lawn und tree und bush."

I meekly answered: "Sure."

My mind was racing. Was I his next victim? What would my buddies think? I had just agreed to work besides the most feared adult in the neighborhood! Would he dispose of me when I finished helping him!? Was I about to dig my own grave in his yard and join the retarded boy?

Summer 1949 had soured again! Any chance of marrying Miss Nelson was fast disappearing, mom was getting drunk almost every day, great-grandpa had died, I feared being called a gardening queer, and the molester was still out there. And to top it off, I had just agreed to rub shoulders with a murderer and maybe lose my life (or at least the respect from my two closest friends in the process)! Goddamn!

Days later, Mr. P. began preparing his yard. A dump truck hauled away the junk from his large corner lot. Mr. P. hired a small bulldozer to spread and level many truckloads of rich loam, transforming a wasteland (and, I thought, ghoulish cemetery) into a fertile plot.

Porky and I watched the whole process from a distance. We waited for the buried body to be unearthed, but saw, to our amazement, only some large boulders, one old tire, and a few bottles unearthed.

"Be careful, Trace," Porky commented on my role in this exercise. "You could end up being one dead chicken."

Swanee called after the preparation for the new work was completed. He reported that early one morning, before the dump truck arrived to clear the lot, he was taking a piss and saw Mr. P. in his yard with a flashlight. He said Mr.P. eventually laid the flashlight on the ground and began digging for something. Swanee was convinced that Mr. P. was removing evidence of the dead retarded child. Swanee said he saw Mr. P. dropping old bones into a large basket and carrying them to his basement.

"Mr. Son-Of-A-Bitch is a crafty monster," Swanee chided. "He's got the dead kid now buried in his basement cemetery. If he had left the body in his yard, he knew the bulldozer would find it."

"Finlander," warned Swanee, "Stay away from his basement. Even though you're ugly, you're still too young to die."

Swanee's feeble attempt at humor did little to lessen my fears. Since Swanee was trustworthy, I had little reason not to believe him. But Mr. P. said he would pay me 50 cents an hour, a fortune compared to my 50 cents weekly allowance. Greed overtook fear. I would just remain cautious around the old guy and make some good money. And I would never go into his basement "death chamber.".

One cold and rainy afternoon a day or so later, mom said Mr. P. called and wanted me to meet him in his basement!

I told mom that I was afraid of that basement and Mr. P. Mom laughed.

"Ducky Bumps," she consoled. "Mr. Phillipovich is a nice man. You have nothing to fear with him."

I was dismayed that mom thought Mr. P. was harmless. I suspected they were drinking pals, and that probably clouded her perception of him.

Reluctantly, I headed over to meet Mr. P. in his basement.

As I entered the dimly lit basement, I found Mr. P. standing in the middle of the earthen floor, holding a long stick!

"Teelaycee, com here," waved Mr. P.

I slowly edged up to Mr. P., preparing for the first painful strike.

Instead, Mr. P. said, "I taught we coult meet in cellar because of rain outside. Here is vaught I vant to do to yard."

Mr. P. began drawing in the dirt floor with the stick. To my surprise, rather than outlining my grave boundaries, the old man methodically sketched a landscape plan for his yard. It was to have carefully placed bushes and fir trees, a large flag pole in the center, and borders with a white picket fence.

I was cautiously relieved!

"You liked." inquired Mr. P.? "You helped me wid dis?"

I told him his plan looked great, although I had only given his dirt diagram a brief glance. I just wanted to leave that dingy basement as soon as I could, and go on living. Mr. P. put his large left hand on my right bony (and shaking) shoulder.

"Tanks, Telaycee, Mr. P. said. "We start when weathers goot.

Mr. P. let go of my shoulder and bent down to rub out his design. I stretched my neck to see an open box behind Mr. P. laying on the dirt floor next to the coal furnace. There was no mistaking what I saw. BONES!

I said a quick goodbye to Mr. P. and ran up his basement stairs. Minutes later, I was knocking on Swanee's back door.

"Hey, Finlander," announced Swanee as he opened the door. "I got a kiss for ya." Swanee let out a loud fart.

"Swanee." I gasped. "I saw them! I saw them!"

"What are ya talking about," Swanee inquired, "your testicles?"

"I saw the bones in the box in Mr. P's basement!" I was out of breath and felt faint. Swanee eyes opened wide.

"You saw the bones?" Swanee seemed shaken. "Are you sure they were bones?"

"YES," I screamed! "They were right next to the coal furnace!"

"The old codger is going to burn them," Swanee said. "He's getting rid of the evidence. I knew it! I just knew it! The Serb is a Nazi. I'll bet that dead kid was either Jewish or Catholic."

I asked Swanee why Mr. P. hated Catholic and Jewish people?

"Well," explained Swanee, "my brother says Catholics think they are superior to everyone else, because their priests take away their sins. Jewish people just take away your money. A lot of Protestants hate both groups, even to the point of killing and burning them. Adolph Hitler did that shit. Mr. P. must be one of those angry Nazi Protestants."

Holy shit, I thought. The world is crazier the more you get to know it.

It took me awhile to convince myself that since I was a Protestant, it was probably safe to work with Mr. P. I was Lutheran. Nobody hates Lutherans! Why would Mr. P. hate me?

I was not back to school yet, so we had time to complete the project. Mr. P. did most of the work. I was his helper. Mr. P. dug all the holes for the trees and bushes, erected the flag pole, and constructed the fence. I planted the nursery trees and bushes and painted the fence. We fertilized and seeded the lawn using a spreader machine. The hardest part of the whole project was covering the newly sewn seed with a hundred gunny sacks. The sacks protected the seeds from erosion and hungry birds, especially crows.

We sweated side-by-side. As we worked, Mr. P. would tell me about his early life in Serbia, what the Wadena Street neighborhood was like thirty years ago, his first car, the job as a crane operator at the steel plant, and so on. I certainly wasn't going to tell him that most neighborhood kids were afraid of him and at least three thought he was a murderer. And I didn't think it wise to mention the "bones" I saw in his basement.

I began to change my view of Mr. P. He was not a monster. He was a nice man. Mom might be right. On one hot afternoon, after we had worked all day, the two of us sat in the coolness of his upstairs porch. Mr. P gave me a small glass of cold beer. I hated the taste but loved the experience. I felt like I had gained an adult friend.

Sometimes, we went to lunch at a Serbian restaurant in Gary-New Duluth. The people at the restaurant were very friendly. It was obvious that Mr. P was a respected and loved patron of the place. Everyone embraced him and, initially, they thought I was his grandson.

The most exciting time of the project occurred when Mr. P. and I went to Nichols Hardware Store to buy a gas driven lawn mower. Mr. P. was the first person in the neighborhood to own one. The machine created almost as much excitement as the soon-to-be marketed Studebaker "spaceship" cars. When Mr. P. first mowed his new lawn, people from the neighborhood lined the fence to watch this strange machine at work.

Mr. P. eventually let me use the mower. I felt pretty cocky strutting across his lawn as my neighbors looked on. Unfortunately, due to its many mechanical failures, we soon resorted to using a more traditional, back-breaking push mower.

Mr. P. had known my great-grandfather. He expressed how sorry he was to hear of his death. He had talked with him many times while they shopped at People's Market.

"He was goot man," Mr. P. said. "He tolded me dat he proud of you. I see why. You goot boy, Teelaycee."

I thanked Mr. P for his kind comments. I told him I wished my great-grandfather had lived longer. It was difficult to accept the fact that I would never see him for the rest of my life.

Mr. P. lowered his head as I lamented about Great-Grandfather Reid. In a quiet and respectful tone, he related a story that I would never forget.

"Many years ago, I was married to vonderful lady." As Mr. P. talked, a trace of a tearful sparkle appeared in his eyes. "Vee vas married 15 year. She was to have baby. But in hospital, someting happen and dey both die. I never tolt too many people dis. I still very sad and miss dem much."

I felt bad for him and expressed being sorry.

"Teelaycee," Mr. P. said quietly. "Vee have chore that I have been putting oft. Come to basement wid me."

My mind and body tensed. What is going on here, I thought? Was this my time to "go?" Was I not a friend of the old man? I wanted to tell him that I was a Lutheran! A fucking Protestant!

When we reached the basement, Mr. P went directly to the basket of bones sitting next to his furnace.

"Come, Teelaycee," commanded Mr. P. "Pick basket up for me. My back sore. Take upstairs to yard."

I was clueless as to what was happening. After all, these were real bones!

Mr. P. had me carry the bones to a spot near a newly planted fir tree in his side yard, next to his house.

"Dis goot, Teelaycee," said Mr. P. "Dig small grave right here." He pointed to a small shovel leaning against his house.

Mr. P. looked at me and, with a slight smile on his face, said,

"Let me explain. Whened my vife, she became wid baby, I bought a dog so new baby coult grow up vid dog. Vend dey died, dey never come home. All I have is dog. Dat dog was loved by my vife and dog loved her. Somehow, as dog live, my vife still live. I bury dog in 1947. He vas 16. I dig him up few weeks ago so he not be taken by bulldozer man. Now time to bury him in better place. You understand, Teelaycee?"

Oh, I understood. I also understood Swanee, Porky, and I were probably the biggest jerks in West Duluth. Because he was hard to understand and very loud and abrupt when he spoke, our juvenile minds had made him into a monster. Mr. P. also walked with a distorted limp, only validating our perception of him.

After the dog was buried, I shared Mr. P.'s story with Swanee and Porky. They were mortified. We had created a neighborhood demon. He deserved our apology.

It took us some time before we had the courage to venture to Mr. P.'s house and, nervously, confess our misconceptions. I predicted we would be kicked out of his place after he heard our cruel impressions of him. I would certainly lose my well-paying job.

Rather than show any anger, Mr. P. told us he had been aware for years of being cast as a child killer by the neighborhood children. (The retarded boy had not died and been buried by Mr. P. He was missing because his parents had sent him to an institution for the mentally handicapped.) The image kids had of him was troubling. He liked children and would never hurt one. Mr. P. felt separated from people and it left him feeling lonely (and a little angry). He said we were the first visitors to his house in over ten years.

Mr. P. limped to his kitchen and came back with four small glasses of table wine.

"Here, my goot boys," Mr. P. said. "Let us to toast dis day of new friendship."

The three of us had never tasted wine before. We stayed in his apartment for at least two hours, talking, and drinking one more glass of wine. Mr. P. told us to keep the wine drinking "our secret." Mr. P. enjoyed our company. Having to live his life alone after losing his wife and child, I could understand his feelings. Sometimes I felt like I had no parents and brother.

I continued to take care of Mr. P.'s new lawn and fencing. Swanee and Porky raked his yard that fall and shoveled the driveway and sidewalks during the winter. They never asked nor took a penny for their efforts. Since I was now Mr. P's handy "kid," I still earned 50 cents an hour for my duties.

We came to appreciate helping Mr. P. not out of pity, but admiration. We realized that he was a man who liked young people. Unknowingly, he taught us to appreciate that just because a person looks and sounds different than you, it doesn't diminish their right to be treated with dignity. I should have exercised that lesson when I was dancing with Nabisco in the second grade.

I hoped that Mr. P's wife, child, and dog were in Heaven living happily together. I thought it would be perfect if the other dog we buried, on our dreadful camping trip earlier in the summer, could somehow join them. And perhaps the dead puppies in Mr. Lund's barn might also be scampering in their presence. (I refused to ask Butch if unborn babies qualify for Heaven. I know he would have spelled out some complicated bullshit answer.)

After I buried Mr. P.'s dog, I made a cross in our basement. I put the cross at one end of the dog's new grave. I wasn't sure what I was doing, but it made me feel better.

A few days later, Swanee, Porky, and I trekked up to the hillside sandpit grave of the collie dog and placed a cross on it. Few words were spoken.

Mr. P. was never again called Mr. Son-Of-A-Bitch by Swanee.

Erection

In Fall 1949, when I was entering the fifth grade, Cousin Sheila began eating lunch at my house during the school week. Sheila was four years older than me and a student at West Junior High School. Her school was located close to our house and some distance from hers.

I adored Sheila. She was smart, had a good imagination, and like me, loved to play make-believe. Sheila was a tomboy, always wearing jeans and a t-shirt or sweatshirt on weekends and all during the summer. The only time she wore a mandatory dress or skirt was at school. I could play with Sheila and not experience the fear I had for most girls. We got along great together. In my mind, she was just another buddy.

At lunchtime, we had forty minutes to eat. Sheila and I invariably "camped out" in my bedroom and pretended we were horses. I was a Palomino named Wildfire and Sheila was Beauty, a chestnut mare. We ate our meal on all fours, lapped our drinks from bowls, and played horse games.

I began to feel something strange happening to me when tussling with Sheila.

"It" happened when I noticed how her long, dark hair smelled so good—like Palmolive soap. "It" happened when we wrestled, our arms and legs all entangled. (I enjoyed grabbing Sheila around the waist of her skirt, throwing her on my bed, pretending to be fighting.) And "it" happened when we were done playing, and she would give me a brief kiss--right on my lips!

Sheila, in the middle

My penis was perking up a bit!

One day, we were having a horse "duel" in the bedroom. Sheila and I got up on our "hind" legs and began to fight. Inadvertently, my hand snagged a front button of her blouse, dislodging Sheila's small brassiere and exposing the nipple of one of her breasts. I was so embarrassed, but my accident didn't seem to bother Sheila. She merely adjusted her bra, and buttoned her blouse. But I was bothered! My button penis was really "perking up." I got a full-blooded hard-on. That never happened before! I felt like a fool—a very guilty fool. Was I becoming physically attracted to my cousin?

I don't think Sheila noticed the strange lump in my jeans. I panicked! I needed out! I lied and told her I had to get back to school early to finish some assignments.

Before returning to Irving, I went into the bathroom to examine my swollen penis. I was scared. Would I develop into a pervert like the redhead molester at our camp the past summer? Would my dink stay like this? But as soon as I stepped outside, the frigid air brought instant relief. I was glad things had returned to normal.

My button penis proved to be short-lived. I had just sat down in Mrs. Shield's fifth grade classroom when my penis got hard again! What was going on? What was wrong with me? I didn't dare ask my school buddies, Dan or Harley.

I couldn't say, "Hey, Dan, you ever had a hard on? What do you do about it?"

Regrettably, I was so confused and desperate that I decided to ask for advice from Butch. He might enlighten me. What a desperate mistake.

My brother had a horrendous explanation.

"The devil is giving you this erection," he exhorted, "because of the sins you are committing with Sheila! It is against God's law to have sexual feelings toward a blood relative. The devil is enticing you! The devil wants you to commit a sin with Sheila! You must stop your rubbing games at lunch time and pray to the Lord Jesus Christ for forgiveness! You have a sexual love toward Sheila and that is a mortal sin! Control your urges through God, my brother!"

Wow! Butch's little sermon would make anyone's pecker limp. Was I a sinner and were my unplanned swellings acts of the devil! My brother wanted me to get down on my knees with him and pray to God for forgiveness.

"No," I said thankfully. "I have to trade funny books with Swanee at his house. I'll be back in about an hour."

"All right," Butch said disappointedly. His voice became grim in tone.

"We'll talk more about this after dinner tonight. You're jeopardizing your privilege to enter Heaven. You did the right thing by coming to me for help. I can save you, Tracy."

Butch's know-it-all attitude made me want to puke. I was a fool to ask him for help. I'd be willing to bet that even Jesus had a boner or two in His youth.

I wasn't trying to be disrespectful. I just viewed Jesus on a personal level, unlike Butch. I wanted my Jesus to be more human in my life. The phrase, "What a friend we have in Jesus," made sense to me.

As I approached Swanee's house, I thought why not ask Swannie about my penis problem? Maybe he can help me? Swanee knew a lot about things I didn't understand.

I met Swanee in his basement, with his comic books spread out on the floor. I did the same with my set and, in about twenty minutes, we were finished trading issues.

"Swanee, can I ask you a question about something that's happening to me? It's kinda bothering me."

"Sure, Finlander," Swanee said as he sat down on the basement steps. "What's up?"

"What's up is my dick," I said. "And I don't know what to do about it. Every time I'm with my cousin, Sheila, I now get a hard-on. I made the mistake of telling my brother. Butch says I am being possessed by the devil and should pray for God's forgiveness. I feel guilty! Am I going to wind up like the fucken redheaded pervert? Should I tell Sheila what's happening, stay away from her or what?"

"Hey, hey, slow down buckaroo," interrupted Swanee. He got up and quietly shut the basement door to the upstairs. "Do you really think the devil is giving you a hard on? If that were the case, I'd be a devil worshiper! Your brother is forever making you wicked. You should be happy that you are starting to get a hard-on. Puberty is beginning, man."

"Pooperty," I said. "What the fuck is that?"

"Your body's changing into manhood," Swanee explained. "Every boy starts growing hair above his balls, gets a deeper voice, and has boners all the time. When I got my first hard-on, I wanted to run up and down Wadena Street and show everyone the good news!"

Swanee was so damn smart. I was feeling a little better.

Swanee continued, "Your brother is feeding you horseshit. That crap will make anyone feel ashamed and frustrated. Ya know: don't do this, don't do that, avoid all pleasure. Two-bits he's whacking his own Mr. Happy every night. Religious monkeys like him love to tell other people how not to live. Then they wind up screwing the minister's daughter behind the church. It's none of his business if you get aroused by Sheila. I would too if I were around her. She's pretty and well-built for her age."

Everything Swanee was telling me made sense, except the part about "whacking Mr. Happy." Who was Mr. Happy?

My questioning, however, turned to another snag that required an answer. I hoped Swanee could further help me.

Swanee," I confessed. "I accidently pulled her bra down."

"WHAT!" Swanee suddenly grabbed me by my shoulders. "You saw Sheila's nipples?"

"I saw one nipple" "I was starting to sweat. "Just one nipple."

Swanee was an inch from my face. "You lucky bastard," he exclaimed. "I would kill to see her nipples. What color was it? Was it pink? I bet it was pink!"

"I told you," I repeated. "I only saw one nipple, her right one. I don't know what color it was. I was too embarrassed to remember."

"Well, I 'm wondering if you two would like a third horse at your "corral" every lunchtime," jested Swanee? "Goddamn!"

"But she's my cousin," I said. "I feel so ashamed."

"Tracy," Swanee said in a comforting voice. "Sheila is the first female that has aroused you like this. You're going through a normal fucken stage. Sheila just happens to be related to you. That doesn't mean you want to climb in the sack with her. It also means you ain't a homo! You'll get erections sitting on a bus, reading in the library, or thinking about Aline up the street. It's natural, not evil. Your brother is a screwball. Don't listen to him. Let nature take its course. Christ, I get a hard-on while mowing the lawn or doing the evening's dishes. It's no big deal. In fact, I'm sure in your case," he chuckled, "it's a very small deal, if you know what I mean."

"Funny man," I said grinning.

Swanee laughed. And then he asked, "Have ya ever thought of jerking off? It will help release some of your tension, plus it feels great, and if you do it right, your dick will get limp . . . at least for a while."

I was lost in left field.

"What is jerking off," I asked? "Does it hurt?"

"MASTURBATION, MAN," Swanee emphasized with a mammoth smile on his face! "What Wayne calls assault with a friendly weapon! 'Stroken' the joint of pleasure."

Swanee put a fisted hand between his legs and made an up and down motion. "Get it now," he said?

"Get what?" I had no idea what he was doing, much less saying.

"Forget it, Finlander!" Swanee said, rolling his eyes. "We'll talk about this later, maybe some time when you're not so fucken stupid. When that time comes, I'll be an old man."

Swanee's mother opened the basement door and asked him to go to People's Market for groceries.

"I gotta help my mom," Swanee said. "Go home and tell your teenage minister that getting a stiffy is normal and sin has nothing to do with it. Okay? And I hope you have a big boner the next time you play with Sheila. You saw her nipple! Be thankful for that!"

I went back home feeling better. Swanee convinced me I had done nothing wrong. It seemed something or someone (especially Butch) was always making me feel guilty. I admired Swanee for his wisdom in dealing with my problems. And, of course, Swanee was one funny son-of-a-bitch.

After supper, Butch motioned for me into our bedroom. I knew what was coming: he was going to cleanse my evil soul! Butch quietly closed the bedroom door and looked at me.

"Tracy," Butch said in a soft voice as though he were my confessor, "let us kneel down together and ask Jesus for His forgiveness of your mortal sin."

My brother fell to his knees in the middle of our bedroom and clasped his hands in prayer.

"Come," he said, "join me my brother."

"Oh, fuck you," I blurted! "Who the hell are you? I'm not praying with you. This is stupid!"

"How dare you speak to me that way! Who do you think you are?! You're not above the Lord! You're a sinner!" Butch was livid!

"No, shit breath," I fired back! "Make me a winner, not a sinner! I'm a lucky ten-year-old kid who just had my first hard-on. I'm finished listening to some holier-than-thou saint who preaches while his thumb is jammed up his ass! I've done nothing wrong!"

I was so amazed by my outburst that I kept it going.

"Swanee," I continued, "said I'm going through pooberty and it is okay for me to start having urges."

My brother fired back. "Swanee only repeats what his older brother tells him. Wayne has no religious core."

That pissed me off!

"Butch," I growled, "you don't know Swanee! He's not controlled by his older brother, like you are trying to do with me. I haven't committed any friggen sin! You're always trying to make me feel guilty. I don't want any more of your stupid interference into my life, hard-on or no hard-on! Besides, Swanee said you're probably whacking off every chance that you get!"

I was still clueless about what that meant, but Butch certain knew.

Butch was incensed! His face got beet red and he began trembling. I darted for the door, but he grabbed me by the neck and started choking me.

"You are such an ignorant little snot," he exhorted! "You think you know so much about life and you know nothing!"

His hands were tightening around my neck and I was having difficulty breathing.

"You're not worth saving, moron," he screamed!

I tried unsuccessfully to knee him in the balls, as he continued to squeeze my neck with all his strength. Luckily, mom entered the bedroom just as I blacked out. Apparently, she slapped Butch in the face. He let go of my neck, and I fell to my knees on the floor.

"My God in Heaven," Mom yelled! "Are you trying to kill your brother, Russell?! He's passed out!"

She abruptly raised me up and held me in her arms.

I quickly came to and began coughing and crying. I thought I was going to die at the hands of my brother. Mom was very angry. She turned and gave my brother another slap on his face. He started crying.

"You almost killed him, Russell," she said sternly. "Is that what your religion teaches you, to kill thy brother?"

Mom began to cry. She grabbed both of us and we all sobbed.

"What is wrong between you boys," she cried out? "Why can't you get along with one another? I am so sick of this squabbling.

Suddenly our dad, who was home early that day, barged into the bedroom.

"WHAT IN THE NAME OF CHRIST IS GOING ON IN HERE," he shouted?! "I'M TRYING TO DO SOME PAPERWORK AND ALL I HEAR IS YELLING AND SCREAMING! ARE YOU ALL LOSING YOUR SENSES?!

"Russ," explained our mother. "The boys had a fight and I stopped it."

"FIGHT OVER WHAT," dad demanded to know!?

Butch got in the first lick, saying. "Tracy has committed a sin and I was trying to straighten him out."

"Ya, dad," I hoarsely piped in. "Butch was using the choking method he learned in church to cure me of my ill ways."

Our father was enraged. "GOD DAMN IT! STOP THIS USELESS FIGHTING! DO YOU HEAR ME? STOP IT NOW OR YOU'LL LEARN WHAT REAL AGONY IS!"

As our father left the room, he was even more pissed. "GODDAMN THE BUNCH OF YA! I WORK MY BUTT OFF AND THIS IS HOW YOU REPAY ME! I'M LIVING IN AN INSANE ASYLUM! YOU'RE ALL A PAIN IN THE ASS!"

That evening our house was in silence. We all tried to avoid one another. Mom decided to go to the "library," a euphemism for bar hopping. Butch remained in our bedroom, reading the Bible. Dad was enclosed in his office. I sprawled out on the front room floor listening to "The FBI in Peace and War" followed by the "Lemac Hour" quiz show. (Lemac was backward for Camel, the cigarette sponsor for the show. The top prize was $64}.

I really dreaded going to our bedroom and facing Butch. I wanted to stay over at Swanee's house. I would even sleep alone outdoors.

Dad came into the living room and ordered, "Tracy, get the hell to bed. It's a school night."

I undressed and got into my bed quickly as possible. I would cancel my house "securing" and knife inventory for one night. I didn't want my pissed-off dad to catch me doing my late evening "chores." God only knows what he might do to me.

Butch ignored me as I struggled to stay awake, convinced I would die if I fell asleep. It was only logical to not trust someone who had attempted to strangle you a few hours earlier. Thankfully, I heard Butch starting to grind his teeth, a signal that he was asleep. (Any time Butch was agitated, he would grind his teeth as he slept).

The next morning, as we lay in bed, Butch whispered, "Tracy, you have to be saved, or as sure as I am your brother, you will go to hell."

"Saved from what?" I cautiously replied.

"Sin," he responded! "You are coveting your body in the manner of the devil!"

I didn't know what covet meant nor did I care. I tried to explain myself.

"What you call sin," I said, "I see as natural."

I knew my defense would never change his mind. I just wanted my say (thanks to Swanee's wisdom).

"You hate Dad," I noted. "Is that Christian. . . hating one's father?"

"It's not as bad as hating the church," Butch retorted, "like you do!"

"I hate the bullshit ritual." I fought back! "I still believe in God and just because I see things differently from you it doesn't make me an idiot. Your beliefs are not the same as mine."

Butch addressed me in an extremely confident voice. "My beliefs are better than yours. They are based on Revealed Truths. I know I'm going to Heaven. I love the Lord and am God fearing. I follow His ways to the letter."

"Well," I said slowly, "I can't love something that I also fear." (My response was somewhat inaccurate, as I loved my father but was often afraid of him). "Your God is a dictator, someone never to be questioned. My God is a friend, a buddy."

"Oh, what a bunch of happy horseshit that is, blockhead!" Butch ranted. "God is not supposed to be your pal! He's the guider of your life! Follow

His dictates by faithfully attending church if you desire everlasting salvation. Wake up, dumb ass!"

Butch could never compromise on any issue.

He got up from his bed and left the room.

We couldn't be farther apart. Butch had found God, and I had discovered erections. Butch and I did agree on one thing. We both wanted our own bedroom.

Dad arrived at breakfast still very angry.

He began, "The three of you are escape artists. You are running from yourselves. I'm getting tired of it. Your behaviors are not helping this family. Russell, you hide behind religion. Your sermonizing and holy attitude is driving all of us crazy! Leave your brother alone! Quit trying to convert him. If he wants to become religious, he will. You're his brother, not his conscience."

It was my turn to be criticized by dad. "Tracy, you escape through frivolous imagination. Your world is a dream world. You can't be a little kid forever. I suggest you start growing up. It is time to put aside your play things. *Sisu*, my son, *sisu*! Start maturing and thinking like a young adult!'"

Looking to mom, dad said, "And Mary, we all know what you use for escape and it is destroying this family! You have got to control your drinking. I did it, so can you! I cannot be mother as well as husband, breadwinner, and father! You've got to stop this nonsense and be a responsible mother and wife! It is time for big changes around here and I want to see them begin to happen TODAY! DO YOU ALL UNDERSTAND!?"

Out of fear, Butch and I replied, "Yes, father."

Mom sat silently as she glared at her husband.

"And you, Mary," dad pointedly asked? "What about you?"

"WHAT ABOUT ME, RUSSELL?!" Mom shouted back! "How can you sit there and address us like we were your misbegotten employees! We don't work for you! You're not our boss! We're a family! We exist for each other. We all have our strong points and weaknesses, including you, I might add!"

"Mary, all I ask is you stop the goddamn drinking. Your boozing is destroying the reputation of the Gran name! People notice and talk and it hurts us all!"

"You mean it hurts you and your business!" Mom was pissed. "You spend little time with the children, or with me for that matter. Everything is about your business and your image! Is it any wonder that the members of your family escape!? We are escaping from you! Our sons want a father, not a salesman! And I want a husband who treats me as an equal and respects what I do for the family!" Mom was now in tears.

Never in my young life had I witnessed mom being so forceful with dad. She was standing up to him and it was refreshing....and frightening. Butch decided to join in the assault.

"Dad," he said trembling. "You accuse us of escaping from reality and doing harm to the family name. Well, what about your suicide attempt? Wasn't that escaping from reality?"

Suddenly dad stood up and, in the process, tipped over the breakfast table on its side.

Dad threw his napkin in my brother's face. "HOW DARE YOU TALK TO ME THAT WAY! THAT WAS AN ACCIDENT AND YOU KNOW IT! I FACE MY PROBLEMS! I DON'T RUN AWAY FROM THEM AND HIDE BEHIND SOME GODDAMNED GOD WHO SUDDENLY CONVERTS YOU TO AN ALL-KNOWING PUNK! YOU'RE LIVING IN A GODLESS WORLD, YOUNG MAN! ONE DAY SOON, REALITY IS GOING TO BITE YOU HARD ON YOUR ASS!"

As he turned to leave for work, father pointed at mom and loudly commanded, "TONIGHT, WHEN I COME HOME, I WANT YOU SOBER! AND, MARY, I WANT YOU SOBER EVERY SINGLE DAY, GODDAMN IT! DO YOU HEAR ME!?

Staring at dad, mom said nothing in reply.

Mom wasn't sober when dad returned. No words were exchanged.

The breakfast incident was never mentioned again. We settled back into our comfortable games of denial and pretense.

Butch and I rarely brought up the subject of hard-ons again. In fact, we rarely communicated at all. I no longer confided in him and he refrained from preaching to me. I don't think Sheila knew about the "growths" she induced.

But who knows, she might have been aware and flattered she had that effect on my button.

I was amazed after taking it all in. A major family fight had evolved over my stiffy.

Butch's attempt at murder left my neck sore, but playing "horsey" with Sheila seemed to make the pain go away.

French Fries

⏤⏥

THERE WERE NO FAST FOOD chains during my childhood. People ate their meals at home, with a rare outing to a diner or restaurant considered to be a special treat.

Usually on a birthday, dad stopped at Bridgman's ice cream parlor in West Duluth and brought home a package of our favorite flavor: butter brickle. The taste was a combination of vanilla ice cream and Heath bars. The store included free cellophane packets of sugar cookies to eat with the ice cream. As Butch and I stirred our Bosco milk drinks, dad served equal portions of the delightfully crunchy ice cream. I let mine melt, and churned it until it reached a creamy consistency to spread over my sugar cookies.

On warm summer evenings, when she was not at the "library," mom walked us down to the popcorn wagon on Grand Avenue next to Bridgman's for a bag of the most delicious popcorn I ever tasted. Sometimes we would sit together on a little bench, near the wagon, and devour our kernels while watching people stroll by. On special nights, mom would buy a large bag of hot roasted peanuts from the wagon man. We ate them at home after they had cooled off. A small bag of popcorn was a dime. The peanuts were a nickel per bag.

In the fifth grade, in 1949, mom would surprise us (that is, Sheila and me, as my brother took lunch to school) and bring home a luncheon meal from Teve's Bar and Grill. Teve's was run by the Pekkala family. They also owned an ice company next to Porky's house. Teve's was known for its excellent food, entertainment, and bar. Usually the lunch was a hamburger, or Coney Island hot dog, and French fries. Mom would never tell us what day she planned to surprise us. I suspect her day of choice centered on how much money she could spare after having a drink or two at Teve's. The treats were so delicious that I never said anything about her being tipsy, although, regretfully, perhaps I should have.

My favorite home-cooked meal was barbequed spare ribs with French fries. Mom would cook two large racks of ribs and baste them with her home-made sauce. The meat fell off the bone. I remember diving into those ribs and getting sauce all over my face, hands, and shirt. I decided ribs should be enjoyed when wearing only a swim suit.

There were no prepackaged or frozen foods available in stores. French fries were made by hand. Mom bought potatoes and sliced them into pieces. She'd soak the pieces in cold water to remove the starch, fry them in melted lard, and spread them on paper towels or newspaper to soak up the excess grease. The fries were served in an oversized roast pan. Nothing tasted better than those fries!

Porky and Swanee were often invited to come over for fries, arriving within minutes of the call after telling them it was "French fry night." The three of us sat on the steps of our enclosed rear porch and devoured a tub of the hot, crispy, and ever so salty, fried potatoes. It was not uncommon to empty a whole bottle of Heinz catsup in the process. Swanee started calling me "the French fry kid." If allowed, I would have eaten them three times a day.

One Friday, in Fall 1949, I came home after school famished. Mom recently had taken a part-time, "long" weekend job at People's Market and was working late. (The employment thankfully curbed mom's drinking on those days). Dad was out of town on a business trip. Butch was somewhere. I found a large bowl of freshly sliced potatoes in the refrigerator that mom had cut up at lunchtime. I decided to fry up a batch. While I had never made French fries before, I had watched mom prepare them many times. My hunger trumped my lack of experience.

I turned the heating element on high and started melting the lard in a deep pan. While waiting, I went to the living room and opened the sports pages of the News-Tribune. I was attracted to an article on the baseball bi-ographies of the 1949 Dukes team (the season was about to end). I became engrossed in the information. I also fell asleep.

I was awakened by the smell of smoke. "Holy shit," I thought! "What the hell have I done?"

I ran to the kitchen and found the lard on fire, with black smoke pouring out of it! I grabbed an oven mitten and picked up the pan, planning to take it to our backyard.

I hesitated when I remembered that the Center family was having a big outdoor birthday party for Ernie next door. Their nearby yard was filled with people! I couldn't go running out there with a pan on fire and become the laughing stock of the neighborhood! So, I placed the blazing pan on the cement floor of our enclosed back porch. A pail of cold water would quench the fire.

After filling the pail in our kitchen sink, I ran down the short set of steps of the back porch to the burning oil and poured the water on the blaze. There was a loud "varoom," and the entire area became enveloped in thick, black smoke. The blast blew me down a connected set of concrete steps that led from the enclosed porch to our basement. For a few panic-filled seconds, I found myself lying prostrate on the cellar floor, certain that I had just set the house on fire. I ran up the basement stairs to the enclosed porch, expecting the worse.

To my relief, the fire was out, but the entire back porch was encrusted in black soot. The gray paint on the inside stair railing was charred, and the window curtains were singed. The labels on the can goods mom stored on the back porch were burned off, and every can was blackened. Two jackets of mine hanging on hooks had numerous burn holes and were smoldering.

I swallowed my pride and opened the porch door to the let out the smoke and acrid smell. Ernie met me at the back door with a look of panic on his face!

"What happened," he said? "What blew up?"

Before I could tell him, Ernie and his friends began laughing.

"What's so funny," I asked? I was getting a little angry at their apparent lack of concern.

"Go look in the mirror," Ernie said tittering. "Just go look in the mirror."

I ran to the mirror above the kitchen sink.

"My fucken word," was all I could say! I was looking at a ten-year-old boy with a blackened, sooty face, singed eyebrows, and burnt hair! And I had burn holes in my sweatshirt. Luckily the explosion missed my eyes.

The neat little porch was now a charred mess and the house stunk of sour odors of smoke, burnt clothing, and singed paint.

I thought, I'm a dead person. Dad will be unforgiving.

Thank God for Ernie Center.

"Hey, boy scout," Ernie yelled to me! "Get some buckets of warm water and soap and we'll help you clean up the mess. Call Swanee and Porky over here too. The more hands we have the quicker we can get rid of the evidence of your stupidity. Your dad best not know of this act of genius. I don't want to be a pall bearer at your funeral."

For the next three hours, Ernie, his school friends, Swanee, Porky, my very shocked mother (who had come home to discover my attempt at cooking), and I, scrubbed the porch. Mom destroyed the curtains (what was left of them) and hung up new ones. My jackets were thrown away along with the can goods. The inside of the back door, and the hand railing, were in bad need of repair as most of the paint had been burned off or bubbled.

My brother exercised his usual moral overtone concerning my error in judgment and refused to help clean up the mess. To him, my mishap was just another indicator from the Almighty that my sinful existence was being punished. The wrath of God had struck again!

Since my father was not due home for two more days, I still had time to finish cleaning the area the next day. Swanee said that I should use some paint remover on the railing and door, sand the areas, and brush on two new coats of paint.

"Look, Finlander," Swanee suggested. "What started out as a disaster can now be turned into a project for the benefit of your father. He'll be proud of your initiative! And I promise not to tell him what a dumb ass you are! Why remind him of something he already knows?

The jabbing quip aside, I thanked God for the friends who were helping me save my ass. I promised my "saviors" French fries for the next decade (cooked, of course, only by my mother).

I took a shower to "de-soot" myself. I was pissed that the hair on the top of my head was singed. I would have to get my hair cut short before dad came home.

On Saturday, I got up early and went to the barbershop on the corner of Grand Avenue and 57th Street. Max, the barber, wanted to know how I burned my hair. I made up a story about getting too close to a fire in my backyard. I didn't need to be told how stupid it is to pour water on burning oil, and I didn't need the local barber joining the "Tracy is a nitwit club." Max was a super gossip and if he learned the truth of my "misdeed," the story would be spread all over West Duluth.

Max nearly gave me a "heinee." (Heinee was a derogatory name for German soldiers. A decade later, it became known as a "crewcut"). I despised short hair. It made my square head look even squarer.

Because it was such a hot, muggy day, I decided to do the scraping, sanding, and painting wearing only my undershorts and sneakers.

My first step was to apply the paint remover on the bubbled door and banister. There was a large can of the stuff in the basement that dad had recently purchased. I planned to pour some of the abrasive liquid into a smaller metal coffee can.

I began struggling with a church key to remove the lid of the larger can, but it wouldn't budge. Next, I braced the can of remover between my thighs and went at the stubborn lid with a screwdriver. I pushed on the screwdriver with all my might, and the lid popped off—followed immediately by a messy glob of paint remover engulfing my genitals!

I was instantly struck with an intense burning sensation, like my crotch was being cooked in battery acid. I started screaming. In desperation, I ripped off my undershorts. I needed to hose the stuff off, fast, from the bathtub faucet! The pain was becoming more severe as I ran upstairs to the bathroom—only to find the door locked!

Butch was in the bathroom enjoying his usual Saturday morning soak.

"Butch," I pleaded! "Let me use the bath! I spilled paint remover on my crotch and I'm in unbelievable pain! Please!"

"Use the kitchen sink, blockhead," he responded! "I'm taking a bath and I won't be out for quite a while! Remember, nonbeliever, God works in strange ways!"

I knew it was useless to beg him. "Thanks, prick," I moaned. "I hope your dick gets stuck in the drain!"

I ran to the kitchen and tried to "water down" my groin area with a wet towel, but there was no relief. My "jewels" were still on fire, and, I started sobbing. Now, with my crotch-torture underway, and Butch's refusal to leave the bathroom and help me, I had to add the embarrassment of calling mom at work and beg her to come home and rescue me.

"Mom," I screamed over the phone! "I need you!"

"Tracy," my mom responded. "I'm busy up to my ears with orders. This is Saturday. You know I can't leave work."

"MOM," I screamed louder! "I spilled paint remover on my 'down there!' Ya gotta help me!" The desperation in my voice must have startled her.

"I'll be right home, honey," mom said urgently.

Our phone was situated in a small alcove next to the bathroom door enabling my brother to hear the conversation. I heard him laugh as I was hanging up the receiver. He was taking great joy in my agony.

"What's wrong, blockhead," he inquired, yelling through the bathroom door? "Has the devil set your balls on fire?" Loudly, he started singing a new Christmas song, "Chestnuts roasting by the open fire. . ." I wanted to drown him!

I went to the refrigerator and got the one tray of ice cubes we had in the freezer compartment. I was sitting on the dining room rug, naked, with a handful of ice cubes on my balls and button, crying my eyes out, when mom came rushing in. The excruciating pain overcame any embarrassment I might have felt from mom seeing me naked (although I still had my sneakers on).

"My God, son," my mother said with her hands on her cheeks! "What on earth happened?"

I quickly explained the circumstances as best I could. She said I must get to a hospital as soon as possible. Since mom did not know how to drive, and our father was at work, she called Ernie next door. (Poor Ernie, it would be awhile before he forgot the likes of me).

Ernie came running over, and carried me to the front seat of his father's Plymouth. Mom sat next to me. He raced to the West Duluth Free Clinic. The doctor on duty applied a generous layer of gelatinous ointment to my now "puffy" genitals. Because the burns prevented me from walking, I was delivered back to Ernie's car in a wheelchair wearing a hospital gown. Back home, Ernie carried me into the house and put me to bed. Mom said the doctor advised I stay off my feet for a day or two and let the swelling go down.

There was no way I could now tackle my painting project. Dad would surely disown me, and I'd be banned from the family, facing homelessness. In less than twenty-four hours, I had managed to burn our back porch, destroy clothing and food, blacken my face and singe my hair (thus necessitating a stupid-looking hair cut), appear as an inept clown to my neighbors and friends, scorch my scrotum (and ensure impotency for the rest of my life), allow mom and Ernie to see me naked while holding ice cubes to my nuts and mini-dick, and face the certainty of being put up for adoption by my father. And all of this happened because of my lust for French fries!

To make matters worse, Porky later said that no hair would ever grow around my pecker.

But there were angels in Heaven. Ernie called on Porky and Swanee again to help. The three of them scraped, sanded, and painted the indoor porch. I watched them while sitting on something called a "doughnut" provided by the clinic. Mom offered them each five dollars but they refused the money. They all agreed that watching the "Laurel and Hardy" act I had put on over the past two days was payment enough for their services. They were good friends and promised not to tell anyone about my disastrous escapade.

When dad came home on Monday, he was spared from the details of the French fry fiasco and resulting firestorm, both on the porch and my crotch.

While dad gave no notice to the "alterations" to the back porch, he did mention he liked my short haircut.

I never attempted to cook anything ever again.

And eventually, I did grow hair "down there."

Mom Goes Cold Turkey

⤚ᴄ⤙

THE YEAR 1949 PROVED PROSPEROUS for our father. He was excelling at his sales job and promoted to district sales manager. Dad was away for days at a stretch. When he was home, he spent his time in meetings, selling encyclopedias, and doing office work. Dad now wore stylish black suits and a homburg hat. Butch thought it made him look like an undertaker.

Dad bought a new 1949 Buick, his first automatic transmission car. I remember him always saying, "Body by Fisher, transmission by Dynaflow, and payment by World Book."

In those days, "educational" sales representatives were often allowed to "demonstrate their wares" in schools to captive audiences of schoolchildren. Any conflict of interest between public education and private enterprise was overlooked. The underlying motive for the salesmen's school visits was, of course, to come away with lists of parents' names and addresses to facilitate future in-home sales.

Dad spoke to our class when I was in the fifth grade. Our teacher, Mrs. Shields, introduced him as the district sales manager for World Book Encyclopedia and, more importantly, as my dad. I was so proud of him! He was wearing his black suit, white shirt, and conservative striped tie, and looked like a movie star. Dad had a nice way of explaining to the class the virtues of learning and, of course, the value of investing in World Book. He handed out take-home literature and showed a short movie on the qualities of World Book.

Dad's sobriety was in sharp contrast to the drunken father who had attempted murder and suicide only a year earlier. Although his public image was now that of an altruistic businessman, dad was still distant at home.

People who liked dad, daresay even admired him, never saw his coarse side. He had become expert at the art of "selling himself." Dad was gaining notoriety in his sales region for being a kind and honest man. Butch saw him as a villain. I viewed him as a man focused almost entirely on achieving success at work—at his family's expense. His job took precedence over his family. We were nearly relegated to irrelevancy unless one of us could somehow make him look good in the community.

Dad was taking a course by the Dale Carnegie Institute called: "How to Win Friends and Influence People." Measured by his business successes, he must have been the star pupil. There was no time for anything except World Book sales.

Dad was rarely just a father. We never played catch together. He showed little interest in my gardening and landscaping, and none of my friends knew him. Butch became a self-imposed stranger. He was relieved dad was gone for much of the time.

I was closer to Paul's father than I was with dad. Mr. Swanson showed me how to grease the pocket of my baseball glove and took me fishing at his camp. He invited me over to listen to the Friday Night Fights on the radio. On more than one occasion, he opened his shop on Saturday so that he could repair my broken bike. He was not without flaws of his own. Mr. Swanson could be a little "rough around the edges." He called Negroes: "niggers," and judged a person's behavior by their race, gender or nationality. But he was never mean or degrading to anyone in his family or their friends, and willingly gave their needs his time and attention. His instruction was always patiently delivered and practically relevant. It was fun to listen and learn from him.

Even though mom was drinking a lot, she managed to join the Irving Grade School PTA in September 1949. She met many people and made a few new friends, and handled the responsibilities given to her by the organization. I began to see a glimmer of self-confidence and enthusiasm for life in mom.

Unfortunately, dad not only refused to support her endeavors, he mocked them. He had no interest in meeting her new friends.

He was especially incensed that mom had volunteered to sing "Abba Dabba Honeymoon" in the upcoming PTA variety show at Irving. In a loud, belittling outburst, he told her she had no musical talent and would only bring embarrassment to the family—and, of course, to his reputation.

Dad informed mom: "A successful salesman must maintain his dignity in the community. Potential customers want to identify with a well-respected person when they are considering making an investment." He emphatically stated: "Singing on stage, out of tune, will not help anyone. I refuse to be a part of it. Mary, if you care for me, and my business, bow out of such silliness."

His deriding comments made mom cry and, predictably, resort to alcohol to pacify the hurt that dad had instilled. Despite our father's criticism and resistance, I was proud when mom did sing in the show. And she received a standing ovation from the audience. Dad, of course, stayed home out of fear of being mortified by his wife's "lack of talent."

We refused to tell him the performance was a complete success. Dad never would have believed us anyway. He treated mom like a third child and denied her the dignity worthy of a spouse.

Mom's lack of spousal support diminished her confidence and damaged her sense of self-worth, and her need for alcohol only increased. It was particularly bad during the holidays when dad was home all day. To him, holidays meant no sales, and the loss of money. He became moody, and the atmosphere in the house was filled with tension, silence, and isolation. We kept away from each other. The atmosphere was like being in solitary confinement of a prison.

When relatives visited to celebrate a holiday, the pretense of "we are all so happy as a family" would be played out for our guests. Mom, Butch and I hated the deceitful game. We were being dishonest with our relatives. Dad was good at the charade. He was used to emoting a "sunny" disposition at work. In the presence of our relatives on a holiday, dad was attentive, sociable, and humorous. He acted thoroughly interested (and in agreement) with every commentary made by our kin.

It was traditional to invite Great-Grandfather Reid (who, sadly, had recently died), Grandma Kier, Aunt Edith, Uncle Ralph, and Sheila to our house for Christmas dinner. Unfortunately, Uncle Bob, my favorite relative, never came to our house at Thanksgiving or Christmas. Grandpa and Grandma Gran spent the winter holidays with Uncle Bob and Aunt Eleanor. Dad's father and stepmother still shared the conviction that we were not the respectable side of the Gran family.

Uncle Bob cared little for his snobbish stepmother. (He once told us the only thing he enjoyed about his war experience was being separated from the uppity woman for four years). But he felt obligated to provide his father a place to go to "enjoy" the holidays. Unfortunately, his stepmother was part of the package.

On early Christmas morning of 1949, mom looked pale, tired, and "hung over." After unwrapping our presents in relative silence, our parents commenced arguing over mom's PTA activities. Dad suspected that the PTA was a front for drinking sprees (to some degree, his suspicion was probably valid). Mom, of course, angrily resented his accusations. Dad stormed off to his home office and the argument was terminated.

Mom began preparing the Christmas dinner and doing some wash in the basement. Butch and I returned to our bedroom, set up the card table, and began a puzzle we had just received for Christmas.

Our relatives arrived around noon and the tension in the house immediately disappeared. It was time for the four of us to begin performing the "happy family" game. When I came out of our bedroom into the kitchen to join in the pretense, I discovered mom was "potted." Her eyes were watery, her speech was slurred, and she had a drunken grin on her face. Mom obviously had done quite a few "washes" in the basement during the morning.

Dad, Butch, and I greeted our relatives and exchanged small talk for about fifteen minutes. Mom came into the living room for "hugs and kisses" and everyone present knew she was "pie-eyed." Nevertheless, we all remained silent about her condition.

When it became time to serve the food, we took our places around the long table in our small dining room. Mom had boiled and mashed the potatoes, turnips, and squash, and I placed them on the dinner table. The homemade cranberry sauce was ready. Other dishes held the celery stuffed with cream cheese and sliced black olives, three or four kinds of pickles, corn relish, and green olives. Grandma and Aunt Edith had brought two dozen yeast rolls along with three homemade pies (pumpkin, apple, and my favorite, raspberry).

At the table, dad began his ritual of sharpening a long, thin handled knife used to carve the turkey. This year's bird was an especially big one, weighing over twenty pounds.

"Mary," my father diplomatically yelled to the kitchen. "Please bring in the turkey for the carving."

"Of course," mom shakily replied in her inebriated state. "It's coming right out!"

We heard the squeaky oven door opening, followed moments later by the noise of mom leaving through the back door.

"Mary," dad bellowed! "What is going on?"

Mom had left the house, walking out without a coat or hat in the frigid December weather! Dad ran to the back door and stepped outside to look for her, but she was nowhere to be seen.

"MARY, FOR CHRIST SAKE," dad screamed! "WHERE ARE YOU?"

There was no response. Mom had disappeared.

Dad returned to the kitchen where everyone now had gathered. He looked like an insane man. "What the hell am I to do," he pleaded?! "Jesus, Mary, and Joseph, her drinking is driving me crazy!"

Aunt Edith, with tears in her eyes, turned to dad and pointed to the oven. She said, "I know why she left. She forgot to turn on the oven and now she's mortified."

We all stared at the giant turkey, sitting completely uncooked, in a large pan. In her "happy," but obviously unfocused state, mom neglected to set the oven temperature to cook the bird. Our Christmas turkey had sat there, in the raw, for hours.

No one had noticed the lack of smell of cooking turkey meat in the Gran household on that fateful day. I think the fighting and isolation throughout much of the day, the cook being drunk, combined with the assorted smells of the vegetables, screened out the now obvious fact that the main course had never been roasted. Sadly, the only thing "roasted" was our mother, who had chosen to disappear.

Dad and Uncle Ralph went to look for mom in dad's car. The rest of us sat around dumbfounded, staring at each other and wondering what to say. What could we say? We all felt concerned for mom. I remember being very scared that mom had run off and might hurt herself.

Aunt Edith continued to cry and blamed herself for not addressing our mom's "problem," as she called it.

"She needs help," Aunt Edith sobbed, "and I have never talked to her about the drinking. She's not a happy person. I have pretended that everything was all right with her. She should be in a hospital under a doctor's care. She's not herself."

I distinctly remember hearing my brother grumble under his breath, "How could she be herself. It's her husband. That man has driven her to drink."

I didn't want to accept what he said, but a part of me agreed with him.

Mom was found about a half block away, at the Moose Hall. She was at the bar with another man and was very drunk. Uncle Ralph and dad brought mom home and put her to bed.

Our relatives gathered to leave. As they awkwardly started for the front door, each of them hugged dad, Butch, and me. The grown-ups agreed that perhaps we could celebrate the holiday on another day, but predictably, it didn't happen.

The calamity of Christmas 1949 curtailed the "let's pretend" games. I think Butch was affected the most by that ugly day. He loved mom very much, and while he did not condone her addiction to alcohol, and other men, he understood why she resorted to such self-destructive and demeaning behavior. Butch's hatred of dad's crassness, insensitivity, and bullishness was growing deeper by the day.

Mom was in fact a sensitive woman, who found herself living with a spouse who was mean, disrespectful, and demanding. Dad's version of love was equated with unilateral duty and obeisance.

Being the baby of the family, mom never spoke to me of her unhappiness. She must have thought her diminutive fair-haired boy could contribute little to easing her domestic struggles. She was probably right.

I knew mom was a decent person. When she drank, or went out with other men, I hated the action, not her. The mess at Christmas was uncharacteristic of mom's true personality. But the debacle left a permanent scar on all of us.

I was growing tired of the dysfunctional family that I existed in, a domestic insane asylum.

So many times, sadly, I wished I could be just an occasional visitor with the people at 5714 Wadena Street.

Mom, PTA Variety Show Night, 1949

The Sutherlands and Boy Loo

‿ᧉ

JOHNNY SUTHERLAND WAS A CLASSMATE in the fifth grade. Johnny was always pissed off. He was a bully, regularly sent to Principal Becker's office for a deserved punishment.

Among his antics was the time he snuck a squirt gun into school. He proceeded to shoot Mrs. Shield's in the ass as she was writing on the blackboard. Another time he threw a lit "cherry bomb" into the girls' washroom, resulting in the school's evacuation. Johnny tied a younger boy to a urinal and repeatedly flushed it, soaking the kid's clothes. He also let the air out of Principal Becker's tires on more than one occasion.

Boy Loo Chin was also in the class. His Japanese family had migrated to America after the war ended. Boy Loo was the only Japanese alien at Irving. He was four years older than me, placed in our class because of his limited English skills. Mrs. Shields had Boy Loo sit at a corner table because he was too big to squeeze into one of the regular school desks. Boy Loo was an incredibly decent person. He was polite and soft-spoken and I never saw him lose his temper or raise his voice. He was happy and thankful for being in America.

Johnny's father had served in the Pacific Theater during the war and hated the "Japs." Johnny felt the same way as his father. It was no surprise that Johnny made fun of Boy Loo by mocking everything he did.

Boy Loo brought a delicious Japanese dinner to class which he shared with us. Everyone filled their plates, except for Johnny. He said the food would make him puke. Boy Loo also brought tea and fortune cookies. Mrs. Shields had each student read their fortune to the other members of the class.

When Johnny's turn came, he held the slip of paper to his face and, in a mocking tone, said, "In one hour, you will all be dead from eating this Jap crap."

Most of the kids laughed, including Boy Loo (and myself). But Mrs. Shields became very angry. She scolded Johnny (and the other members of the class) for being rude. Reluctantly, Johnny had to apologize to Boy Loo. I felt ashamed for laughing. I knew better. Mom was always saying, "Treat people with dignity and never be disrespectful." (I found mom's rule to be impossible to follow around my brother.)

Apparently, when Johnny informed his father about the luncheon cuisine, Mr. Sutherland called Principal Becker and was outraged that Mrs. Shields allowed her pupils to eat "Jap food."

When Boy Loo came to class dressed in a traditional Japanese outfit, Johnny burst out laughing. The outfit was made of silk and very colorful. I thought it was quite beautiful. Boy Loo gave a talk on the meaning of the colors and symbols on his clothing. It was a fascinating presentation and we all learned a lot about Japan. Johnny showed no interest at all.

"He's a slit-eyed queer," exclaimed Johnny as we broke for afternoon recess. "Rice paddy wears a silk blouse and dress to school and everyone goes gaga over it! If he ain't a faggot, my name ain't Johnny Sutherland! I wonder if he wears silk panties and nylons under that fag outfit?"

I was afraid of Johnny. He was big for his age and I worried that he might, for no reason, beat me up on the playground. Fortunately, Johnny never harassed me. But I kept my mouth shut when I was around him. I never felt comfortable in his presence. Johnny was a very nasty kid.

Mr. Sutherland worked with dad as a projectionist. In addition, Uncle Bob and Mr. Sutherland served in the same South Pacific unit during the war and were fellow members of a VFW Post. I suspect Johnny was told by his father to "leave the Gran kid alone."

I became acquainted with Mr. Sutherland as he came to our Little League practices and games. He drove me home after every contest. (My parents never attending a game). Sitting in his beautiful Cadillac, he invariably commented about the Japanese.

Mr. Sutherland admired President Truman for dropping A-bombs on Japan, but he said: "the entire nation should have been wiped out." He claimed that Japs in America still could not be trusted and "the sneaky bastards should be back in relocation camps."

Mr. Sutherland related that: "During the war, American prisoners captured by the Japs were fed rats and rice filled with maggots and turds. Japs tortured our troops. They are evil people who still hate Americans. And I hate them."

His comments made me wonder if other American servicemen also despised the Japanese, four years after the end of the war? Did the Japs still hate Americans?

THE BLAME GAME

The arrival of Spring 1950, after another hard, long Minnesota winter, signaled the time for the fifth graders at Irving to play softball during afternoon recess. The game was familiar to us, and required no special equipment. Mrs. Shields intended the game to be a fun exercise. She made sure each side was balanced in ability and gender.

When Mrs. Shields assigned Boy Loo and Johnny to the same team, I knew it was only a matter of time before something bad would happen. It began when Johnny sarcastically commented: "Oh great, we got soy sauce who is about as athletic as my grandma, and she has Parkinson's disease! Boy plays right field and bats last! I don't want Mr. Jappo wrecking my chances of winning!"

Boy Loo had never played ball. He knew nothing about the rules of the game. His ignorance of the sport fed Johnny's rage. Boy Loo stood on the plate when he batted and held the bat cross-handed at his knees. Mrs. Shields corrected him, but never once did he hit the ball, not even a foul ball "tick." He struck out very time. Johnny derided Boy Loo and called him "old faithful" because of his predictable failure.

Boy Loo had never learned to throw a ball, and always rolled it to a player. Although his lack of skills and knowledge of the game was obvious to us all, including Mrs. Shields, his performance was tolerated (except by Johnny). He was doing his best to contribute, having fun himself, and cheering on his teammates.

On the last day of the school year, it was a tradition at Irving Grade School for Mrs. Shields' fifth grade class to play a game against Miss Tangwall's fifth graders. The contest was held on the softball diamond at Irving Field.

Mrs. Shields class had won for years. No one could remember the last time Miss Tangwall's team had been victorious.

Each teacher selected nine players (boys only) for their team. Mrs. Shields put Boy Loo on our team, perhaps as a gesture of fairness. Even with Boy Loo, we had a strong lineup, and were sure to win. My teammates included the LeDoux brothers, Dan Carich, Bob Sisto, Harley Gellatly, Ron Hicks, Johnny, and Boy.

Miss Tangwall;s class included both fifth and sixth graders, but since only the fifth graders were allowed to play, their talent pool was much smaller than ours. Miss Tangwall's players were inexperienced at softball. Only two had played in the summer cadet hardball league. We had six players who regularly participated in organized ball and were very adept at playing softball. We were assured of victory and would easily "play around" the automatic out that Boy Loo represented.

Several parents were in the stands to watch the annual competition including, of course, Mr. (and Mrs.) Sutherland. Things started out well when we won the coin toss and were named the "home" team. Mrs. Tangwall's players had first "ups" in the five-inning game. A five-run rule was in effect: five consecutive runs by either team ended that half inning.

At their first "at bats," Miss Tangwall's team when down in order. Johnny was our pitcher and no one could hit him. He struck out the side in nine pitches. I remember thinking this game would be a "breeze" to win.

It was my team's turn to hit. Mrs. Shields assigned the batting order. Art LeDoux, the smallest kid in our class, was to bat first. I was second and Johnny was third. Boy Loo was the "clean up" hitter, much to our surprise! The fourth placed hitter was usually the best batter on a team, and Boy Loo was, to be kind, terrible!

Johnny could not believe Boy Loo was "hitting" fourth! He quickly ran over to his father and informed him of Boy Loo's place in the batting order.

"WHAT," Mr. Sutherland screamed?! "IS THE WOMAN NUTS? JAPPO IS USELESS AND IS BATTING FOURTH! MY GOD IN HEAVEN!" Mrs. Sutherland demanded that he "hush up and calm down." Mr. Sutherland reluctantly complied but his face was beet red.

In the bottom of the first, we scored three runs when Johnny hit a home run with Art and me on base. When Boy struck out on three pitches, Mr. Sunderland just shook his head, making another jeering (but quiet) comment to his wife. They both laughed so everyone could hear them. Mrs. Shield's glanced over at Mr. and Mrs. Sutherland. She was disgusted by their behavior.

Miss Tangwall's team went scoreless for the first four innings (in fact, they had yet to have a base runner). Meanwhile, we added another run. Starting the top of the fifth, and last inning, we were ahead four to nothing. When Johnny started for the pitching mound to begin his final inning, Mrs. Shields called him back and announced that it was Boy Loo's turn to pitch! Johnny almost fainted! He couldn't believe Mrs. Shields was letting Boy Loo pitch! To be truthful, I was as stunned as the rest of the team. Boy had never pitched a ball in his life!

Mr. Sutherland was so incensed he left the stands and went to his car, probably for a deep swig of the whiskey he kept in his glove compartment.

Boy Loo took to the mound. His first "pitch" was rolled to the catcher! His next pitch went well over the catcher's head! His third pitch hit the batter in the rear end! In no time, Miss Tangwall's team scored five runs, the consequence of eight consecutive walks by Boy Loo. Miss Tangwall's team was now ahead by the score of five to four. Her players were crazy with excitement! Because of the five-run rule, the teams changed sides.

Our team was now up. Except for an enraged Johnny, we didn't blame Boy Loo for the score. Mrs. Shields, understanding the weakness of the opposing team, was just trying to give the other side a chance. But in the stands, Mr. Sutherland, his face bright red, was nearly insane with anger!

We needed two runs to win the game, and were confident our team could do that because our best hitters were due up. We would retain bragging rights and continue the string of wins by Mrs. Shields teams (and undoubtedly save Mr. Sutherland from a heart attack).

I led off the bottom of the inning with a single to center field. After taking a few pitches, Johnny hit a double down the left field line. I ended up at third base and Johnny was on second. There were no outs.

Boy Loo was up next. We knew he would strike out and be followed by two of our best hitters, Harley Gellatly and Dan Carich. We had the game in the bag. One of those guys would surely knock us home.

Boy Loo stood at the plate, batting cross-handed with the bat being held down by his knees. True to form, he swung and missed the first two pitches. One more, and he would strike out, and we could go on to win the game.

I never believed in miracles, but what Boy Loo did next, changed everything.

On the third pitch, Boy Loo hit the ball, and not only did he make contact, he crushed it! The ball went high into center field and over the outfielder's head! It was the longest hit of the game! Boy Loo had finally "connected" and his hit would easily bring home two runs! Our team was jumping up and down on the bench!

Holding his bat in one hand, he ran up the baseline, and I trotted toward home plate, still watching the ball sailing high in the air. On my way to score, to my horror, there was Boy Loo, running straight at me, on the same third baseline!

The collision occurred about midway, with Boy Loo's bat hitting my face. We both went down in a tangled heap, blood starting to run from my nose. Johnny rounded third and ran by the two of us on his way to home plate. The opposing pitcher yelled for the ball. He took the relay from the shortstop and tagged me with the ball.

"GAME OVER," yelled the umpire! "GAME OVER!!"

Mr. Sunderland ran from the stands to the umpire and screamed in his face, "WHAT DO YOU MEAN, GAME OVER!? THERE'S ONLY ONE OUT, YOU DUFUS!"

The umpire backed away from Mr. Sutherland and loudly addressed the teams and crowd.

"The game is over," the umpire explained. "The batter is out for running down the wrong base line. The runner who tried to score from second passed the "live" runner in front of him, and therefore is out. And the pitcher just tagged out the runner who fell down on the third base line." (That runner being me.) "It was a triple play. Miss Tangwall's team wins five to four."

As the umpire was leaving the field. Miss Tangwall's players went bananas! They could not believe what had just happened! Neither could I, still lying on the ground. I had never seen a triple play before, much less been involved in one. My team stood motionless, struggling to understand how a sure thing had turned into a nightmare. We were defeated, humiliated, and zombie-like, unable to act or speak or know what to do.

The first to respond was Mr. Sutherland.

Mr. Sutherland stormed over to Boy Loo who was sitting on the base path. Boy Loo had no clue what had just taken place. Mrs. Shields began to attend to the accidental wound that I had just received. I was bleeding profusely. (I wound up with a bloody and very sore nose.) Boy Loo was unhurt in our collision.

I should say that Boy Loo was unhurt until Mr. Sutherland began kicking him in the legs and back. Mr. Sutherland grabbed the bat that Boy Loo had finally dropped and was in the process of swinging it at Boy Loo's head.

"Fucken idiot Jap," screamed Mr. Sutherland! "I'm gonna knock some fucken sense into you!"

Luckily, the umpire reappeared just in time to grab the bat from the raving Mr. Sutherland. He held onto Mr. Sutherland long enough for Boy Loo to get up and limp off the field. Mr. Sutherland continued to threaten Boy Loo, yelling loudly, "Rice patty! Beware! I'll get you, and when I do, you'll wish you were back in Japland!".

I decided to abandon any thought of hitching a ride home that afternoon with the Sutherlands. In fact, I vowed to never be around Mr. Sutherland again.

It wasn't the loss that would become an ugly memory. It was Mr. Sutherland's sickening display of hate and vengefulness toward Boy Loo that would last in my mind.

I also knew Boy Loo wasn't at fault for what happened. Johnny and I should have stayed at our bases. With only one out, Harley or Dan surely would have plated us.

As I was walking home from the game, I thought again about what Mrs. Shields was teaching us by picking Boy Loo for the team, having him bat "clean up," and then pitching the final inning. I think she wanted Boy Loo to feel part of the team, and to show the whole class and their parents what fair play really meant, win or lose. Given her team's history of winning, Mrs. Shield's probably concluded that we would win anyway.

Mrs. Shields couldn't have predicted Boy Loo's incredible hit, the subsequent humiliating collision that resulted in a triple play, and loss of the game. And she didn't expect Boy Loo being kicked by an enraged, racist parent. Not everything goes as planned.

I never saw Boy Loo play softball again. He did limp for a while. His family refrained from taking legal action against Mr. Sutherland. Boy Loo was subsequently fast-tracked through the higher grades and graduated high school three years before I did.

Thankfully, the Sutherlands moved to the West End of Duluth that summer. Like Nabisco's moving away to Two Harbors in the second grade, I was relieved the Sutherland's were no longer "players" in my life.

A few years later, Uncle Bob told me Mr. Sutherland was killed in the Korean War.

Kotex

⤚

I HAD BEEN WHINING TO Porky and Swanee that I needed a new baseball glove. Mom promised to get me a mitt for my birthday in late August, but selfishly, I wanted one now. After all, my mitt was a tattered five-fingered rag dad used in high school, when Babe Ruth was playing.

One night in June 1950, when the Dukes weren't in town, Swanee called me on the phone after supper.

"Hey, Finlander! Get yer ass over here," commanded Swanee! "We're going to Wheeler Field to watch fast pitch softball. Okay?"

I enjoyed watching fast pitch. The games were lively-paced and the plays required split-second timing There was little "dead" time during the contests.

"Sure," I said happily. "I'll be right over on my bike."

Wheeler Field was located across Grand Avenue from Wade Stadium, where the Duluth Dukes played baseball. It was a neat complex with stands, outfield fences, and well-manicured grounds. There was no cost to watch the contests, and, every night during the spring and summer months, there were league games.

It was getting dark as we headed for the stadium, so we turned on our bike lights. It was a cool thing to have bike lights on at night, almost as if the light switch gave the bike more power. Swanee was riding an expensive hand-me-down bike given to him by one of his uncles. It was a pristine Elgin sold by Sears and Roebuck. It was made sometime in the 1930s. His uncle told him it retailed then for $35—more than most people earned in a week's work at that time. Swanee's bike was even nicer than Sheila's new J. C. Higgins model my Uncle Ralph had given her. I was jealous of them.

When we arrived, the game was in suspension due to heavy fog that had drifted in from Lake Superior. Swanee and I parked our bikes behind the right field stands. We approached the grassy area between the stands and the foul line. The field was empty. Without saying a word, Swanee suddenly lifted me off my feet and threw me down on the soft turf. I felt a lump under my chest. Before I could do anything, Swanee wrapped his arms around me, picked me back up, and carried me—lump and all, to our bikes.

"Put me down, Swanee!" I softly yelled, feeling helpless. "Why the hell are you carrying me like a sack of flour?"

"Shut up, idiot," Swanee whispered as he dropped me to the ground. "You want a new glove, don't ya!? Take a gander, Finlander!"

As Swanee released his arms, the lump on my chest fell to the grass. It was a fielder's glove, clearly left on the field by one of the players as the teams ran to their dugouts.

"Jesus, Swanee," I said quietly, but forcefully. "You're stealing that glove?"

Swanee replied. "You've been complaining for weeks about wanting a new glove, haven't ya? Well there it is, mental midget. Now let's pedal our asses outta here!" Swanee began getting on his bicycle.

"But that's stealing," I said. "It's not my glove."

As Swanee started to ride off, he said, "It's your glove if you put it in your basket and bike home. Come on! It's a gift from the city. This is a "team glove" covered by the league budget. It's not really stealing. The fucken taxpayers paid for it. Our parents pay taxes so we have a right to the mitt."

I climbed on my bike and rode off after him back down Grand Avenue. I felt uneasy about taking the glove, but I was excited to "own" such a quality mitt. Along the way home, Swanee kept repeating that we had done nothing wrong, and I began to "sort of" believe him.

"That right fielder will just get a new glove from the city," explained Swanee. "Don't sweat the small stuff, Finlander. Enjoy the new mitt. Tell the neighborhood that it was a gift from me to you. That way, your mother won't have to buy a glove for your birthday. She'll be happy."

"Okay," I responded cautiously. "If you think it's all right."

I so wanted to accept Swanee's justification for what we had just done. I loved the glove.

Swanee's arguments always seemed so logical. If the glove really was community property, then our taking it wasn't stealing. I began to feel relieved and my uneasiness ebbed by the time we reached his driveway. .

"Come on," said Swanee. "Let's go in the garage and look at your new glove."

We turned on the inside light of the small garage and sat down at the work bench to examine the mitt. It was dyed red and made of real leather. Because it was a softball glove, the pocket and webbing were large. Eddie Stanky's signature was stamped near the heel. The well-known second baseman had just been traded by the Boston Red Sox to the New York Giants.

"Wow, cool autograph," exclaimed Swanee. "You know Stanky's one hell of a ball player."

In those days, the assumption was that if your glove displayed the signature of a famous major leaguer, you became a better player. Since I played second base on my organized teams, I could not have picked a better glove to help me hone my skills. Our little escapade was turning into a good thing.

"The glove is going to need some padding as the pocket is too big for hard ball," instructed Swanee. "I know just what will fix it. Kotex."

"Kotex," I said somewhat baffled? "Why Kotex? That's what women use to powder their faces."

Swanee looked at me with crossed eyes.

"I swear you are even dumber than most Finlanders," he said. "You are a retarded Finlander—the dumbest of the dumb." He uncrossed his eyes and informed me, "You don't use Kotex for powdering! Kotex is a sanitary napkin, a cunt rag!"

"What the hell are you talking about," I asked, thoroughly baffled?

Shaking his head over my ingrained ignorance, Swanee explained: "Kotex is used to sop up blood when a woman has her time of the month. During this period, and it's a bitch of a time for guys, blood is let go through the vagina. A sanitary napkin is used to mop up the flow. Girls go on the rag around twelve or thirteen, just when guys start getting hair on their balls. The napkins are great for padding gloves. My catcher's mitt is filled with cunt rags." Swanee paused and looked at me as though I was a complete idiot. "Do you understand what I am saying, Einstein?"

I decided that Swanee was not only condescending, his explanation was absurd. I was annoyed. "You're playing games with me, Swanee," I said, with a look of anger on my face. "Why would any ball player want to stuff their mitt with blood soaked rags? I don't recall seeing much Kotex floating around any ballparks I've ever been to. Does Ted Williams or Joe DiMaggio use these rags? Cut the shit!"

"I'm not playing any goddamn game with you," insisted Swanee. "This is a softball glove! Stuffing Kotex around the pocket of the mitt will make it better for hardball because the napkins will soften the blow. The smaller pocket and larger webbing will make it a perfect baseball mitt. And you don't use blood-soaked rags, moron! You use fresh napkins. They're soft as a rabbit's ass, just like your brain."

Perhaps this Kotex idea was a good one after all, I thought.

"Okay, okay," I responded. "But just how in hell do we get the Kotex? I'm not going to the store and buy it! I couldn't do that, no way! You expect me to walk up to Mrs. Bengston at People's Market and inquire where she keeps the Kotex? Never in a million years could I do that!"

"No, no," Swanee said adamantly. "You'll just have to get some from your mother."

Now I knew he was jerking my chain. "WHAT," I yelled! "Oh, now I get it! First the condom trick and now you want me to ask my mother if she'll give me some of her sanitation napkins! Well, you ain't going to fool me this time! This Finlander's onto you! Christ, my mother would ring my neck! Why don't we ask your mother, smart ass?"

I had him now and it felt good.

Swanee put his right hand on my shoulder and said slowly, but clearly: "Look, shit-for-brains. First, they are sanitary napkins, not sanitation napkins. Second, I am not trying to trick you into another embarrassing moment with your mother! That would be too easy, you nitwit! Third, I would be more than happy to use my mother's rags, but she's dried up! She doesn't bleed anymore! She's gone through menopause!"

"What the hell is menopause," I cautiously inquired? "Another bullshit term to make me feel stupid?"

"You don't need my trickery to make you feel stupid," Swanee exclaimed. "Just act natural. You're already stupid!"

He pissed me off again, but before I could respond, Swanee continued: "Menopause occurs to older women when they stop flowing blood from their vagina. They no longer can have kids. They dry up. My mother is 52 years old and she has already gone through menopause. So, my ignorant little friend, the result is no blood equals no-need for napkins, simple as that. So, that being the case, how old is your mother?"

"Well," I calculated out loud. I was good at math. "She was born in 1914, and this is 1950, so she's almost 36."

"She's still on the rag," Swanee confidently concluded.

Swanee paused and looked a little ashamed of himself. "I'm sorry, Finlander. That last comment sounded a might bit crude. You know that I respect your mother very much."

"I know. You didn't mean the way it sounded," I responded.

I was now pissed for getting pissed at Swanee. He was my best friend and cared about me knowing things. Swanee usually steered me in the right direction. He was my hero, although I would never say that to him. Guys just don't say such things like that to other guys.

I was lucky to have him as a friend.

"I think I know where mom keeps the Kotex," I said. "She usually stores that stuff under the sink in our bathroom, near her lotions. I guess that's why I thought Kotex was a powder puff or something."

I didn't feel so stupid anymore. But I had no idea women bled "down there." Females were so complex.

The next night, mom was at the "library," dad was away working, and Butch was at church. The coast was clear. I entered our bathroom and took five napkins from mom's box under the sink. I wanted to make sure the mitt, which I had left in Swanee's garage, was well-padded for hardball. With the pads jammed into my pockets, I ran to Swanee's house, in a heavy rainstorm, to have him show me how to stuff my new glove. He met me at his front door.

He said quietly, "You got the rags, Finlander?"

I proudly responded, as though I had accomplished some great feat and was expecting accolades, "Yah, I got five of them! That should do the trick, heh?"

"C'mon," said Swanee. "Let's go to the garage and fix your mitt."

I placed the Kotex napkins on the bench next to the mitt.

"Okay, Finlander," instructed Swanee. "The first thing you can do is to unlace the glove. Start at the glove heel so that we can stuff the rags in from there. We'll probably need all five. Your mitt will be soft and cushiony as a nun's ass. You'll never get stung by a hard ball. And you can thank your mother for the padding, although I wouldn't suggest you do that!"

We both laughed. If my mother knew what we were doing in Swanee's garage, my face would likely get a "good slap" from her. But I wasn't worried about the missing napkins. Mom would probably assume Sheila took them.

To make it easier to access the rawhide lacing, I unhooked the wrist strap, and when I turned it over, I discovered a name etched on the underside. I read the name three or four times before I screamed aloud, "HOLY SHIT! HOLY, HOLY SHIT! HOLY SHIT!"

Swanee looked at me as though I had lost my senses. "Are you all right, Finlander," he asked?

In a panic-stricken voice, I replied: "Look! This is Uncle Ralph's softball glove!"

"What," Swanee shouted! "Are you kidding me?"

"I wish I was, but I ain't," I lamented, stretching the strap for Swanee to read. My heart sank into my stomach.

There it was, deeply etched in black ink: RALPH OLSEN SR. This was my uncle, Aunt Edith's husband, the man who took me to the Dukes ball games, bought me hot dogs and soda, included me on fishing trips, gave me Christmas and birthday presents, and played catch with me when I was at his house.

Swanee stared at the name and whispered, "Well I'll be a son-of-a-bitch. What are the chances?"

I had no answer. I was stunned. The mitt was now tainted, no longer a great "find." A feeling of intense guilt overtook me. Uncle Ralph was a spectator at most of my games. There was no way he wouldn't recognize his stolen red glove on my hand.

"Swanee," I pleaded. "What the hell are we going to do?"

I felt horrible and dirty. "I can't keep this glove," I cried. "It's even got Uncle Ralph's phone number written below his name, Calumet 4-4361."

Swanee thought for a moment. "Are you certain the glove is your uncle's? It could be somebody else's. Olsen is a common name. The phone book probably lists all kinds of Ralph Olsens'.

Swanee was grasping for straws.

"With the same fucken phone number as my Uncle Ralph," I screamed! "What goes here, Swanee? Do the Ralph Olsens' of Duluth have a common phone? Do they all live together? Jesus, Swanee, I knew this was a wrong thing to do! I don't want this goddamn glove! It's obvious that my uncle was playing in the league last night and left his mitt in right field during the fog break. I know for a fact that when he is not pitching he's always in right field! Shit, shit, double shit!"

The was the first thing I had ever stolen in my life and the item belongs to a close relative who treats me like I was his son. To add to my misery, I didn't feel all that great sneaking Kotex pads from my mother, especially since I often criticized her for underhanded behavior. In less than twenty-four hours, I had mistreated two members of my family. Maybe Butch, the asshole, was right. I was nothing but an outright sinner.

For a long while, Swanee and I said nothing, staring at each other like two goons stuck on an elevator.

Swanee broke the silence. He had a plan. It couldn't have been more foolish or desperate. "We'll bring the mitt to your uncle and tell him we found it on Grand Avenue. Someone must have taken it from him and lost it as they were going down the street. Someone must. . ."

"Swanee," I interrupted. "We steal a mitt, then I steal some rags, and now you recommend that we lie to my uncle with a goofy story about his glove. I'm not good at lying. Every time I lie, or fib, my voice rises and gets jittery, and I'm a dead fish in the water. Do you really want me to lie to Uncle Ralph? He's always been so good to me and I know he likes you."

For a moment, Swanee stared down at his feet. He took a deep breath. We both came to the same conclusion, but Swanee expressed it best.

"If a guy is a prick, then he deserves to be treated as such. If a guy is a nice guy, he warrants respect. Your uncle is a nice guy. To not return the glove to him and tell the truth is wrong."

Swanee put his hand on my shoulder and looked me straight in the eye.

"Trace," he confessed, "the stealing was my idea. You didn't go to Wheeler field with the idea of copping a glove. I'll take full blame for this caper."

"Nah," I said, disagreeing. "Remember, I sure loved your logic for keeping the mitt.

I thought of Butch and his lecture on how the truth "would make you free." I was beginning to understand what he was trying to say, although I hated to admit it.

"We're equally guilty," I had to keep talking to stop myself from crying. "Neither of us wants to be known as a thief. We ain't choir boys, but we ain't crooks."

Swanee nodded in agreement. He began to quietly re-lace the glove.

As he laced, Swanee asked: "Well, if we are going to tell him what we did, when and where do we return it? He must have a game coming up, so sooner the better. Shit, I wish I didn't have a conscience! All this church stuff has a way of rubbing off on ya."

Swanee turned to me and knowingly inquired: "Isn't he a bartender at the Kom On Inn?"

Everybody in West Duluth knew that Uncle Ralph worked at the popular local tavern and restaurant, and it was two blocks from our houses.

We looked at each other and nodded our heads. There was only one correct thing to do. I grabbed the mitt and stuffed it under my shirt to keep it dry. We were off in the pouring rain to the Kom On Inn. My stomach was fluttering with butterflies, my legs felt weak, and I couldn't catch my breath as my heart was beating so fast.

Swanee was silent. I kept hoping that he would come up with some other miracle solution to avoid having to face my uncle, but it didn't happen.

When we reached the tavern, I peered through the entrance door window and saw Uncle Ralph behind the bar. He was cleaning glasses with a towel.

"He's working, Swanee," I said in an unhappy voice. I was hoping that Uncle Ralph wouldn't be at the bar, but there he was, in plain sight, smiling as usual.

Swanee opened the door and I followed him in. I was shaking.

Uncle Ralph immediately greeted us as we approached the bar. His smile became brighter. "Howdy, boys," he said in a welcoming tone. "Get in out of the rain. You guys look soaked to the gills. What'll it be, beer or whiskey?" He took out two glasses and gave us each a small bottle of coke. "On the house as guests of the Kom On Inn! Is this a social visit or are you interested in buying the place?"

We laughed, albeit nervously, at my uncle's welcome. He had a great sense of humor, certainly honed over the years by being a barkeep. We sat down on stools next to the bar and took sips of our cola. "Well, here goes," I thought, "the end of my uncle ever respecting me again. I am such a sinner! My brother is right!"

Despite sipping the coke, my mouth was cotton dry. I began, hoarsely: "Uncle Ralph, Swanee and I have something to tell, and give you. The other day at Wheeler field, we . . ."

Uncle Ralph quickly finished my sentence with "stole my softball glove." Swanee and I looked at each other and then back at my uncle. He was no longer smiling.

Swanee stuttered, "But, but, how did. . .did you know?"

"Why didn't you come after us," I said, on the verge of fainting?

Uncle Ralph placed his hands flat on the bar and leaned toward us. I thought he was going to grab us by the ears and knock our heads together. Instead, he spoke in a quiet tone.

"My team was playing last night. I was in the clubhouse waiting for the fog to lift when I saw you rascals ride up on your bikes. I must say it was a clever trick to wrestle and fall on my glove and then scoop it away. It's a good thing the game was postponed. I would have had to finish playing barehanded."

In a quivering voice, I said, "Uncle Ralph, I feel so embarrassed and guilty." With my head lowered, unable to look him in the eye, I muttered: "It was a stupid thing to do."

Swanee quietly interrupted me and confessed: "It was my idea, not Tracy's. I'm really the one to blame. Tracy didn't know what was going on. I feel bad about this. You've always treated me nicely and I go and do something like this to you. I deserve a kick in the rear end."

"I went along with it, Uncle Ralph," I admitted. "It wasn't just Paul. I planned to keep the glove for hardball. There's no excuse for what we did, especially to you. I guess you have the grounds to tell our parents and I wouldn't blame ya if ya did."

Uncle Ralph straightened up, and I was fully expecting him to tell us to get the hell out of his workplace. Instead, he crossed his arms, and surprised us by what he said next.

"There is no excuse for what you did," said Uncle Ralph. "Stealing anything is wrong. When I witnessed your little exercise last night I almost ran after you. I was also going to inform your parents. But then I thought, let this be a test of their honesty."

"Huh," I said? "I don't get it."

"If you didn't feel guilty about stealing the glove," Uncle Ralph explained, "the two of you wouldn't be standing here, in this bar, soaking wet like two swamp rats, confessing your dirty little secret. At least you had the balls to come and tell me, no pun intended."

Uncle Ralph continued: "Now let me ask you this. If the name on that glove was Ralph Johnson, Pete Smith, or whomever, would you have still returned the glove and apologized to the rightful owner?"

Swanee and I thought for a moment and, in unison, responded: "Probably not."

"Then your sense of honesty is a little flimsy." said Uncle Ralph. "It seems to depend on whether you know the victim or not. Honesty is honesty, boys, no matter the situation. Do you understand what I'm saying, or am I out in right field, no pun intended again?"

"We understand," Swanee responded, and, in truth, we did.

"People deserve to be treated honestly. No one likes to be short-changed, lied to or stolen from," Uncle Ralph advised us.

Uncle Ralph had made his point. I truly felt like a jackass. Slowly, I opened by shirt and took out his glove. When I started to hand him the mitt, he gently pushed it back to me.

"Tracy," he said, "keep the glove. I've got a dozen other mitts at the house."

Suddenly, the atmosphere in the room brightened. Uncle Ralph said, "You are good kids. Everybody makes mistakes and I think you have learned from this one. That's not to say I didn't think about wanting to kick both of you shit heads in the ass."

My uncle lifted the bar section and walked out to us. "Give me a big hug instead, you turkeys, and then get home into some warm, dry clothes."

Swanee and I were engulfed in Uncle Ralph's huge arms, both of us feeling remorse for our stupidity. After separating, he gave us both a kiss on the forehead.

As we started to leave the tavern, Uncle Ralph said: "Now Tracy, that is a softball mitt. You'll need to modify it for baseball. Here's some practical advice."

"Yes sir," I said.

"Unlace the glove and pad it. The pocket should comfortably fit the size of a hardball and...." Uncle Ralph hesitated, looked around the bar to see if any women could hear what he was about to say, and turned back to us and whispered, "use Kotex for the stuffing. It works like a charm."

Swanee and I looked at each other grinning broadly. We thanked Uncle Ralph for the "secret" information.

I returned my mother's sanitary napkins. Mom never noticed the napkins were missing or that I had a new mitt. She also forgot about buying me a glove for my birthday.

We covertly got some pads from Mr. Bengston at his store. He kiddingly asked if Swanee and I were planning on a sex change. Of course, he knew about the practice of using sanitary napkins to stuff baseball mitts. I used the glove through high school. I did change the "stuffing" periodically---secretly aided by Mr. Bengston.

Privately, for a while, and always chuckling, he called me the "Kotex kid." In a way, I liked the nickname. The moniker reminded me of Uncle Ralph and the kindness and wisdom he extended to Swanee and me.

Uncle Ralph--a kind man

Grey Man

∽

IN THE WANING DAYS OF Spring 1950, I began to take notice of him. On my way to and from Irving, I would see him walking the streets or standing on a corner near an intersection. Sometimes, he would be peering into a store window. He was always alone.

A very tall and cleanly dressed man, he walked with his hands clenched behind his back and never looked up as he traveled the sidewalks of West Duluth. He was elderly in years, surely retired, and I surmised the old man filled his time observing others actively living their lives. He was unassuming and peripheral, and yet why did I take such an interest in his presence? Why was I intrigued by him?

Never once did I see him address anyone, or smile, or join a group of people. He was almost invisible to others who were around him. He was not good looking, what with the many warts and indentations on his face, and he possessed a pronounced bulbous nose. But the old man had kind grey eyes which contributed to a gentleness that was very settling—at least to me.

I wondered if his indistinctness made him lonely? What was it like to never utter a word to anyone for days, not be warmly touched or smiled at— separated from the world you were living in?

I felt sorry for him. I wanted to know more about him—his past life. Where was he from? What kind of boyhood did he experience?? Did his mother sing to him at night? Did his father play with him? What had he done for a living? Had he been married? Did he have children and grandchildren?

What happened to his friends and relatives that led to seemingly such an isolated life?

These questions made me reflect on how horrible it must be to be trivial in the eyes of others. I vowed that I would never allow myself to exist in a time where I had no one. To be loved and give love had to be the greatest goals in one's life. I thought of my mom and the utter hell she must be enduring with dad. She was married to a person who made her feel lonely and unappreciated.

I think this old man had my attention because I was fearful that, one day, I could be like him. I never wanted to be an irrelevant and meaningless person. I needed friends. My ultimate fear was being so lonely that I resolved life was no longer worth living. Being alone, devoid of friends, was living death.

I remember thinking what my life would be like without the presence of Swanee and Porky, and my school teachers at Irving? The thought frightening me.

One day, I decided to take a bicycle ride to my old neighborhood to get some stick matches from the dump yard at the Diamond Match Factory.

As I was riding past the Northland Hotel on 51st, out of its front door came the old man. As usual, he was neatly dressed, with his hands behind his back, and his head down. He began to slowly walk toward the center of West Duluth. I decided to follow him on my bike. I could get the matches some other time. I wanted to see how the old man spent his day.

The man walked the side streets and avenues of West Duluth. He methodically looked in the shop windows along Central and Grand Avenues. He watched the fuzzy test patterns on the recently introduced Magnavox television sets at the local appliance store next to Joe Blasaak's gas station. His noon hour was comprised of having a coffee and doughnut at the bakery next to the Doric Theater. He trekked all the way to the Duluth Zoo to view the animals, and returned home in mid-afternoon to the Northland Hotel.

He had talked to no one (even the waitress at the bakery gave him his order without either one of them saying a word). I wanted to ride up to him and say something, but I was too shy, and a little scared. My heart ached. What a sad and lonely human being that I had just followed.

A few weeks later, as I was trudging along one rainy morning to grade school, I passed the doorway of the drugstore on the corner of Grand Avenue and 57th. The old man was standing alone in the doorway. Probably because his presence startled me, I quickly said to him, "Hi, sir. Nice day if it wasn't raining."

He immediately smiled at me and responded, "Hello, good boy. Have fun at school."

My heart began racing with excitement! I had acknowledged him and it felt exhilarating! He had smiled and responded to me! I convinced myself that I was the first person to say hello to him in years. From now on, I vowed, I would say "hi" every time I saw him. We would become friends! He would no longer be alone! I would adopt him as my new great-grandfather!

I never saw the old man again. For weeks, I biked every day in West Duluth looking for his familiar figure. He was nowhere to be found. Swanee thought he had probably died, or moved out of the area, or maybe was in the hospital. Whatever happened to the old man, after our brief (and only) verbal exchange, at the drugstore doorway, in the pouring rain, that spring day in 1950, would always remain a painful mystery.

I would never forget the anonymous old man, with the kind grey eyes, who instilled not only a sadness in my heart for him, but also a lesson that being loved and loving others, were the most important ingredients for a happy, satisfying life. I remember him to this day and the tender insights he unknowingly gave me.

Camp Constipation

$\sim\!\!\!\sigma$

I HAD NEVER GONE TO an "organized" camp. A few of my buddies who were Boy Scouts attended something called "jamborees" during the summer. I lacked any real interest in scouting, dressing up in a uniform, getting badges, making bird feeders, and tying knots. It all seemed so silly and regimented. The only uniforms I liked to wear were the ones I wore playing baseball and basketball.

Swanee once said the Boy and Girl Scouts were just "fronts" to control America's youth. He believed the organizations should be called the "Youth Fascist Leagues of America," and avoided at all costs. I guess I agreed.

Butch was still trying to save my soul by enticing me to go to Bible camp to "see the light." I couldn't fathom spending a second of my time at such a place. I was not comfortable with organized religion nor worshipping in a group.

Swanee said Bible camps were brainwashing centers. He had been forced by his mother to attend one when he was ten. "At a Bible camp, there's nothing but boring lectures, praying sessions, and mind-wrenching rules. You're more a prisoner than a camper," Swanee said. "The camp is always trying to mold you to their way of thinking. They teach you the ways to save your soul, get to Heaven, and avoid Hell. It's horrible! That stuff is not camping. The only good thing about a Bible camp is there are usually girls, and they don't all look like Reverend's Scrotters' mongrel daughter, Hope. You get to smell them and fantasize about their tits and what it would be like to screw every one of them. But believe me, Finlander, I still would never go to any organized summer bullshit camp, and especially a boys-only bullshit camp! You sleep, eat, and shit with strangers. And they ain't no pussy. I know you would hate the experience."

Mindful of Swanee's opinions, one early summer day, Porky invited me to go to "railroad camp" with him.

Porky's late father had worked for the Duluth Mesabi and Iron Range Railroad (the DM&IR). As a fringe benefit, the sons and daughters of employees (dead or alive) could attend the company's "railroad camp" free for one week each summer. Qualified campers could bring a friend for a charge of $25.

I was excited! From what little I knew about the camp, it did not propagandize attendees to become railroad workers. It was only interested in entertaining children.

I wanted to go with Porky and asked mom and dad if I could attend the camp. They said going to camp with kids my age would be good for me and a wonderful learning experience.

Mom called up Mrs. Herstad to confirm Porky's offer. It was agreed that Porky and I would attend the camp the first week of August. Mom and dad were pleased when Mrs. Herstad assured them that the camp was very well supervised by adults. She said the food was healthy and deliciously prepared. The lake bordering the camp was protected by experienced life guards and the sleeping quarters were in safe and clean cabins.

Mrs. Herstad explained that there were two camps, a boys' camp on one side of a lake, and a girls' camp on the opposite shore. The boys were separated from the girls the entire time. Mrs. Herstad said we would take a free train to the camp but it was the responsibility of the parents to pick their kid up at the end of the week.

Since the camp was only about 50 miles from Duluth, mom said it would be no problem for dad to drive Porky and me home after camping was over.

I was going to a real camp! One with no stupid indoctrinations or group guilt sessions! I told Swanee about it, and his only comment was. "You'll be sorry, Finlander."

I thought the month of August would never come. By late July, I had packed a WWII duffle bag, given to me by Uncle Bob, with my sleeping bag, three changes of clothes, a jacket, two pairs of shoes, underwear, tooth brush and powder, writing paper, pre-stamped envelopes and pencils, socks, swim trunks, and my trusty baseball glove (aptly stuffed with Kotex). My mother also gave me some spending money that I hid in one of my shoes.

Porky told me we would do a lot of swimming and boating, play baseball and basketball, learn how to make bracelets and rings, eat like pigs, go hiking, build campfires, roast hotdogs and marshmallows, and just have fun. Porky said the week would go by fast. We were to go to the camp on Sunday and return on the following Saturday.

The day before I was to leave, dad sat me down at the kitchen table, after supper, and gave his traditional "grunt and brush" lecture.

"Son," he began, "it is important that you grunt regularly at camp, especially if you plan to swim a lot. Without grunting, you will develop cramps and possibly drown. Make sure that you pass your stools everyday—every single day. Do you understand?"

I, of course, said that I did understand. (I had been hearing Dad's "sermon" since I was a toddler.) I promised to follow a precise daily regimen of grunting.

"Remember, Tracy," dad warned, "you are going to a strange place for a week. You may find it difficult, at first, to grunt. Drink a lot of liquids and you should have no problem with elimination. Do you understand what I am now saying?"

Again, I assured him that I would drink a lot of water and was confident that I would adjust to "foreign" grunting rather quickly. Porky told me that the toilet facilities were very clean and private, so I had no big worry about crapping in a different facility.

"And please, Tracy," my father added, "brush your teeth at least twice a day, three times if you can, okay?"

"Okay, dad," I replied smiling. "I'll brush until my gums bleed and all my fillings fall out!"

We both laughed. My father gave me a rare hug, and twenty dollars to use for spending money. I was in seventh heaven. For the first time in my life, I had received money from both of my parents on the same day. I felt rich!

That night in our bedroom, my brother threw some forewarnings at me that had nothing to do with shitting or brushing.

"Blockhead," he began. "I'm not going to say much about your excursion to this godless railway camp except be on your toes. Beware of the older boys playing tricks on you. They will try to take advantage of your youth, and naivety, and make you do things that are stupid."

Oh, here we go, I thought. The teenage reverend is trying to save my soul again and instill fear in my veins. Please forgive me if I have some fun!

"What are you talking about, Butch," I inquired? "Am I going to be tarred and feathered or be forced to eat dog shit? Is someone going to cut my balls off? Maybe if I'm lucky, I'll participate in a Bible burning around the good old camp fire!"

"Listen to me, wise ass," he yelled! "Did you ever think that you may be talked into smoking cigarettes or a smelly cigar; that you may be caught in a situation where you are blamed for setting off a stink bomb in your counselor's cabin? I guarantee you, blockhead, you will be tested. Remember, the brain God gave you isn't the brightest one on the block. Don't be a patsy and make an ass of yourself. Beware!"

"Don't worry, Butch," I said as I turned on my side facing the wall to go to sleep. "Speaking of asses, Butch, verily, verily, I say unto you." I then lifted my top leg and let out a loud fart!

"You're such a cocky little jerk," my brother exhorted! "You'll never learn until the day you enter Hell!"

Defiantly, I let out another fart. I had made my commentary. No further words were spoken (nor farts produced). We both soon fell asleep.

Early the next morning, my father and mother drove Porky and me to the downtown Duluth station where the special DM&IR passenger train was waiting to take us to camp. I had never been on a train before. I was so excited! This was the first time I would be separated from my family for any length. The camping trip somehow made me feel more mature. I would be on my own for an entire week. Before mom and dad gave Porky and me a hug and kiss, I promised them I would send a letter from the camp (and once more assured my father I would grunt and brush faithfully).

The train ride was fun. After about an hour, we arrived at a small railway station in the country. Around 150 campers stood on the platform with baggage in hand. Most of the kids seemed older than me. Many were from the Minneapolis/St. Paul area. Porky was the only kid among the campers that I knew. I stuck close to him.

We were approached by some camp counselors who had walked down a long road to the station. The counselors welcomed us and shook our hands. One of the counselors, a woman, addressed the group as we stood around her.

"Boys," the woman began, "we here at the DM&IR camp are so very happy to welcome you. We know this next week will be one filled with many joys and wonderful memories. Our staff is dedicated to serve you. Think of us as your big brothers and sisters." (Christ, I thought. I did not want this camp to remind me of my pestering brother!) "Now let's get to the camp," continued the counselor, "and begin our adventures." We began walking in pairs back up the hilly road to the entrance of the camp. Porky was my partner.

The camp was situated on a beautiful crystal blue lake. Near the lake were the cabins – each one identified by a letter of the alphabet. A large pavilion was located across from the cabins where we would be engaged in group games, skills development, and rain day activities. On a small hill overlooking the camp was the mess hall and kitchen. Adjacent to the mess hall was a hobby and souvenir shop. Somewhat farther away were the athletic fields and a large campfire area. The bathrooms and showers were located at the edge of a wooded area just beyond the cabins.

I could see a sandy beach and a long wooden dock, beyond which was a diving platform about fifty yards from shore. Every structure was newly painted and the athletic fields and expansive lawns were neatly groomed. What a place, I thought--fun, fun, fun!

Porky and I were scheduled for cabin B. Made of logs, the building was identical in style to the other cabins. Each cabin slept eight campers. Porky and I were given a two-tiered bunk bed near the rear entrance of the cabin.

Porky let me have the top bed as he didn't like climbing up the small ladder to the upper level. The bed was comfortable and had three pillows. I laid out my sleeping bag right away and put my clothes and accessories in the closet next to our bunks.

I went out on the back porch and could see the bathroom/shower facility about 40 feet from our cabin.

"Perfect," I thought to myself. "I won't have to walk a long way to take a dump or squirt. I can quickly go in there and do my duty when no one else is around. Grunting and pissing will be a piece of cake."

There was no way I could shit or piss in a crowd. (Porky poetically portrayed the process as "checking for rats"). I would clam up in an instant. I was not like a neighborhood buddy of mine, Jimmy Jensen, who could take a crap while riding on a float during the Duluth Memorial Day parade. Nothing bothered him. When I was at his house and he had to do a number two, Jimmy would leave the bathroom door wide open and carry on a conversation with me. I needed privacy to eliminate. I didn't want anyone to see me or hear me (or smell me, for that matter). Swanee said that being under the sign of Virgo, during my life "I would be ruled by my bowels." I think he might have been correct.

Porky had to take a leak and I went with him to the toilet building. When we entered, I almost fainted from shock and utter disappointment! The "facility" reeked from the smells of urine and feces! There was little, if any, ventilation to the place. The urinal was one long trough, and the ten crappers were lined up against a wall. The toilets had no enclosure walls nor doors! There were no privacy barriers at all! Guys were sitting on the toilets, in public view, while "yet-to-go" campers were lined up directly in front of them! Everybody could see you grunting and urinating. Horror of horrors! This was barbaric! How could I possibly "go" when everybody was watching me? I began to feel sick to my stomach.

Even at Irving, I could never piss in a urinal if a kid was standing next to me. I always plugged up! Here at camp, there would be guys standing in line, almost on top of you, anxiously watching you fart a string of farts, grimace, and hopefully produce a dump, and wipe your ass! I doubted if even Jimmy Jensen could perform under these conditions! I knew I couldn't.

I was only fifteen minutes into my camping experience and already I was facing a fucken nightmare. How could I grunt under such caveman conditions! I was fair minded! I was open to compromise! A lumpy bed, fine. Bad food, fine. Dumb ass kids, fine. But come on, people! Wide open and revoltingly smelly toilet facilities, NEVER!

My deep longing for a secluded, odorless toilet abruptly brought on my first, and only, case of "home sickness." Much to my surprise (and dismay), within minutes of arriving, I was thinking about going home. The sudden strangeness of the camp, and its "tribal" shit facilities, scared me. I felt lifeless and isolated. Why did I consent to come here? What was I thinking?

I began to feel guilty. My father had spent a sizable amount of money for the camp fee. There was no way I could call him and ask to be picked up on the first day! Dad would endlessly lecture me on my lack of *sisu*, the failure to adjust to a difficult situation, and the wasted expense. Mom would not be allowed to express her opinion. Swanee would wear an "I told you so look" on his face for weeks (and Butch would never shut up about attending Bible camp as they offered private, clean restrooms)!

I had no person to confide in about my fears and inhibitions. (What was I to say to the head counselor? "I'm sorry. I despise this camp for I cannot shit or piss here?") Why, why did I not listen to Swanee?

I resolved to build up my courage. Since I was stuck here, I would just have to "*sisu* it." Maybe there would be an opportunity to dump in the woods or crap in the lake. But my gut was tied in a knot. How and where would I piss and shit over the entire week without being watched or caught? Could I die from lack of shitting? What if I crap in my pants? Will I get the "runs" and spend hours in that "we're all watching you, Tracy" shit house? I amazed myself at how quickly I could become so miserable. I wanted to die, preferably alone and quickly. I hated this place.

In my anticipation of the morning trip to the camp, I had neglected to grunt prior to leaving home. I now had to go bad! I began to panic. I had again committed the "gruntless" error reminiscent of my first day of kindergarten!

Porky took his leak and, as we were leaving the smelly barn, an announcement came over the camp loudspeaker. It was time for an hour's swim in the lake. All boys were to get into their swimming trunks and report to the beach area at once.

"Here's my chance," I thought. "I'll wade out up to my neck in an unpopulated area of the lake and do a number two. No one will be the wiser. I won't even have to wipe my rear end. The water will easily perform that function. And urinating should be a breeze."

I was excited! A spurt of hope surged through my veins. Luck was with me for once. The timing of the announcement couldn't have been better!

Porky and I rushed to our cabin and got into our trunks. We scooted down to the beach area and were met by the director of the camp. His name was Mr. Washburn, but he told us to call him "Spike."

After telling us about water safety, Spike concluded his lecture with a warning. "Boys," he said, "please do not urinate in the lake." (I swear he was looking straight at me!) "Especially do not, under any circumstances, perform an underwater number two." (He must have read my mind!) "We do not want to leave the lake because of what we call a 'brown out.' That stuff floats. If we catch anyone going in the water, the person will be restricted to their cabin for the rest of the day and will lose all swimming privileges for the next day. Is that understood, boys?"

Everyone (except me), yelled "Yes sir!"

"There goes Plan A," I lamented. "Plan B will be the woods."

When I got into the water, I still held out hope that if I got alone for a few minutes, I could pull off a quick crap. Unfortunately, I waded to the deepest area possible and found myself surrounded by other kids. There was no way I could grunt and get away with it. My plan to "aqua-shit" was foiled. My stomach ached and I was underwater farting like crazy. (I was not alone with this practice as there were bubbles erupting everywhere in my vicinity.) I managed to slowly urinate and felt a little relief, but the thought of needing to dump was uppermost in my mind. I had to find a way to get to a secluded spot in the nearby woods.

The dinner bell eventually rang for lunch. We were told to line up at the large mess hall in our swimming trunks. Hamburgers and French fries were on the menu—my favorite meal—yet I didn't enjoy the food. I was on guard to physically ward off a burst of good old number two within the dense confines of the lunch room. As it was, "one cheek sneaks" took place as I was downing my meal.

After lunch, we were instructed to go to our cabins for a short rest. As we settled into our beds, still in our trunks, I now had a chance to visit the woods and do my duty.

I climbed down from my bunk. Porky wanted to know what I was doing. I lied to him that I was off to the bathroom. I made my way out the back door of the cabin and tiptoed into the woods. I took an extra pair of undershorts with me to wipe myself after I finished. I would leave the soiled shorts at my crap site.

The woods were very thick with pine trees and dead brush. It took me awhile to find a clearing that allowed me enough space to squat down and grunt. I carefully positioned myself (I didn't especially desire a stray stick being jammed up my ass), and waited. No production was forthcoming. I strained and strained, yet I could not go. I must have remained in that awkward stance for twenty minutes. I was cemented up! The mosquitoes were beginning to have a blood banquet on my ass cheeks. Reluctantly, I stood up, pulled up my swimming trunks and cautiously walked back to the cabin.

I thought to myself. "Maybe bears can do it, but this animal cannot shit in the woods."

"Jesus," exclaimed Porky as I entered the cabin. "Where the hell you been? One of the counselors came to the cabin for a headcount and found you missing. I told him you were at the crapper. He went and couldn't find you. The counselor returned panic stricken and organized a small search party. Why did you disappear? What, were you pulling your pecker somewhere?"

Yikes! I suddenly felt the need to crap again!

"I couldn't sleep so I took a short walk into the woods, that's all," I lied again. No way was I going to reveal my real purpose in leaving.

"Well," countered Porky, "you'd better go find a counselor and tell them you're okay. They probably fear you're dead at the bottom of the lake, or that you ran away."

I wanted to run away—right back to my bathroom in West Duluth.

I went looking for a counselor. No sooner had I left the cabin when two of them came walking from the woods toward our building. With fear in my heart, and a million butterflies in full flap in my stomach, I approached them. I squeaked, "Are you looking for me?"

One of the counselors was the woman who had welcomed us at the railroad station earlier in the day. She responded to my question by asking, "Are you Stacey Gran?"

"Tracy Gran," I softly corrected her. "I'm Tracy Gran."

The woman counselor put one hand on my shoulder and asked, "Were you just in the woods, Tracy?"

"Yes, ma'am," I replied, in a voice that I could hardly hear myself.

"And are these yours, Tracy?" The same counselor had my shorts clasped in her other hand. (I had forgotten to take them back to the cabin). Thank God, they had no crap on them!

Again, I responded, "Yes, ma'am." I had the feeling of being in a courtroom and Hope Scrotters was conducting an inquisition.

The counselor then asked me the question I feared the most, "Did you go to the bathroom in the woods?"

I was mortified! It was bad enough to be caught trying to crap in the woods, but I was discovered by a woman counselor who had my shorts in her hand! I wanted to crawl into a hole and, for the second time that day, die.

Attempting to answer the counselor's embarrassing question, I began crying, "I tried to go, but I couldn't. I'm so sorry. It's just that. . ." I hesitated.

"It's just what, Tracy," questioned the other counselor?

Sobbing, I muttered, "I'm not used to public toilets where everyone can see you."

The two counselors looked at one another. Then the female counselor looked back at me.

"Tracy, honey," she said in a quiet voice. "We cannot allow our campers to go to the bathroom in the woods. It is not sanitary. I can sympathize with your problem. Believe me, you are not alone with these feelings. But you're just going to have to adjust to the facilities. We did at one time have enclosed toilets, but too many of the older boys were doing things in those enclosures that had nothing to do with going to the bathroom." The counselor hesitated for a split second. "Need I say more, son?"

"No ma'am," I responded. As usual, I had no clue what the counselor was accusing those boys of doing.

The female counselor stepped closer to me and gave me a hug.

"It's okay, Tracy, we all make mistakes." Her voice was very understanding. "Let's learn from this one and, from now on, use the correct toilet facilities, all right?"

"Yes ma'am," I promised. "It won't happen again."

"Good boy." The female counselor gave me another hug and handed me my shorts. "Now go to your cabin," she instructed, "and finish your rest period."

I went back to the cabin and climbed up to my bunk. I was convinced all the kids would know what happened. Soon, I would likely be called "the wood-shitter" or "Tracy shit-in-the-woods" or some such nickname. (Thankfully, my failed attempt at forest defecation was never revealed to the other campers.)

I did keep my promise to not dump in the woods. In fact, I never did a number two the whole time I was at camp! I became constipated! I regularly peed in the lake while swimming. But, as the week went on, I feared countless stools were packing my intestines and transforming into immovable concrete blocks. Consequently, I ate little food for fear that my accumulating crap would poison me. My stomach became bloated and hard.

I was so tense. For the first time in years, I wet my bed. Luckily, I woke up before I flooded the sleeping bag (but the front of my pajamas was soaked).

I hid them in my duffle bag. I put on another pair of bottoms that mom had supplied.

I was homesick. I missed a home that was already "sick." But it was a "sick" I was familiar with and had learned to handle. The camp was threatening to me. The kids were older and I knew none of them. The counselors were strangers (except for two of them who had discovered my shorts), the cabin setup was foreign in smells and sounds, the bathroom facilities were disgusting, and I was slowly poisoning myself.

I did enjoy the time playing basketball and baseball (the games took my mind off being constipated), but something negative even developed during one of those activities. In the early part of the week, Porky and I were playing two-on-two basketball against a couple of brothers from Minneapolis. As I was going in for a layup, a brother inadvertently scraped my cheek with one of his long finger nails. On early Thursday, I began to break out in scabs all over the area where I was scratched. The scabs were itchy.

A counselor noticed what was developing on my face and took me to the camp nurse. She said I had something called impetigo—a skin irritation of yellowish, pus-filled, scabs or crusts. The nurse had me stay in the little hospital area over the last two days of the week. I was not allowed to be among the other campers for fear that I could spread the disease within the camp. The nurse gave me some salve to curb the itching and told me that the scabs eventually would have to be picked off.

It was the best two days at the camp. The little room I was in had a private toilet (I still couldn't work up a grunt), and was extremely clean and quiet. Plus, I felt relieved that none of the kids would see my scabs.

To be fair, there were some fun camping experiences during the earlier part of the week. I learned to make wrist and neck bracelets by following a rather simple weaving pattern. Using plastic straps, I made a wrist bracelet for myself and a necklace for my mother.

I also was chosen by my cabin members to represent them on a counselor chaperoned night hunt for "snipes." (Snipes did not exist in northern climates. The hunting was a ruse). Such animals, I was told, were very hard to catch because of their speed. Apparently, a snipe was the size of a small cat and related to the raccoon family. Each chosen hunter was given a flashlight and butterfly net to help them bag one of the critters. Whichever cabin caught a snipe first would get free ice cream sodas the next day.

Some older guys in my cabin said that if I was the first kid to catch a snipe, I would be inducted into their secret "circle jerk" club. I was puzzled as to what the club did but the cabin members said it was very prestigious to be a member of the organization. Porky said that he had heard about the exclusive club last year. He said only a few boys were members. They had a "mystery hand shake" and met late at night after the counselors had gone to bed. I so wanted to be a "circle jerker." I would try my best to catch a snipe.

Early Tuesday evening, each chosen hunter had a counselor accompany them into the woods where snipes could be found. I looked for over two hours and never once did I see a snipe. I felt I had let my cabin campers down. When we returned to the cabins at around 9pm, all the hunters and counselors met as group. It was announced that no one was successful in netting a snipe. The contest was considered a tie. All of us would be receiving sodas the next day! I felt so much better. I no longer considered myself a big loser.

The guys at my cabin were happy to hear about the sodas. But to my dismay, the older campers told me my membership in the "circle jerk club" was no longer possible since I had not caught a snipe. I felt disappointed but understood the reason for my rejection: no snipe in hand, no "circle jerk club" for me.

On Thursday, within in my room at the camp hospital, I mailed my parents the letter that I had promised to send them. I portrayed my experiences at camp as fun-filled, exciting, and rewarding. I could never convey that I hadn't shit in a week, urinated principally in the lake (and once in my sleeping bag), got caught trying to grunt in the woods, contracted a case of impetigo, was quarantined at the camp hospital, and was hopelessly homesick. No, my letter was very positive, and thoroughly fictitious.

My mother and father were told that I was having a ball. I was developing countless friendships, eating and sleeping well, and grunting regularly. I related to them I had caught a snipe and won a contest for being the sole camper to capture one of the little varmints. And, because of my unbridled success at "sniping," the older boys in my cabin, via permission of the counselors, elected me into the renown "circle jerk club." Proudly, I bragged I was now a "circle jerker." I couldn't wait for their reaction.

Saturday finally arrived. My little hospital room had a window that peered out to the main entrance of the camp. I anxiously waited to see that big, shiny, black Buick drone up the steep incline that led to the nearby parking lot.

I vowed to never go to an organized camp again. Of course, I would re-frain from telling Porky how I felt. I didn't want to hurt his feelings and, in some indirect way, dishonor the memory of his father who qualified the two of us for this six-day nightmare. Mr. Herstad had probably turned over in his grave numerous times because of my fiascos.

Mrs. Herstad had phoned Porky and said her boyfriend and she would pick him up. This was a good thing as I was sure my father (and certainly my brother) would ask me a thousand questions about camp on the way back to Duluth. Since I would have to answer many of the questions with lies, I did not want to be mortified in the presence of Porky.

Around eleven in the morning, my parents and brother pulled into the camp parking lot. I had packed my bags the night before and was ready to go. I said goodbye to the camp nurse and ran to my parents' car. Never was I so glad to see my family! As they got out of the car, I hugged mom and dad. I felt as though we had been separated for years. Even Butch received a brief hug from me. Apparently, they failed to notice my scabs.

My family was here to take me home! A sense of freedom had returned. The "ordeal" was over! Soon, I would be able to grunt again within a private, familiar bathroom. A restful sleep would return in my own bed. I could romp in a neighborhood that I knew and loved. I had beaten the odds by not dying from my crap abstinence! Victory was mine and, in some unexplainable way, I was proud of myself.

But, my ordeal was not over. The worst was yet to come.

"Tracy," dad's voice sounded very cold and stern. "I demand to speak with the head of the camp. There are a few things I must get straight. I want to know what the hell is going on at this place."

Dad scared me. What was wrong? What does dad want to get straight?

"Why, dad," I responded? "Why do you want to see him?"

"I want to speak to the head man!" Dad was mad. "Never mind the goddamn questions! Where is he?"

Dad was pissed at something.

Mom also seemed concerned, but refrained from saying anything. She had a worried look on her face. Her silence added to my sense of fear. Why all this tension? On the other hand, Butch had a shit-eating grin on his face.

He couldn't resist chiming in, "Nice complexion, blockhead. That's the worst case of acne I have ever seen. What a pus puss. You should wear a bag over your fat head. I thought circle-jerking was supposed to make you insane, not ugly."

"Butch, stop your wise ass remarks and shut up," dad spurted out! "You're no help in this matter! Tracy, take me to the individual who runs this camp now! I don't have all day to spend here!"

What "matter" is dad talking about? My fear heightened.

Did dad interpret my scab-filled face as a sign of carelessness and weakness? Maybe he somehow found out about my non-grunting for almost a week—a cardinal sin in our family? Was dad informed about my being caught attempting to crap in the woods, by a female counselor no less!? Have I embarrassed the Gran name? I now felt like puking on the parking lot.

Unfortunately, for my sake, Spike was walking toward our car. He had been greeting other parents as they were arriving and we were next in line.

"Hi, folks," Spike said with a large, welcoming grin on his face. He extended his hand to dad and, as they shook hands, acknowledged, "I'm Spike Washburn, camp director. And you are, sir?"

"Russ Gran," dad coldly responded. "I'm Tracy's father and this is his mother, Mrs. Gran, and his older brother, Russ Junior."

Spike immediately sensed my father's ire.

With now a guarded smile on his face, he began to address my family. "Tracy caught a case of impetigo during his stay. I recommend that you take him to your family doctor for a prescription to cure the infection. Impetigo is. . ."

Dad coldly interrupted Mr. Washburn in a condescending voice we were very familiar with.

"I'm well aware of the disease and of course will take care of it."

Dad had one thing on his agenda and got right to the point.

"Mr. Washburn, could you please tell me how your camp can endorse group masturbation?! And how in the name of Jesus can you justify the solicitation of young boys into a club that emphasizes such behavior?! I find it intolerable that a summer camp for children, that is sponsored by a reputable company, condones such a practice. I plan to...."

"Mr. and Mrs. Gran," Spike interrupted my father and looked a little taken back by dad's characterization of the camp. "Please," he continued, "this camp does not condone such behavior nor does it sponsor a club for the exercise of the activity. We are dedicated to the physical and moral well-being of our young people. Our snipe hunting escapade is done every week and meant only to get the boys out in the woods. The act in question has absolutely no part in our agenda. What was your source of this false information?"

Suddenly, eight eyes were on me.

Dad was the first to demand an answer from me, "Son, did you not tell me that you were inducted into a circle-jerk club and that it was sponsored by the camp counselors?"

I was mortified. From the detailed conversation between dad and Spike, I quickly put two and two together and realized that circle-jerking must have meant group masturbation. The older kids had played a joke on me.

I had embarrassed myself not only in the presence of my parents, but also managed to include the camp director and my self-righteous brother in the debacle. Spike must have thought I was a "nut" case.

"Son," dad icily repeated. "I'm waiting."

A little voice within my shaking brain prudently told me it would be wise to try to explain myself. I could never bullshit my parents.

My mind was racing and I couldn't control the trembling of every part of my sweaty body. I let my discombobulated explanation overtake me and, with complete panic in my dying heart, fired away. "I thought circle-jerking was a good club and I wanted to impress upon you I was having a great time at camp and I was elected to the club for getting a snipe and really enjoyed myself and I got homesick and I'm sorry, dad, but I hated the toilet facilities and I didn't grunt once, and I peed in the lake and had trouble eating and I caught impetigo and I wet my bed and tried to crap in the woods but a woman counselor found out because she discovered my undershorts and I was put in the hospital, and...."

"Wait a minute, son. Slow down!" Dad mercifully interrupted my babbling confession. "Jeepers creepers, what are you saying? You sound like a crazy person! Have you lost your mind, son?"

"Mr. and Mrs. Gran, I think I can help here." Spike put one of his hands on my shoulder. He must have felt the pounding vibrations emanating throughout my body.

In a consoling voice, he explained, "Let me clear up a few things. Tracy was placed in our small hospital after we determined he had contracted impetigo. He was under a 24-hour nurse's care and received ointments for his sores. We attempted to call your home but never received a contact."

Spike continued. "The sniping adventure is simply a well-chaperoned, evening exercise into the woods. Please, believe me, no one has ever caught a snipe nor have we as counselors inducted any camper into such a disgusting, but mythical, club. A few older campers enjoy playing tricks on younger campers. The "club" has, unfortunately, remained as an unwanted tradition at the camp. We have tried to stamp it out and, for the most part, been successful. Obviously, the hoax still exists and for that, I am at fault. I would be willing to refund your money for the past week. It doesn't sound like Tracy had much fun, and I feel partly to blame."

Dad paused for a moment before addressing Spike.

"Mr. Washburn," he said apologetically. Dad's accusatory tone had vanished. "After hearing my son, and listening to you, I now realize the fault lies not with the camp. I guess our son was just not prepared for an organized camping adventure and chose to lie about his experiences. Unfortunately, Tracy is to blame for his miscommunication and lack of maturity. I do apologize to you for my rather rude behavior and I want to thank you for taking care of Tracy in the hospital. If I owe any money for the nursing care or drugs, please send me a bill. I would be more than happy to repay you."

"Oh no, Mr. Gran," responded Spike, "the treatment is all part of the camping package. There is no extra charge."

Dad extended his hand to Spike. "Well, then we are off. I trust the rest of your day will be better than the past ten minutes."

Spike laughed and proceeded to shake the hands of my parents and Butch. "Goodbye to you folks. Tracy, take care of yourself. I hope to see you next year."

Spike smiled broadly as he turned away. I was left with my family on the hot parking lot. I was now dead in the water. My fate had been sealed.

No sooner had we entered the car and began to drive off when the interrogation and lecture began. Butch was in nirvana as he awaited the beginning of the paternal spotlight being shined on me. Butch was rubbing his hands together, like some vindictive ghoul in heat, anxiously anticipating the inevitable admonishments from our father.

As we sat in the back seat of our car, Butch cockily pronounced "I always knew you were full of ca-ca--now it's official." My brother began laughing. I wanted so to squash his nuts. "You got a week's full of shit in ya. You're going to die! The official cause of death: shit overload!" He began to shriek in raucous laughter. "Look," Butch pointed to my head. "I see poop coming out of your ear!"

Mom instantly turned around in the front seat and, in her well-known threatening voice, offered my brother her oft used option, "Russell Victor Gran, Junior, either you shut up or I'm going to give you a good slap!"

Butch became mute, but the shit-eating grin remained on his face.

Then the emotional drum roll began, signaling the beginning of the "trial," with dad as the presiding judge.

"Tracy." (Here comes chapter one, verse one. I thought). "I am very disappointed in you. Goddamn it! *Sisu*, son! *Sisu!* You try to do your best, no matter the circumstances. A winner never quits and a quitter never wins! You quit, Tracy, and look what happened to you."

My brother had to pipe in, "Yeah, you became a constipated pus puss!"

Butch no sooner had the last word out of his sneering mouth when our mother swung around in the front seat and slapped him straight across his face. He began crying. His tears were the consequence of shock and not pain.

Mom had finally carried out her repetitive threat of a "good slap." It was satisfying to see my brother get what he deserved.

"Damn it, Mary," our father yelled! "Would you fucken let me handle this?!"

It was the first and only time I ever heard our father use the "F" word in sobriety. He pulled over to the side of the dirt road and stopped the car. Speaking to us via the rearview mirror, the tirade commenced:

"Russ Junior, keep your mouth shut! Stay out of this conversation! This talk pertains only to your brother and me. One more word from you and you will face dire consequences. Do you understand?"

My brother squeaked, "Yes, father."

"Tracy," dad cleared his throat. "You lied about your camp experiences – that hurts the most. If you weren't enjoying camp, you should have called us. We would have come and got you. I spent good money, almost half a week's pay, for you to experience homesickness, constipation, impetigo, hospitalization, being the object of a stupid joke in hunting for a nonexistent animal, and to top it off, induction into a mythical masturbation club. In addition, you wet your bed and got caught attempting to grunt in the nearby woods by a female counselor. Are there any other gems of wisdom that you forgot to tell us or is my summary accurate? Good god!"

I assumed dad's last question did not require an answer. I desired not to add more episodes to my nauseating saga.

No one talked during the rest of the trip home. A father-induced moratorium of silence was instilled within the car. A Gran had failed. The camping experience was never mentioned again. Even Butch kept his fat mouth shut—an abnormality I never thought possible.

Dad gave me a large portion of cod liver oil to assist my constipation. The horrible solution worked. I grunted as a Gran was intended to grunt.

Porky and I talked briefly about railroad camp. I made sure he was left with the false impression that I had a wonderful time. Thankfully, the following year, Porky decided not to go to camp. I was relieved of the burden of making up an excuse for my never repeating the "experience."

Swanee, as usual, was right all along. Upon my return from camp, I told him of my "adventures."

His only response was: "If something looks like shit, smells like shit, and tastes like shit, then it probably will be shit." I agreed with his disguised "I told you so," although given my prolonged constipation at the camp, I wish he would have used a different substance to make his point.

One interesting tidbit on public grunting did intrigue me. When I frequented that dungeon of a washroom at camp for the sole purpose of brushing my teeth (at least I did fulfill one part of my father's "grunt and brush" edict), I noticed a behavior so common I wondered if it was instinctual. Fat males, both boys and men, always stood up to wipe their asses. Thin people remained on the toilet and wiped their cracks from between their legs. I wisely never relayed this grunting trend to dad. Perhaps, however, I had discovered a law of human elimination based on body weight! Fascinating!

The Top Of The Mountain

On top of the Mountain

"Good morning, Americans! Stand by for news!" The staccato-like voice of Paul Harvey, a new Chicago-based radio broadcaster, woke my brother and me out of an early morning sleep. We slept adjacent to the kitchen, where our mother cooked breakfast. She had just opened our door to get us out of bed. Mr. Harvey's energetic vocal declaration already had accomplished that task.

It was the first Monday of September 1950--time to start my last year of elementary school at Irving. My brother, now a ninth grader, would experience his final year at West Junior High School. Mom always softened the

229

blow of going back to school on the initial "day of return" by serving us our favorite breakfast (i.e., the expensive cut of Hormel bacon and butter-laden toast). We gulped down the delicious food while mom assembled our new school clothes on our beds.

A week earlier, at J. C. Penny's, we had picked out new coats, shirts, pants, socks, and underwear. (Since dad was "making money," no longer did Butch have to justify new clothing purchases. And my wearing second-hand clothing days were finally over.) We next went to our favorite store in West Duluth, Mike and Sam's, to once again buy Keds and street shoes. I loved the fresh "shoe polish smell" in the small store. I was always excited to hear that not only had my foot size increased, but I could wear my Keds home! My new Keds always made me feel taller than when I entered the shoe store.

As we finished eating and dressing, we heard the soon-to-be-famous sign off, "Paul Harvey. . . Good Day!" I went to the bathroom to carry out my fatherly-mandated functions of grunting and brushing. As my brother left via the front door, I exited out the back.

I would be a "senior" (the top of the mountain) at Irving Grade School. I was anxiously delighted over a status I knew would automatically bring me prestige, and respect.

Ever since starting school, I was in awe of the sixth graders. I was never comfortable around them, yet I felt "blessed" to be in their company. But sixth-graders only had other sixth-graders as friends.

As a sixth-grader, I was an heir apparent, cocky, full of confidence, about to take my place "on top of the mountain." From now on, it will be an honor for any kid from the lower grades to speak to me.

I practically ran to Irving on that first day, glowing with self-centeredness. Then, as I entered Miss Tangwall's classroom. I remembered the room would include, God forbid, fifth-graders! I had to rub shoulders with the "unwashed!" I wanted to be on top of the mountain in a room comprised only of sixth graders. I thought of asking to be moved to the "pure" sixth grade down the hallway, but this was Miss Tangwall's class. She was the best teacher in the school. I quickly abandoned that idea. (Miss Tangwall was the finest teacher, on any level of education, I would ever have.) My concern about being in a mixed-grade class soon changed.

In her quiet way, Miss Tangwall captivated her students--and the "capture" lasted from day one in early September until our final class in mid-June.

Miss Tangwall made everyone in her class feel special. She said each one of us possessed unique abilities that, if exercised, would serve as a successful formula for a fulfilling life. She said we had to be our own best friend, but not be egotistical at the same time. No one likes to associate with self-centered people, Miss Tangwall warned. She was aware of the "top of the mountain" mentality whereby sixth graders felt superior to the students in the lower grades.

"Treating people as though they were less valuable is self-centeredness," said Miss Tangwall. "You'll never have a fulfilling life if you shun others because you think they are not up to your standards. Treat people in the manner you desire to be treated. It's a simple formula for a happy life. We are human beings," she said, "and should share the top of the mountain."

Early in the school year, Miss Tangwall held up a picture of a man who looked like a cowboy.

"Class," she began, "this man is the late Will Rogers, an American actor and humorist. He once said he never met a man he didn't like. What do you think he meant by that statement?"

Her comments stumped me. I was only eleven years old and already I didn't like my brother, and I certainly hated Adolph Hitler, Mussolini, "Uncle" Mac, the German soldier who killed Sonny Daniels, and especially the redheaded perverted drunk who tried to molest Porky, Swanee, and me. How could I like any of them?

After a minute or so, students began listing people they didn't like.

Miss Tangwall listened patiently and then replied that we were wasting our time hating a person or groups of people. Will Rogers, she reminded us, believed everybody has "good" in them. She said he enjoyed discovering the positive characteristics of people.

"To forgive people is to care for them," she taught. "We all belong to the human family, no matter your age, sex, race, religion, or nationality.

Throughout your life, do your best to be kind and caring, and respect others that are different from you."

My priorities began to change for the better—thanks to the teachings of that wonderfully wise lady. And it was soon clear that she was having the same impact on all the students in the class.

Miss Tangwall truly loved us and the feeling became mutual. We not only enjoyed experiencing math, English, literature, writing, and geography in her class, but we learned to be thoughtful and caring youngsters.

Miss Tangwall never yelled, lost her temper, or appeared bored. She took us on field trips, brought in guest speakers, introduced imaginative reading, and assigned creative homework projects. She instilled a set of core values. Every assignment she gave, story she read, trip we undertook—all had meaning. It is safe to say that every student in room 308 relished the school year 1950-51. Because she believed in us, we learned to believe in ourselves. There was no "clock watching."

Since half of the students in our room were fifth graders, Miss Tangwall was a master at teaching both grade levels without either feeling left out or ignored. No one felt marginalized. She made us all feel comfortable in her "one-room schoolhouse."

The two classes read Laura Ingalls Wilder's, "Little House on the Prairie," (a story set primarily in a one-room school in Minnesota) and we put on a class play using the same theme.

One of our "guest speakers" was Mr. Albert Woolson, a Civil War veteran. He was 103 (he lived six more years and was the last surviving Union Army veteran). Mr. Woolson told us about his past and what it was like growing up in the nineteenth century, including his time spent in a one-room schoolhouse. He talked about the numerous one-room schoolhouses that existed back then and the good memories he had of that style of education.

We were mesmerized by Mr. Woolson's stories, particularly one about seeing Abraham Lincoln. He said he was very tall, wore a "stovepipe" hat, and his voice was high-pitched.

Mr. Woolson said President Lincoln was a good man and was very honest and hard working. Colored people loved him because he freed the slaves, and white people loved him because he ended the Civil War. When Lincoln was killed, people were shocked and saddened.

Mr. Woolson said he was born in 1847 and was a drummer boy during the Civil War. I got to shake his hand and it felt like touching a century of American history! His visit made the past come alive, and we were proud to be members of the only multi-grade class at Irving. It was fun knowing that most of early America was schooled that way.

During the school year, we visited two museums, a bakery, the West Duluth fire station, a hospital, an enormous mansion where rich people once lived, a rest home, the steel plant in nearby Morgan Park, a bottling factory, and our own kindergarten. We saw and met many kinds of people. The experiences helped us to better understand what Miss Tangwall called "walks of life."

By far the two most rewarding trips we took were at a local rest home and with our school's kindergarten. In both instances, the elderly and the kids were so happy to talk with us. By meeting both the old and young, we broadened our tolerance of others different from ourselves "on top of the mountain."

I also loved Miss Tangwall because she chose me to be one of the school's police boys. Police boys watched over the safety of other children as they crossed the roads surrounding the school. Each police boy was assigned a street to monitor. My responsibility was the school crossing at 57th Street. I was assigned as a "boy" for the lunch hour and dismissal periods. It was the duty of each police boy to walk out into the center of his street, halt the traffic by holding up an octagonal STOP sign, and allow children to safely cross to and from the grounds of the school.

It was considered prestigious in the school community to be selected for the police boy assignment. There were no adult crossing guards, and this made our jobs much more important. We had several practice sessions with the vice principal, who taught us proper decorum and safety rules.

I remember running home after school anxious to tell my family of my assignment!

Thankfully, mom was not drinking and truly happy for me. She agreed being chosen a police boy by Miss Tangwall was quite an honor.

My brother did congratulate me (to my surprise). But he ended his remarks by saying, under his breath, "Miss Tangwall must be hard up for police boys this year." I flipped him the middle finger out of mom's view.

When dad came home from work, I waited for him to settle into his evening chair to read the Duluth Herald. I prepared myself for another lecture on *sisu*.

"Dad," I said, approaching him shyly. "Guess what? I was chosen to be a police boy by Miss Tangwall."

He immediately lowered the paper to his lap, looked at me, and said, "What! You are going to be a police boy at Irving? Son, that's wonderful! I am so proud of you. You betcha! That Miss Tangwall lady knows what she is doing, by golly. When she chooses someone to do something, it's because she knows you will do it correctly. That's great, Tracy. That's great."

He then extended his right hand to shake mine. I was floored. This was the side of dad I had never seen before. My heart raced at his reaction to my news.

I was, for a brief time, in heaven (above the top of the mountain)! Both parents were proud of me. Only a few days earlier, I had embarrassed them and myself with the railroad camping escapade. I felt as good as when I got my first bike or when dad made me a Jap Zapper machine gun at our "old" house.

It was exhilarating to have your parents tell you they were proud of you.

A few weeks later, I was happy again when our family was the first in the neighborhood to get a television set. Dad arranged to have a huge console with its 12" screen delivered to our house. It was made in Canada by the Travelers Company. The immense console nearly overwhelmed the small picture, but we didn't care. I was simply excited to have what I called a "movie screen" in my own living room!

As soon as the deliverymen left the house, I called Swanee and Porky. I told them to get over to my house as soon as possible for something far more exciting than mom's French fries. Swanee said he already knew we had a television set. He watched it being delivered, and as I later discovered, so did many of our neighbors.

After waiting out the four-minute warmup, the three of us sat on the couch and stared at the test pattern for an hour. Just having the thing in the house was entertainment enough. The set made our room smell "electrical."

Available programming was rather limited. Initially, we watched everything broadcast on the Dumont channel. Five-minute coverage of news was followed by fifteen minutes of entertainment. The first movie appeared in October. It was a one hour, 1930's era western starring Bob Steele. After the snowy-screened movie ended, I ran outside to tell my neighborhood friends what I had just seen on "our TV."

In my naïve vanity, I just loved saying "TV," instead of "television." Swanee predicted (correctly) that the impact of television would be greater than that of the automobile a half century earlier.

People certainly were fascinated by our television set. Every late afternoon, when many of our neighbors were walking home from work, they would stop and gaze through our front window at the console. If it happened to be on, and Dad was home, he would invite them in for a closer look. In jest, I told dad we should charge admission and make a little profit from the "lookers."

With more families soon acquiring television sets, even with limited programming, leisure time habits began to change. Kids still played outdoors after school, but only after watching their TV kid show in late-afternoon. And television provided new heroes and celebrities.

The "set" was primarily a visual device—you could see people and things in real time. Radio, on the other hand, required you to use your imagination. It was a lot easier to be a passive watcher than an imaginative listener. Radio became less popular. (Certain celebrities like Jack Benny, Milton Berle, and Bob Hope, began appearing on both mediums.)

The days of quietly relaxing on the living room floor listening to a favorite radio program, evolved into whole families staring at the television set for three hours every night. In the early days of television, Americans had the best of both mediums as radio and television programming offered many interesting and worthwhile shows. But radio entertainment would experience a slow, steady death.

Because of the experience in Miss Tangwall's class, being a police boy, and watching television, my last year at Irving was most memorable. I also received a certificate from the principal for being the outstanding police boy! And I was especially happy when my parents surprised me with a Gilbert's Erector Set as at graduation gift.

I would always remember Miss Tangwall and the experiences I had as one of her sixth-grade students. She was born "on top of the mountain."

Retribution

⤴

THE DAY AFTER SCHOOL ENDED was exhilarating. Better than Christmas. The sun shined brighter and everything smelled fresh.

The season of outdoor play, staying up late and sleeping in, long bike rides, going to Dukes games, playing ball, hiking and camping, gardening, swimming at Park Point, and harassing the adult scoundrels had arrived.

In September 1951, I would be a seventh grader at West Junior High School. Swanee, Porky, and I would be enrolled in the same school. Swanee was going into the ninth grade and Porky into the eighth. I looked forward walking to and from school every day with my two best buddies.

During the summer 1951, an unexpected event occurred that was particularly satisfying.

Swanee, Porky, and I decided to go to a Sunday afternoon Dukes game. Swanee's mother was sick, so he had been pardoned from mandatory church attendance. We decided to ride our bikes to the stadium, and play catch prior to the contest.

The three of us arrived at the ball park well before game time. We chained our bikes, and ran to the grassy area beyond the left field foul line fence. With almost no traffic, there was little fear of an errant throw hitting someone. We played catch for a half-hour and decided it was time to get our tickets and watch the teams warm up.

As we walked toward the ticket booth, a Ford convertible entering the stadium parking lot. The beautiful car had its top down, and carried two people—a man and a woman.

"I'd give my left nut for a car like that," commented Porky.

"Ya," I added. "I bet Miss Nelson would go on a date with me in that car."

"She's a beauty," Swanee commented. "Someday that'll be my car."

"In a pig's ass," kiddingly noted Porky. "That Ford was meant for me and only me."

As the gorgeous vehicle slowly rolled by us and parked nearby, the identity of the driver was unmistakable. Our chins dropped in unison!

In perfect harmony, the three of us blurted out: "It's him!" We stared at the tall man with the bright red hair in the driver's seat. It was the pervert who tried to get us to suck his dink at our campsite in the Duluth hills two years back! The guy whose nuts were crushed by Swanee! The pervert who ripped Swanee's tent to pieces! Now, here the asshole was, less than twenty feet away.

As the two of them exited the car and headed for the entrance to the stadium, Swanee whispered, "Guys, face the wall so we're not recognized. Let that prick and his lady friend go by us." The two of them passed by and stood in line to buy tickets.

"Okay, let's follow them in and see where they sit. I'm going to call dad and Wayne and tell them to come to the stadium. I want them to meet that redheaded cocksucker."

We were excited, but truth be told, full of fear. There was no question in our minds about the identity of the guy. I was almost sick to my stomach remembering how close we were to death two years earlier. The three of us didn't want anything to do with the pig-fucker and agreed it would be smart to let Swanee's father and brother take control of the situation.

The pervert and the lady found open, unassigned seats in the bleachers along the third base line. (I always sat in that area with my mother and grand-mother.) Once we knew where they were, we ran back to the pay phone in the stadium's lobby. Wayne answered Swanee's phone call.

"Wayne," Paul said excitedly. "Guess what? Tracy, Porky, and I have just run into the pervert who tried to get us to suck his thing at our campsite two years back! He's at the game!" Swanee paused and listened to his brother. He then responded in anxious voice, "OK, OK, we'll be sitting in the third base bleachers! See ya then! Bye!"

Swanee hung up the phone and punched his right fist into the palm of his left hand. "Dad and Wayne are coming, guys," exclaimed Swanee! We began walking back to the bleacher section. "Dad and Wayne are going to confront the asshole," said Swanee.

"This should be good!"

The pervert and his lady were in low seats near the grandstand. We went to the opposite end of the bleachers and sat on the top row. From there, we could watch for Wayne's and Mr. Swanson's arrival. The three of us paid little attention to the game. We focused on the man who almost slit our throats.

At the end of an inning, the lady got up and began walking toward the lobby. Even from our height, we could see a diamond ring and wedding band on her finger. She was the pervert's wife!

I whispered to Swanee and Porky: "Is that lady in for a surprise or what? I feel sorry for her."

"Ya," Porky added. "She's probably innocent of what the pecker-head does for a hobby."

Swanee sensed that Porky and I were losing our resolve. "Look, guys," he said. "Remember this asshole was going to kill us if we didn't follow his instructions. I think the jerk would have done so even if we had sucked him dry. The cocksucker deserves what he's going to get from dad and Wayne."

Porky and I nodded our heads in agreement. Swanee was right. The prick was a child molester. He needed to be reminded of what he attempted to do to us.

During the middle of the sixth inning, Swanee spotted his brother's truck pulling into the stadium parking lot. Mr. Swanson and Wayne exited the truck and began walking toward the ticket gate. Because it was after the fifth inning, they wouldn't have to pay. Swanee went to get them, and soon they were sitting with us. We pointed out the culprit to them.

Wayne said, "So, that's the child molester. I wonder if the lady next to him knows that "sicko" threatens to murder kids if they don't polish his tool? I'd like to cut his nuts off and jam them down his throat!"

Mr. Swanson interrupted his oldest son.

"Wayne, for God's sakes! Let's keep our heads." Turning to Swanee, Porky, and me, Mr. Swanson asked us: "Boys, are you absolutely sure this is the man who did what you said he did a couple of years back? Can there be any doubt? We don't want to confront an innocent man."

We all assured him the man was the guy who tried to molest us.

"Okay, then," Mr. Swanson said. "I suggest we leave the game and confront him when he exits the stadium. We want to be out in the parking lot before him. Let's go and wait by his car. There's no way we'll miss him doing that."

The five of us left the stadium and walked to the convertible. Swanee checked the odometer. It registered just over 400 miles. The car was a cherry. It still had that new car smell.

Wayne said, "Let's really piss the redheaded donkey off and wait for him in his car! Won't he be overjoyed to see the five of us sitting in his shiny new Ford!"

We all laughed, even Mr. Swanson.

"A funny idea," suggested Mr. Swanson, "but we'd be inviting legal trouble. Let's just wait by the car."

We didn't have to wait very long.

The redhead and his wife were leaving before the game was over. As they approached their car, the man began running at us, yelling, "Hey, goddamn it! Get the fuck away from my car!"

Wayne quickly confronted him.

"Look, shit for brains," Wayne's face was a few inches from the redhead's face. "Before you start shooting your fucken mouth off, I want you to say hello to the three kids leaning against your car! You remember them, Red? You showed up at their camp a couple of summers back and tried to make them suck your faggot cock!"

Wayne then roughly grabbed the man by the throat and dragged him right up to the three of us. Wayne's aggressiveness frightened me. I had never seen him so mad.

"And I'm sure you must remember this guy," screamed Wayne as he pointed to Swanee. "His name is Paul, remember, dick-fuck!? He's my younger brother; the one who smashed your balls with a flashlight just as you were about to force your filthy woody into his mouth! How did the flashlight feel, asshole? And you threatened to kill these kids, remember that too, douche bag?"

Wayne's questions were obviously not meant to be answered. The man could not have responded to Wayne anyway. Wayne's tight hand grip was making it hard for the redhead to breath, much less speak. He was no match for the muscular Wayne.

The tension eased slightly when the redhead's wife, now starting to cry, said, "Oh, Marc. Why? I thought we were done with this sick behavior? I can't trust anything you promise me!".

It was obvious that the lady was not hearing about her husband s sick behavior for the first time.

Even though his neck was still in Wayne's grip, the redhead managed to reply to his wife in a weak, raspy voice, saying: "Julie, I was drunk! I didn't know what I was doing!"

I couldn't believe this asshole was looking for sympathy from his shattered wife! The guy still had balls.

Mr. Swanson cleared his throat to get everyone's attention, and told Wayne to release his grip. The redheaded man bent over in pain and coughed repeatedly.

"We're done here," said Mr. Swanson. Then he spoke directly to the man's wife: "Ma'am, I'm very sorry for you. You seem like a nice person. To be honest, we had planned to mash your husband's brains a bit, but I think your hearing what he tried to do to my son and his friends is punishment enough for this shell of a man. I gather it's not the first time you've heard such stories. I'm not surprised he feels no shame for what he's done."

Mr. Swanson then slowly walked up to the redheaded man and pointed a finger in his face.

"As for you, if I ever see you again, it will be too soon. If you try to harm these boys in any way, I will hunt you down and, believe me, you will pray for death. And make no mistake after I'm done with you, slime ball, your body will never be found, at least not in one place!"

As we started to walk away from the couple, the redheaded man screamed at us in a scratchy voice: "Kiss my ass, you mother fuckers! I'll slit all your throats one day!"

Wayne quickly pivoted around and rammed his right steel-toed boot directly into the man's crotch, lifting him off his feet, and leaving him writhing on the ground in a fetal position.

A crowd was gathering around the man. We could hear him groaning as we rode away on our bikes. Mr. Swanson and Wayne followed us in the truck.

On the way home, Swanee predicted that the pervert's voice would probably go up a few octaves after Wayne's vicious kick to his balls.

We all laughed…even though again I didn't understand what Swanee meant.

I was continually afraid that one day I might see the pervert at another Dukes game. I went to many home games that summer (and over the ensuing years), always on the lookout for him. My worst fear was that I would run into him alone, perhaps in the men's room. Happily, I never saw the man again.

Mr. Swanson did not tell our parents what had happened at the stadium. He felt justice had been served (or kicked), and nothing would be gained by talking about it. But throughout that summer, and for some time afterward, I thought about the pervert's wife and what might happen to her. I personally hoped she chose to leave her husband, the bastard.

Sadly, it reminded me of a similar hope often expressed by Butch when he was reflecting on mom's situation.

One Rainy Day

—♭

JUST PRIOR TO THE START of school in 1951, mom and I had returned home from my checkup with our family physician. It was a warm but wet day, so I decided to stay inside and start gluing together a balsa wood model of a World War II B29 bomber.

I carefully laid out the individual plane parts and directions on our dining room table. At some point, I paused from working on the model and found myself staring across the table at one of the large windows.

I got up and walked closer to the window, staring intently at the thin, watery rivulets creeping down the outside of the glass. Standing transfixed, I saw how several miniscule streams were transforming themselves into a story book. It was as though the path taken by each stream reminded me of the life course of someone who was or had been important to me during my short lifetime.

One path was transient, falling only an inch or two and veering off to the side of the pane and abruptly ending. Sonny Daniels' life was like that, terse in existence, suddenly gone forever. The rivulet might mirror my beloved Great-Grandfather Reid who, while only in my life briefly, would always be with me in spirit and inspiration. Or it could symbolize the "grey man" that I had followed, lonely in his ways, who, unbeknownst to him, taught me the importance of human attachment.

Two paths interspersed as if battling one other, all the way to the bottom of the window, reminiscent of my parents' marriage, and, perhaps, the duel among God, Butch and me.

In one corner of the wet window display a rather large blotch of rain collected before trailing off in all directions. The intricate dispersal reminded me of my Irving Elementary School teachers whom I would forever cherish.

I smiled to myself when I saw three close-knit streams running slowly all the way to the bottom sill. My good buddies, Swanee, Porky (and me), prominently on display in my window picture book, like stems from a common seed following parallel yet unique courses. How does one measure the contribution of precious childhood friendships?

My reverie was broken by Porky's voice yelling "Traayceee!" from the backyard. The rain had begun to let up as I opened the porch door to let Porky into the house.

"Let's go see Swanee," he said, seeing my unfinished model. "You can work on that later."

After I got my jacket and hat on, we ventured over to Swanee's house. His garage door was half open. Swanee was inside polishing his father's car. The new green Kaiser was a beauty. Porky and I each grabbed a soft rag and helped Swanee remove the remaining wax. The wax smelled like bubble gum.

Swanee's father would be pleased when he came home from work, in the late afternoon, and saw the fruits of our labor.

An Afterward

⤴

ON SEPTEMBER 20, 1961, MY parents, brother, and I stood in the cavernous lobby of the Hartford, Connecticut, train station. Mom and dad had driven with me out east, to Amherst, Massachusetts, where I was entering my first year of graduate school at the University of Massachusetts. My brother Butch was an underwriter for the Traveler's Insurance Company in Hartford. Our parents were leaving on a train back to Duluth, Minnesota.

It was the last time the four of us would be together.

In 1962, soon after I married my wife, Jan, dad sued mom for divorce. Our mother had been under a private nurse's care for months preceding our wedding. She had been drunk daily after returning from the New England trip, and on a few occasions, run away from home.

My parents were married for 29 years. Following their divorce, they neither saw nor communicated with one another again. For the next 43 years, mom lived alone in a small, third floor apartment in West Duluth. She never remarried. Mom worked as a cleaning lady at a local hospital, retiring in her late seventies. She later volunteered at the same hospital until she was ninety. Still plagued with excessive drinking, she was hospitalized periodically for her disease. Her later years were also plagued with cancer, culminating in a lower jaw removal when she was 84. Mom died on October 11, 2006, while a resident of the St. Benedictine Health Center in Duluth. She was 92.

Our father remarried in 1963 and moved to Bellingham, Washington. He became employed as a county tax assessor and retired in 1979. His second wife passed away in 1995 after 32 years of marriage. In 2002, at age 90, he married for a third time. He was an active member in the Shrine and earned his 33rd degree in the Masons. Our father became a member of the Episcopal Church and eventually was a deacon and lay minister. He died on September 7, 2011, a few months shy of his 100th birthday.

Prior to moving east, my brother and I graduated from the University of Minnesota, Duluth (UMD). Butch renounced his devotion to his religious calling in college. He taught briefly in high school and then migrated to New England and remained in the insurance industry until his early retirement in 1990. He then moved back to Duluth and earned an advanced degree in studio art at UMD. (I find it ironic that my brother and father experienced a diametric role reversal in their lives: my brother transitioned from a "church monkey" to an atheist, while our father opted for the opposite direction.)

My brother died from a heart attack on June 14, 2017. He was 81. He never married and had no children. I regret that our lives were characterized by friction and distance. I loved him very much. I hope he loved me.

After attending graduate school at the University of Massachusetts, and State University of New York at Buffalo, my wife and I eventually settled in Maine. I worked for the University of Maine System for 33 years, retiring in 2005. My wife retired the same year from a position at a local hospital. We have two children, one grandchild, and reside in Winterport, Maine. My wife and I have been married 55 years.

Alcoholism tends to be intergenerational. Our family was no exception. In 1977, at age 37, I was admitted to the alcoholic ward at Eastern Maine Medical Center in Bangor. I "slipped" a few more times and, hopefully, had my last drink in 1978. Thanks to the fellowship and collective wisdom of a specific 12 step program, and support and understanding of my family and friends, I have stayed sober, relatively serene, and very grateful.

After our parents divorced, mom made periodic visits to our home in Maine. My brother would join us during those times. I never saw my father for 32 years (from 1963 to 1995). We did communicate via the phone and by letter. My brother had no contact with dad for over 40 years. Eventually, and independently, Butch and I did visit our father in Bellingham. I enjoyed the visitations, but I know my brother was very unhappy in dad's presence.

Grandpa Gran passed away in 1964 at the age of 85. His wife—the grandmother we never knew (nor wanted to), died in 1956. (After his wife's passing, Grandpa Gran married for a third time at age 81. A year or so later, grandpa's new wife filed for divorce!)

Our father's brother, beloved Uncle Bob, died in 1970. He was only 62. Dad never attended his brother's funeral due to lack of money for travel back to Duluth. Uncle Bob's wife, our Aunt Eleanor, never forgave our father for his non-attendance and severed all communications with him. Aunt Eleanor would live to be 107 and died in 2014.

Mother's mother, our treasured Grandmother Kier, passed away in 1976 at age 84. Mom's crazy, fun-filled sister, Aunt Edith, lived to be 69. She died in 1986. And Uncle Ralph, the very gentle man, experienced a fatal heart attack at age 47 in 1963. Emphysema was the cause of Sheila's death in 2000 at age 64.

Porky, Swanee, and I remained close friends in junior and senior high school. My childhood chums never went on to college. When I entered UMD, we began to distance ourselves from one another.

After high school, I would see Swanee far more than Porky. In fact, Swanee and I double-dated on a few occasions. Swanee no longer called me Finlander. My new moniker was "college boy." I know he was proud of my going to the university. I was equally proud to still be his friend.

Paul Swanson (Swanee) married in 1960 and had three children. He became an electrician. Ironically, he was a lifelong member and trustee of the Duluth Gospel Tabernacle—the church he barely tolerated as a child. He also owned a flower shop, Paul's Petunia Pad, and served with the Army Reserve. I would last see Swanee, and his wife, Marie, at our wedding in 1962. After I went east to graduate school, we would never communicate with one another again. He died in 2000. He was 63. Part of me died with him.

Swanee's brother, Wayne, was killed in a motor vehicle accident in the early 1960s. Mr. and Mrs. Swanson are long since deceased.

George Phillipovich, the beloved Mr. P, succumbed to cancer in the early 1960s. Mr. and Mrs. Center and their son, Ernie, have all passed away.

Gerald Herstad's (Porky) life remains a mystery. I cannot find an obituary for him. After high school, our paths rarely crossed. Occasionally, he would drive by our house and honk or wave, but we almost never spoke to each other. Our final meeting was a brief encounter at a local drugstore in the summer of 1962. He died in 1999 at the age of 61. I will always cherish his friendship.

Another mystery is the fact that I have been unable to find pictures of Porky and Swanee for the years covered by this memoir. This absence haunts me.

Miss Tangwall, my favorite teacher, spent over 40 years at Irving Grade School. She lived to be 96 and died in 2008. Miss Tangwall was a remarkable person. I was so fortunate to have her as a teacher.

I do not know what became of my teacher, the gorgeous Miss Nelson. Even after seventy years, I still desire to date her (and I now own a car)! What a lady. I bet she was "eye candy" all her life.

The duplex house, at 219 North fifty-first Avenue West, where I was born, has been razed, as has the entire neighborhood. A fenced-in, gigantic wood processing plant now occupies the area. Our second house on Wadena Street still stands. My garden is gone and the adjacent yard of Mr. P. is, once again, a mess. People's Market closed in 1960 and was torn down. The "mom and pop" owners, the Bengstons, have been dead for years. The boyhood houses of Swanee and Porky have changed little. The Petersons' house has been demolished. Wadena Street looks much the same as it did in the late 1940s. But the West Duluth of my childhood is no longer to be found.

Irving Grade School closed in 1982. The building is now an apartment complex. A large vehicular overpass parallels the structure. The playground has been replaced with private homes. Irving Field is still in existence. A consolidated school presently serves the children of West Duluth. Bussing has replaced walking and kids have their "institutional" lunch (and sometimes breakfast) at the large complex. Teachers rarely live in the neighborhoods of their students.

The Doric and West movie theaters are closed. Numerous cozy mom and pop stores and small businesses are now boarded up enclosures or vacant lots. Big box stores are everywhere, their gawky presence somehow awkwardly disrupting the familiar turfs of my youth. I feel unwanted in that new environment. The modern surroundings lack definition for me and there are few touchstones left for reflection and reminiscence. It's a truism that you can't go home again. Change is constant, but not always better.

I do feel comfort in knowing that Swanee and Porky will forever remain my best buddies. Their memory is entrenched in my heart. They were the "sweet birds of my youth." Perhaps, one day, somewhere, we can again go camping. If that day transpires (the sunrise is already in my heart), I trust our campsite won't be visited by some red-haired pervert.

And I hope Nabisco had a good life.

Brothers in life, and death

Special thanks to Jacob Gran, Diana Huckins Bartlett, and Paul Sherburne for their computer and editorial assistance.

80268081R00145

Made in the USA
Lexington, KY
31 January 2018